WITHDRAWN

Making Sense of Collectivity

Social Sciences Research Centre
Interpreting the Modern World

Series Editors: Ricca Edmondson and Mark Haugaard
National University of Ireland, Galway

Many key problems now facing humankind demand multidisciplinary analysis, but at the same time academic specialisation is on the increase. Hence this series encourages original research which challenges conventional disciplinary divisions. This interdisciplinary approach is not merely a matter of combining existing views that have been kept apart by arbitrary institutionalised divisions. More significantly, it also aims at reshaping existing research paradigms through a process of open dialogue.

Also available

Ideology After Poststructuralism
Edited by Siniša Malešević and Iain MacKenzie

Making Sense of Collectivity

Ethnicity, Nationalism and Globalisation

Edited by
Siniša Malešević and Mark Haugaard

Pluto Press

LONDON • STERLING, VIRGINIA

First published 2002 by Pluto Press
345 Archway Road, London N6 5AA
and 22883 Quicksilver Drive,
Sterling, VA 20166–2012, USA

www.plutobooks.com

British Library Cataloguing in Publication Data
A catalogue record for this book is available from the British Library

ISBN 0 7453 1937 8 hardback
ISBN 0 7453 1936 X hardback

Library of Congress Cataloging in Publication Data
A catalogue record for this book is available

10   9   8   7   6   5   4   3   2   1

Designed and produced for Pluto Press by
Chase Publishing Services, Fortescue, Sidmouth EX10 9QG
Typeset from disk by Stanford DTP Services, Towcester
Printed in the European Union by
Antony Rowe, Chippenham, England

Contents

Introduction: The Idea of Collectivity   1
Mark Haugaard and Siniša Malešević

1. Different Societies? Different Cultures? What *are* Human Collectivities?   12
   Richard Jenkins

2. The Construction of Collective Identities and the Continual Reconstruction of Primordiality   33
   S.N. Eisenstadt

3. The Fundamentals of the Theory of Ethnicity   88
   John Rex

4. Nationalism and Modernity   122
   Mark Haugaard

5. The Morphogenesis of Nation   138
   Gordana Uzelac

6. Cultural Variety or Variety of Cultures?   167
   Zygmunt Bauman

7. A Disagreement about Difference   181
   John A. Hall

8. Identity: Conceptual, Operational and Historical Critique   195
   Siniša Malešević

Notes on Contributors   216
Index   218

Introduction:
The Idea of Collectivity

Mark Haugaard and Siniša Malešević

The concept of collectivity is the basis for the sociological enterprise as defined by both Durkheim and Weber. This insight is premised upon the idea that society is more than the sum of its parts. Contrary to the assertions of Margaret Thatcher, once individuals are in inter-action with one another (as they invariably are) they contribute to the creation of collectivities which both transcend and supersede the interacting agents.

The process of collectivity creation can be either intentional – resulting in the creation of groups and organisations, or uninten-tional – resulting in social systems where collective membership and ends are more diffuse. In this instance the term social system should not be interpreted in a structural-functionalist sense but rather as an area of social life characterised by a loosely defined 'local' social order. The difference between intentionally and unintentionally created collectivities is essentially one of scale. At one end of the scale there are specific groups created for the purpose of collective goals, while at the other end of the spectrum there are large complex systems which are almost entirely the consequence of the uninten-tional effects of intentional action. In the centre of the scale there are collectivities which are a hybrid of intentional and unintentional action, organisation and system. The paradigm instance of such a hybrid is the nation state, which is both an intentional construct (as in nation building) and, simultaneously, a political creation which presupposes foundations in culturally constituted societies that have come into existence through forces which nobody controls or directs. Indeed, one of the central legitimating claims made by nationalists is that nations just 'are', that is, they exist simply as the unintended consequence of actors reproducing their local collective system of meaning and identification. The actual form which col-lectivities take can be multiple, including, starting at the intentional end: athletic associations, corporations, nation states, empires, tribes, ethnic communities, civilisations, etc. Indeed, the contemporary claim that we are entering a global era is a claim to the effect that the globe itself constitutes a collectivity – a collectivity which is super-seding the nation state. While the global collectivity is largely at the unintentional-effects end of the spectrum, it is also, like all collec-tivities, partly a hybrid; there are agents (largely an elite group) who embrace the global vision of the world and who act upon it.

The concept of collectivity can be analysed at three levels: in its generality; in its particularity; and in terms of derivative concepts. The first concerns problematising the idea of collectivity itself – what is a collectivity? The second is centred on the analysis of particular collectivities – nation states, empires, global communities and so on. The third has to do with concepts which only make theoretical sense relative to collectivities (either general or specific) including, for instance, identity and culture.

At the general level, a collectivity is a bounded area of social order which is reproduced and recreated by actors who have a sense of membership of that social order. Collectivites are subsets, or special forms, of social systems. What distinguishes collectivities from social systems in general is that the latter do not necessarily presuppose a conscious sense of membership. Social life is made up of many over-lapping social systems that are routinely reproduced without a sense of membership as a prerequisite, for instance: all the minor social conventions which constitute part of the predictability of routine interaction form part of the 'local' cultural system, words are part of language systems, and any minor economic exchanges contribute to the re-creation of economic systems. An actor going into a shop and saying 'Could I buy a pound of sugar, please?' is contributing to the reproduction of four systems (the Anglo-Saxon cultural conven-tions of politeness, the imperial system of weights and measures, the English language, and the capitalist economy) without, necessarily, having any sense of membership of these systems. In contrast, col-lectivities are social systems which entail a sense of membership – the nation or the ethnic community. Using Marxist terminology, it is possible to compare a social system to a class-in-itself (a class without class consciousness) and a collectivity to a class-for-itself (one with class consciousness) – it should be noted that within the general category of collectivities, groups or organisations are the subset which are most definitively classes-for-themselves.

In general, social order is largely reproduced through tacit knowledge. This tacit knowledge is termed 'habitus' in the work of Bourdieu (Bourdieu, 1990) and 'practical consciousness' knowledge in Giddens (Giddens, 1984) – we will use the terms interchangeably. This knowledge is vast and complex in its extent. While routine interaction presupposes that most of our knowledge of social life remains a practical habitus-type knowledge, this knowledge is not insulated, or hermetically sealed, from our discursive knowledge. If a foreigner asks for the 'correct' way (i.e. the norm according to the 'local' social system) of addressing a shopkeeper or using a particular word, it is possible to give a relatively accurate discursive answer. However, the 'local' may have to think hard in order to formulate an answer, and this 'thinking' is essentially a process of conversion, or translation, of practical knowledge into discursive consciousness knowledge. While conversion is possible, smooth routine interaction presupposes that most of our knowledge of social life remains practical consciousness – which explains why it is that it is possible to pass a written examination in a foreign language while simultaneously being unable to speak it with any degree of fluency when confronted with native speakers.

While collectivities presuppose a sense of membership, what constitutes the essence of that membership, and the sense of collectivity, may largely be practical consciousness knowledge. As argued by Jenkins (Chapter 1), nation states are possibly some of the most clearly defined forms of collectivity – they are bounded in space by geographical borders, in time by history (independence, constitution day, etc.), and there are rules of membership in the form of criteria for nationality. Yet on close examination, what constitutes the defining criteria of, for instance, Danishness (to use Jenkins' example) is relatively discursively obscure. Not only does it entail discursively readily available official bureaucratic criteria (birth certificates etc.) but there is also a complex array of practical consciousness knowledge that constitutes the essence of 'Danishness' – for instance: a special relationship to the flag, and a shared knowledge of myths, legends, stories and histories.

When analysing particular forms of collectivity (the second level), it is important to bear in mind that while nation states are the most obvious forms of collectivity in the modern world, collectivities are not synonymous with nation states. Nation states are a form of collectivity which is of relatively recent origin. In Eisenstadt's chapter (Chapter 2) we are introduced to Axial civilisations, which constituted a form of collectivity that endured for longer periods than nation states (yet?) have. As has been pointed out, if the globalisation thesis is to have any substance, it is a claim to the effect that the globe itself constitutes a form of collectivity. The image of the 'global village' implies a sense of collective membership. Between the national and global levels, the European Union is a new form of collectivity in the making. However, while the discursive criteria of 'Europeanness' exist bureaucratically, the practical consciousness knowledge of 'Europeanness' is less developed (Eurosceptics would say not developed at all!). In this instance (and more generally so in the case of large collectivities), practical consciousness knowledge is considered more significant than discursive criteria to the essence of collectivity membership. While bureaucratic criteria may be a necessary condition for 'Europeanness' the absence or presence of practical consciousness knowledge of 'Europeanness' is central to the falsification or verification of the hypothesis that there exists a European collective identity.

Because small intentionally created collectivities are created for particular purposes (organisations) they tend to be different from larger collectivities in a number of respects. Firstly, due to the fact that they owe their existence to definite objectives which lend meaning, hence legitimacy, to their existence as collectivities, the essence of collective membership tends to be less mysterious. Consequently, appeals to practical consciousness knowledge is of less significance to the definition of membership and the constitution of the collectivity. However, this is not absolute; even in highly instrumental organisations appeals to 'local' habitus may not be entirely absent (the ubiquitous knowledge of what constitutes a good 'team player') and attempts are frequently made to create local practical consciousness knowledge through company social events, weekend activities, personality development courses and so on.

The second significant contrast between organisations and other forms of collectivity is the tendency of the larger less well-defined collectivities to place some mysterious, quasi-sacred, element at the core of the collectivity. It is for this reason that civilisations, nations and ethnic groups frequently claim primordiality. This substitutes for the *telos*, or ultimate end, of an organisation. A tennis club exists to promote tennis, a computer company to sell computers. A nation does not have an ultimate end that justifies its existence in the same instrumental way. So in order that it may itself become an end, the nation may claim to embody something that transcends the merely arbitrary practical contingencies of everyday life. The nation state exists in order to preserve this primordial essence – the 'destiny of a people' or the 'spirit of a nation' becomes the ultimate end for the nation state. Again this is not absolute; 'civic nationalists' claim that their membership does not entail such transcendental claims. However, it is subject to debate whether or not civic nationalism, in anything approaching a significantly pure form, actually exists as a social force in the modern world – the United States is frequently cited as an example of civic nationalism but when one reads and hears George W. Bush's constant references to the United States as 'God's country' there is a clear sense of sacredness which is inconsistent with the principles of 'civic nationalism'. As Hall argues and documents well (Chapter 7), civic nationalism does not automatically translate into civil nationalism, just as its ethnic counterpart can equally take a hostile and exclusionary form.

This contrast of types of ultimate ends mirrors Tönnies' distinction between *Gemeinschaft* and *Gesellschaft* (Tönnies, 1963) and Durkheim's analysis of mechanical and organic solidarity (Durkheim, 1933). In both the former (*Gemeinschaft* and mechanical solidarity) the membership of the collectivity is less discursively conscious and has sacred elements which the latter do not – *Gesellschaft* and organic solidarity take place because of instrumentally rational needs to collaborate. Implicit in the former there is also a claim to the effect that the self is not constituted as an individual who 'chooses' collectivity membership based upon any utilitarian calculation to find the most efficient means to realise a particular end, but the self is constituted externally through membership of the collectivity. In this way the meaning of self gains a foundational essentialism, possibly an aura of sacredness, from association with the collectivity. This rarely articulated premise lies at the core of many identity claims. As argued by Malešević (Chapter 8), this makes the concept of identity deeply problematic as a source of sociological analysis – in itself it explains nothing because it is a reified concept the occurrence of which is in itself in need of scientific explanation.

The analysis of identity brings us to the third level where we analyse particular social phenomena inextricably associated with collectivities. While identity has reference to the being-in-the-world of individuals, it is not the unencumbered self of methodological individualism which is being referred to. Rather, it is the encumbered self of collectivities: individuals who are defined by their membership of 'ethnies', nations, and so on. Consequently, the concepts of identity and collectivity are inextricably tied to each other, one being inexplicable without the other.

As we have seen, collectivities presuppose large areas of practical consciousness knowledge or habitus. In essence this is a culture. Of course the word 'culture', as Bauman reminds us (Chapter 6), has two usages, the anthropological meaning and the other 'elite' usage which has reference to some form of distinction. The former refers to the habitus or tacit knowledge of a collectivity and to the visible manifestations of such collective consciousness (artefacts and customs). This practical consciousness knowledge makes interactive agency possible and is a key ingredient in making collectivities more than the sum of their parts. The latter usage of the term refers to the practice whereby social actors hierarchically order the tacit knowledge of different groups within society – as in the assertion that 'so-and-so is a cultured human being'. This usage implicitly presupposes the claim that there is a collectivity of people within the larger collectivity, whose local culture is superior to that of others. Looking at identity and culture together, an identity claim is, in many instances, also a cultural claim to the effect that those who share identity also share culture – local culture is what makes them different.

The chapters in this book all seek to analyse the concept of collectivity in its generality (what are collectivities?), in its specificity (how are nations constructed? how is a particular collectivity changing?) and/or address manifestations of collectivity (in particular, identity and culture). Accordingly, the chapters are grouped within this threefold classification. At the general level: in Chapter 1, beginning with Durkheim, Weber, Marx, Simmel and Mead, Richard Jenkins takes us back to the sociological basics of the concept of collectivity. He argues that the use of the collectivity in current social and political theory either tends to take it for granted as a given or fall back on the attenuated, diffident model of the collective. To counter these prevailing views, Jenkins sketches an outline for a new concept of collectivity that goes beyond the more-than-sum-of-the-parts understanding and interpretation of societies and cultures. For Jenkins, collectivities are not 'things' that 'just happen', nor are they primordial entities that ultimately determine the course of individual action. They are symbolic complexes that emerge in social interaction, which occasionally can be objects of individual manipulation. Their boundaries are flexible and constantly reproduced through social interaction. Collectivities are generated through shared knowledge, common behaviour and 'established and recognised ways of doing things' (p. 19), that is through institutions. But most of all, collectivities are always meaningful (to individuals involved in the processes of social inter-action) and material (in institutions, in patterns of interactional behaviour, and in the substance of individual human beings).

In Chapter 2, S.N. Eisenstadt puts forward a particular theory of collectivity based upon his research into Axial civilisations. He firstly develops an analytical framework for the study of the construction of collective identities and then provides a comparative and historical analysis of how collectivities have been developing in pre-modern societies, in Axial age civilisations, in non-Axial civilisations such as Japan, and in the modern era. Eisenstadt argues that the con-struction of collectivity is, like the construction of political and economic power, an autonomous and fundamental constituent in the construction of social life. The processes of collectivity con-struction are seen as universal and omnipresent in all known societies and civilisations throughout history. Collectivities are his-torically built and reconstructed around certain fundamental but recurrently changing thematic blocs tied together with the notion of primordiality. According to Eisenstadt, the incessant construction of collectivity has a foundation in the continual reconstruction of pri-mordiality (around such themes as ethnicity, race, language, kinship, territory, generation or gender) which is articulated differently in different Axial civilisations. Because these articulations tend to be specific and relatively unique to particular civilisational circles Eisenstadt concludes that humanity's answer to primordiality, even in modern times, does not have a single form but emerges in multiple ways.

Moving to the second level: in Chapter 3, John Rex outlines a general theory of ethnic relations. He argues that as yet there is no systematic interpretation of ethnic phenomena the analysis of which would include the historical and geographical variety that ethnicity takes or the stronger connection between the macro- and microlevels of analysis. Rex provides a skeleton for an integral theory of ethnic relations that links ethnicity in small communities, larger ethnic groups ('ethnies'), ethnic nations, modernising nation states, minority nationalisms with the establishment of empires, post-imperial situations, transnational migrant communities, as well as with the social and political problems confronting modernising nation states in managing minority nationalisms and migrant ethnic minorities. Rex also revisits the arguments put forward by primor-dialists and instrumentalists and analytically compares this debate to the classical sociological distinction between *Gemeinschaft* and

Gesellschaft. He explores the way in which the modernising nation state and pre-existing forms of communal bonding have become subordinated to the purpose of the state's rulers.

In Chapter 4, Mark Haugaard theorises the motivational causes of nationalism. Building on his work on power, Haugaard aims to explain how and why nationalism is associated with modernity. Starting from the striking paradox of nationalism as an essentialist ideology that operates very successively in the environment of instrumentalist modernity, Haugaard aims to go beyond Gellner's account of nationalism to identify why nationalism has such a powerful appeal to many. He argues that nationalism is a modern form of collective *Gemeinschaft* which answers ontological needs created by the uncertainties of modernity and its attendant power structures. Nationalism draws its appeal from the individual's necessity for continual reification. As Haugaard puts it: 'The desire for ontological security by avoiding either the potential infinite regress of arbitrary meaning or the interactive failure of nonconfirming structuration is an internal force which feeds the ideological cravings for a nationalist primordialist certainty' (p. 136). Haugaard argues that in contemporary society agents find themselves in the contradictory position of being caught between the demand to create themselves reflexively and the pressure of simultaneously being socialised within state-sponsored disciplinary regimes.

In Chapter 5, Gordana Uzelac offers an alternative interpretation of nation-formation by drawing on the main assumptions of realist social theory as developed in the work of Margaret Archer. She argues that most theories of nationalism suffer from the fallacy of 'conflationism', that is they conflate structure, culture and agency. Gellner's modernist account of nationalism was criticised as an example of 'downwards conflation' since it reduces agency to structure and culture, while van den Berghe's sociobiological theory of ethnic nationalism as well as Hobsbawm's theory of invented traditions are rebuked as examples of 'upwards conflation' since both approaches reduce culture and structure to agency. Uzelac argues that realist social theory with its theoretical and methodological tools provides not only a good basis for the critique and reassessment of existing theories of nationalism but more importantly a nucleus for a new and more comprehensive theory of nationalism that focuses on morphogenesis, or on an analytical history of the emergence of a nation.

Bridging levels two and three, in Chapter 6, Zygmunt Bauman analyses the relationship between the newly emerging global collectivity (globalisation) and the creation of corresponding cultures. Bauman starts with the historical origin of the concept of culture, which from its inception stood for two different, but with the birth of modernity rather complementary, processes – the hierarchical ordering in relation to meeting an aesthetic ideal (to be more cultured) and the collective difference of groups (culture as a distinct way of living). With the birth of the nation state these two understandings of culture have amalgamated into the concept of 'national culture' which became perceived as clearly demarcated, homogeneous, stable and tied to a specific territory. According to Bauman, globalisation is dismantling this image of culture; cultures are now perceived more as 'hybrids', products of 'creolisation', patchworks of different elements. Globalisation does not create 'global culture' but rather 'globality of culture' ('worldwide "virtual travel" and worldwide display of locally born forms of life', p. 175) Globality of culture sets the new key choices of contemporary life: opting between cultural variety and variety of cultures, that is between multicultural (individualist) and multicommunitarian (collectivist) policies. Bauman finds both options deeply problematic, arguing that 'what is needed is to optimise the conditions under which choices are made' (p. 179).

At the third level: in Chapter 7, John Hall gives us a model whereby we analyse the tolerance of nationalism and difference. Contrary to widely held belief that plurality and difference are necessarily good, he argues, distinguishing between ethnic, civic and civil nationalisms, that some level of cultural homogeneity is a necessary precondition for political stability and economic prosperity. For Hall, cultural difference has to be limited by a degree of commonly shared values to ensure that belonging to a particular culture remains much more a matter of free will than a group right over individuals. Focusing on the examples of American society and the history of nationalism in Europe, Hall aims to demonstrate that in each case the building of the state or nation was accompanied by fierce resistance to difference. To get to where it is now, a united Europe had to go through processes of ethnic cleansing and forced homogenisation, whereas the United States was conceived as, and remains, a giant melting pot that discourages genuine cultural difference (accepting form at the expense of true cultural content). The rest of the world may have more luck in this respect but, as Hall concludes, civil nationalism and the recognition of real diversity will be extremely difficult to achieve.

In the final chapter, Siniša Malešević assesses the analytical strength of the concept of 'identity' by tracing it back to its prior mathematical meaning. He argues that 'identity' is conceptually a weak notion allowing for either vague and all-inclusive or reified and excessively inflexible use. The conceptual deficiencies in defining and understanding the notions of 'identity' and 'ethnic identity' are reflected in the quality and type of the research strategies used to assess empirical claims to ethnic identity. Using the examples from his previous work, Malešević illustrates how such a conceptual aloofness directly creates deep methodological problems when attempting to operationalise and employ this concept in empirical research. The final part of the chapter sketches some possible historical and sociological reasons why the concept of identity has acquired such a hegemonic position today, both inside and outside academia. Malešević argues that 'identity' has filled the vacuum created by the departure from the historical scene of three other master concepts – 'race' (after the collapse of Nazi project), 'national character' and 'social consciousness' (with the end of the Cold War). In the contemporary environment of dramatic social, political, economic and cultural changes, 'identity' has become an umbrella term for anything and everything, a short cut for avoiding proper explanation.

Taking an overview, the task of making sense of collectivities is a subject which lies at the core of sociology, anthropology and political science but which, because it is so central, is all too frequently taken for granted. With the exception of works on nationalism – which is only one form of collectivity – there are few, if any, contemporary works dealing with this subject.

Part of the legacy of the classics – Marx, Durkheim and Weber – is to argue that modernisation entails a move from traditional collectivities to ones dominated by economically rational criteria of efficiency and instrumental logic. Since Gellner and Anderson's analyses, nationalism has been taken seriously but largely within the paradigm of modernisation as an outcome of the rationalising logic of industrial capitalism. Given the rise of essentialist nationalism and religious 'fundamentalism' and of resistance to the neoliberal discourse of globalisation, this perception is no longer tenable. Traditional societies were held together by social forces that entailed loyalties transcending the merely instrumental, and so, too, are contemporary collectivities. In this work, we analyse what it means to make sense of collectivities in a way which takes account of this need for new conceptual tools.

References

Bourdieu, P. (1990) *The Logic of Practice* (Cambridge: Polity Press).
Durkheim, E. (1933) [1893] *The Division of Labour* (New York: The Free Press).
Giddens, A. (1984) *The Constitution of Society* (Cambridge: Polity Press).
Tönnies, F. (1963) [1887] *Community and Society* (London: Harper Torchbook).

1 Different Societies? Different Cultures? What *are* Human Collectivities?

Richard Jenkins

Among the goals which sociology and its cognate disciplines have set themselves, the theorisation of human collectivity, the quest for a working understanding of that sense of a 'more-than-the-sum-of-the-parts' which is the distinctive reality of the human world, stands out as particularly elusive. Since the claim to be able to penetrate the mysteries of human collectivity – groups, organisations, societies, cultures, or whatever – is arguably sociology's main intellectual distinguishing feature, this may also be the most important item on its agenda. In the guise of the individual–society debate, in its many guises, this difficulty continues to haunt sociology and social theory, without resolution or working consensus in sight.

A discipline whose practitioners cannot agree on the ontology of their fundamental subject matter might be thought to be in poor shape. What, exactly, is the nature of their – or our – problem in this respect? It boils down to a simple difficulty, rooted in the observable realities of the human world. In our everyday lives we participate, as embodied individuals, in a world which is populated by other embodied individuals, who are easy to see, to touch, to taste, and so on. They are tangible, three-dimensional, distinct from each other, and very material. They act, they speak, they eat, they copulate, they dance, and so on. Collectivities, however, are much less visible or tangible. They do not 'act' in the same way. Other than in the shape of their constituent individuals, they do not eat or copulate or whatever. Thus in a number of respects collectivities have a distinctive ontological status; they simply do not exist in the same way that individual humans can be said to exist.

In *which* respects? Most obviously, with the exception of small face-to-face collectivities, such as families, friendship groups, sports teams, or military regiments, for example, a collectivity's individual members – if the roll can actually be called with any accuracy, that is – are hardly ever, and in many cases never, to be found gathered together at once. For the largest collectivities such a gathering is not actually a possibility: they have too many members to assemble in the same place at the same time, and, besides, deciding who counts as a 'full' member is never straightforward. Even if one could identify and muster in one place all of the members of, for example, the United Kingdom or General Motors, the resultant logistical problems of communications and co-ordination would militate against the successful mobilisation of meaningful collectivity, and, simply in terms of area, the concept of 'one place' would be problematic.

Nor are size and observable presence all there is to this problem. Even when they are in the same place, the mere spatial coincidence of all the individual bodies that constitute its membership cannot be considered 'all there is' to a collectivity. There are bodies of knowledge and tradition, appropriate collective symbolism, appropriate artefacts, constitutional procedures, and so on, all of which must also be in place, and operational, in order for collectivity to be 'there', and which are at least as significant as the actual membership at any point in time.

Furthermore, the boundary of a collectivity's membership is always fuzzy, due to the availability – in birth and selection – of differing avenues of recruitment, depletion as members die or leave, and, in many cases, uncertainty or vagueness about the criteria of inclusion and exclusion and the procedures for resolving contested cases. In other words, human individuals can be said to be embodied in ways that human collectivities are not. The individual, in an immediate definite *physical* fashion stops at the skin (and I know that this puts the matter much too simply, but since the focus of this discussion is collectivity, I will not explore the matter further here: see Jenkins, 1996, pp. 39–53). The epidermis is a good guide to the boundary of embodied individuality. Where, however, is the 'skin' of a collectivity? Even a small one, a face-to-face community, for example?

This point suggests something else that we should take into account when we are conceptualising collectivity. As biological organisms, individuals have a definite shelf life: we are born and eventually we die. These are the only certainties that humans have. While there is a sense in which individuals can continue to have a presence in the human world long after the worms have finished their job, the post-mortem maintenance of an individual's identity, reputation and influence depends on the uncertainties of collective and individual memory, and the vagaries of reputation, not on cheating the Reaper. In other words, it depends on the work of people who are still living, and the uses which they have for the dead. Such 'immortality' is necessarily fragile. By contrast, collectivities routinely persist in the very long term, sometimes surviving many complete turnovers in their membership. This may, in fact, be one of the defining features of collectivities, that they continue despite the coming and going of their constituents (although we should not forget that this is collective longevity rather than immortality).

Collectivity in social science

So the problems in conceptualising the collective dimensions of human life are real enough. As genuine problems, they have evoked four kinds of response from social scientists. Borrowing Kuhn's terminology, the first is 'the normal social science paradigm', which characterises what most sociologists and others in the related 'social disciplines' do. It amounts to a taken-for-granted background assumption that there *is* something called 'society', that it resides unremarkably in a bounded domain of shared institutions and culture, that it is definitively different from individuals, and that the most important thing to do is to get on with the business of sociology without spending too much time worrying about metatheoretical, or even metaphysical, questions about the nature and ontology of collectivity.

Taking the collective for granted in this manner can manifest itself in different ways. Historically, it has often encouraged a reified, distant and determining model of 'society' or 'societies', as somehow existing 'over the heads' or 'behind the backs' of real people and acting on them, as a different level or dimension of human reality. The necessary abstraction inherent in theorisation has often been embraced to the point where it becomes difficult to connect substantively the collective and everyday life, and has frequently been allied to an emphasis on social integration and reproduction, on system and social structure. Another version, which has become more common recently, takes collectivity for granted in the context of a general rejection of structural and systems models which has almost become conventional wisdom, and which encourages what is, effectively, an assumption of collectivity in its absence. Sociological heads are kept down, and specialist empirical furrows enthusiastically ploughed, to the exclusion of general theory: *of course* there's 'such a thing as society' – *obviously* – but it's neither an important nor relevant issue. In whatever fashion this assumption appears, however, Urry's characterisation of those who take the existence of society for granted as 'smug' (2000b, p. 5) seems entirely justified.

The second social-theoretical approach to the problematic onto-logical status of collectivity has been to downplay its role in the human world; to work, at best, with a weak or atrophied model of the collective. This is effectively a closeted positivism or realism, in which collectivity is reduced to its visible and tangible manifesta-tions: discourse, artefacts, and so on. A model of collectivity as 'culture', this response is found in much anthropology, in a range of microsociologies – ethnomethodology and conversational analysis are classic examples, but the same comment applies to much work inspired by symbolic interactionism – in sociologically informed cultural studies, and in the sociological literatures that have nailed their colours to the mast of postmodernism during the 1990s. The emphasis on culture in this approach often leads to a further emphasis, on difference – as in different cultures and cultural diversity – as the sine qua non of collectivity.

In the third place, it is, of course, possible simply to deny the problem, and deny the existence of collectivity per se. I don't know of any actual sociologists – not even the most rigorous of method-ological individualists – who would go quite this far. The end product is an essentially arithmetical model of the human world as an assemblage of individuals that is loosely conglomerated by the tactical need for combination in the competitive pursuit of self-interest. It's a model of collectivity as warfare – Hobbes would recognise it – and its most articulate recent expression is probably to be found in liberal economics, or political philosophy in the shadow of Hayek and Popper. It is so remote from the discussions we are engaged upon in this volume that there is no need to say more about it here.

Finally, and maintaining a focus on individuals, there is a tradition of thinking about the 'problem of collectivity', which – to declare an interest, if not a prejudice – has, for me, been the source of all the really interesting thinking about collectivity. This take on the problem is rooted in an understanding of collectivity as the emergent product of interaction between individuals, and – though this is not the focus of the discussion here – of individuality as the emergent product of collectivity (which is emphatically not another way of saying that individuals are collectively determined).

Traces of this point of view can be discerned from the beginnings of systematic sociological thought in the nineteenth century. In

Marx, this perspective can be discerned in his distinction between classes in and for themselves, and his understanding of the circumstantial constraints on human historical agency. Weber's distinctive contribution was to conceptualise group identification as an emergent product of the pursuit of shared objectives, of co-ordinated collective action, by individuals. Durkheim, in *The Division of Labour*, suggested that the nature of relationships between individuals has consequences for the nature of collective solidarity, while in *The Elementary Forms* the *conscience collective* emerges from the coming together of individuals, during ritual, for example, into something-more-than-the-sum-of-the-parts. *The Division of Labour*'s argument resonates with Simmel's well-known demonstration that increasing the number of people involved in interaction, even if only from two to three, qualitatively alters the situation: that collectivity is *really* more than the sum of its parts. Simmel's exploration of the distinctive possibilities offered by metropolitan life and overlapping webs of group affiliation is also to the point here.

Moving on to Mead, his interest in the collective was largely overshadowed by other concerns. Even so, he was emphatic that his 'generalised other' arose during interaction between Self and Others, while the sociological implications of his proposal that selfhood and mind should be understood as distributed rather than individually localised are still rarely realised. After Mead, a broadly interactionally founded model of collectivity continues to be present in social theory, most obviously perhaps in Goffman's notion of 'the interaction order' (1983), but also in a wide range of social-constructivist sociologies. Within anthropology, this perspective can be found most definitively in the work of Fredrik Barth, as well as in Anthony Cohen's notion of the 'symbolic construction of communities' (1985). Barth, in his (these days somewhat neglected) masterpiece, *Models of Social Organisation* (1966), no less than his more celebrated argument in *Ethnic Groups and Boundaries* (1969) that the boundaries of collectivities are perpetually renewed interactional constructs, offers one of the most thoroughgoing attempts to put this understanding of the collective on a solid, research-based theoretical footing.

This generic understanding or model of collectivity as an emergent product of what people do, all day and every day, can be synthesised concisely into a number of connected propositions, thus:

- Human collectivity is not primordial or natural, in the sense of a 'herd instinct', or whatever.

- Human collectivities are not 'things', and they do not 'just happen'. They emerge as a consequence of actual individuals doing things together, in mutually meaningful and co-ordinated ways.
- Individual behaviour thus cannot be understood as determined by membership of collectivities (although the constraints and enablements attendant upon membership are relevant for the understanding of behaviour).
- The boundaries of collectivities are not fixed and are continually produced and reproduced during social interaction between members and non-members.
- Collectivities exist in, and as, symbolic constructs and complexes, which are, necessarily to some extent, known about, understood and manipulated by individuals.
- Collectivities are, definitively, something more than their individual constituent parts. Expressed in terms of simple mathematics, collectivities are products rather than sums, geometric rather than arithmetic constructs.

This is an understanding in which, while the collective and the individual may not be 'the same', they are not in any sense opposites either. Each conditions, and is inconceivable without, the other. However, lip service is more often paid to this principle than anything else. It requires a kind of sustained conceptual effort which the other options outlined above do not. I want to spend the rest of this chapter exploring something of what it might mean to take this model of collectivity seriously.

Collectivity as an emergent product of interaction

More meat and sinew can be put on the bones of this somewhat abstract set of propositions about human collectivity as an emergent product of interaction between individuals, by asking the blunt question: in terms of the observable realities of the human world, where are collectivities to be found?

In the first place, shared *knowledge* is important. Collectivities are something that individuals know at least something about. If collectivities are emergent products of interaction then – unless we are to surrender the pass to a model of 'society' as existing behind people's backs or over their heads – individuals must know at least something about them. They know at least something of what being or becoming a member entails, in terms of ways of doing things, use of language, and so on. In other words, they know how to *do* membership (whether they can explicate all of this knowledge or not). What is more, they identify themselves and/or other individuals in terms of collective affiliations or characteristics. They identify collectivities in terms of their perceived characteristics and those of the individuals who constitute them.

This applies equally, although in very different senses, to groups and to categories (Jenkins, 1996, pp. 80–89; 1997, pp. 52–73; 2000a). A group is an explicitly self-conscious collectivity, the members of which recognise it and know about their membership of it. In other words, the basis of group identification is collective internal or self-identification. A category, however, is a collectivity that is defined from the outside, constituted in its recognition by Others. Defined according to a criterion or criteria that its members share in the eye of the external beholder, without their recognising the fact, it is thus definitively non-members who know about categorical identity. As Marx's distinction between a class-in-itself (a category) and a class-for-itself (a group) illustrates, a category is always, at least in principle, capable of transforming itself, or of being transformed, into a self-aware group.

The second place to look for collectivity is in *behaviour and interaction*: their knowledge of collectivities influences what individuals do, and collective membership is brought into being in part by doing appropriate things. Collectivities are also phenomena in terms of which individuals act towards each other. Unless they are to be completely irrelevant – and therefore of no sociological interest at all – collectivities *must* have at least some consequences for individual practice and experience, and for the nature of interaction between individuals. What those consequences are is a matter for discovery in any particular situation, but they are as likely to involve enablement as constraint. Group membership opens some doors and closes others; it renders some courses of action highly recommended and others controversial; doing or not doing some things will simply be taken for granted. And so on. This is not complicated, and it is, in large part, what we mean when we talk about collectivities being constantly produced and reproduced in interaction. If individuals stopped acting as members of Group X, or if they stopped treating other individuals as members of Category Y, it is difficult to know in what meaningful sense either X or Y could be said to exist.

Finally, there are *institutions*, defined here simply as established and recognised ways of doing things (Jenkins, 1996, pp. 126–153). Institutions can vary from the very simple and localised, such as 'proper toilet etiquette' or 'the queue', to the very complex and extensive, such as the United Nations or the networks of international air travel. In the terms of this definition, collectivities are themselves institutions, and are also in part made up of institutions. Some collectivities – states, for example, or clubs – are also organisations. An organisation is an elaborated and complex institution characterised by apparently definite boundaries, criteria of membership and procedures of recruitment, explicit purposes and objectives, and internal structures of positions and identities, occupied by embodied individuals. While organisations are always collectivities, collectivities are not always organisations.

It can easily be appreciated from the above that knowledge, behaviour and interaction, and institutions are at best only analytically separable. Bearing that in mind, two very general propositions can be offered about human collectivities. First, collectivities are always *meaningful*: to individuals, in their interactional consequences, and as established ways of doing things. Second, collectivities are also definitively *material*: in the embodiment of individual members, in observable interactional patterns, and in the materiality of institutions (in what their members do and say, in buildings and other structures, in artefacts, and so on).

With terminological acknowledgement to Erving Goffman (1983), the above discussion leads to a three-cornered, or three-legged, model of collectivity. By this token, the human world, and any collectivity, can be understood as three orders.

- An *individual order*, which denotes embodied individuals: what-goes-on-in-their-heads.
- An *interaction order*, which denotes the relationships between embodied individuals: what-goes-on-between-people.
- An *institutional order*, which denotes established pattern and organisation: settled-ways-of-doing-things.

These are classificatory orders: they are not to be understood as different or definite and discrete empirical realities. They are ways of looking at the world of humans, developed for analytical purposes. As such, they are only conceptually distinct: in observable reality, what they represent overlaps totally, and can, in fact, be difficult to disentangle. They constitute the human world as a trinity. These 'orders' occupy the same physical and social spaces: embodied individuals, interacting with each other, on the basis of accepted ways of doing things. Each has consequences for the others in terms of constraint and enablement, and in terms of the process and progress of change.

These classificatory orders allow us to think about collectivities as emergent products of what people do, without positing different 'levels' of reality – whatever that might actually *mean* – and without prioritising either the individual or the collective as determinate or most significant. The terminology also reminds us of the reality of order, that all that is solid does not melt into the postmodern air, and that one of the defining features of collectivity is persistent pattern.

Before leaving this part of the discussion, there are two other things to be borne in mind. Perhaps most important, and to revisit my opening paragraphs, this is not a model of collectivities as necessarily possessing sealed, definite boundaries (although some may *appear* to). As Barth argued about ethnic groups, three decades ago (1969), collective boundaries are necessarily osmotic and somewhat imprecise, negotiated and constructed in interaction at or across them, and prone to change. Collectivities are thus *not* 'hard-edged' (by definition, as it were). However, it is frequently the case that a great deal of work is put in, by insiders or outsiders, in order to produce an image of hard-edgedness and clarity. It is precisely the absence of clarity and definition at the borders of collectivities that necessitates this work of boundary-maintenance.

The other point is that the emphasis on knowledge points us firmly in the direction of the cognitive, and what Berger and Luckmann (1967) called 'symbolic universes'. What requires emphasis here is that working collectivity does not depend on consensus or normative integration. As Anthony Cohen has convincingly argued (1985), collectivities are, at least in large part, symbolic constructions: the symbolisation of collectivity depends – as indeed does the power of symbolisation in general – on condensation and imprecision, on its capacity to mean many things to many different people. The collectivity of groups, for example, *is* necessarily meaningful. Some of that meaning is shared among members, but not all – or even most – of it. The appearance of sufficient consensus is what matters, not its reality. The collectivity of a group is the creation of an umbrella of imagined similarity, under which members can stand shoulder to shoulder without having to explore their potentially divisive differences.

With respect to both boundary maintenance and symbolic construction, collectivities are imagined, products of the human imagination. Although Benedict Anderson (1983) got it right when he introduced us to the notion of 'imagined communities', he got it wrong in failing to push the argument to the realisation that *all* communities are, of necessity, imagined. That they are imagined, however, does not mean they are imaginary, which is essentially my restatement of W.I. Thomas's famous 'first law' of social constructivism: if someone believes a thing, it will affect what he or she does, and it will therefore be real in its consequences (for a recent reformulation of this theorem, see de Swaan, 2001, pp. 27–33). To repeat one of the central arguments of this chapter, individuals orient their behaviour in terms of collectivities, and in that their consequences are seen and experienced.

So far, I have proposed two different versions of what is essentially the same conceptual trinity: collectivity as constituted in knowledge, behaviour and interaction, and institutions, and as analytically imaginable in the individual, interaction, and institutional orders. I have also suggested that it is possible to discover immanent collectivity in the observable realities of everyday human life. To further emphasise this point, I will explore briefly five – and there are certainly others – of these substantive, observable dimensions of collectivity.

The first is inseparable from the diffuse and distinctly human sense of collectivity – the 'more-than-the-sum-of-the-parts' – without which I wouldn't be engaging in this discussion at all, but it is not necessarily confined to it. The inability to accept the visible, physical world of appearances as 'all there is' can be found everywhere: in religion, politics, science, romance, literature, and so on. It suggests, first, that imaginative powers are part of our distinctive human nature, and second that Weber was, for example, mistaken about the inevitability of the 'disenchantment of the world'. Without our imaginations – our capacity for enchantment – there would be nothing but ourselves, and whoever we could see or remember at the time. That would be all. It probably wouldn't even amount to the sum-of-its-individual-parts.

Second, identification with others, within actually existing groups, is obviously important. Group membership provides us with the experience of concrete collectivity that is the template for ever more abstract collectivities: large-scale corporations and polities. In terms of size, membership of groups stretches from family, friends and lovers, to the vagueness of nations or enormous business organisations. Small or big, however, group identification requires maintenance work – construction in every sense of the word – if it is to continue.

Which brings me back, third, to the shared symbolic universes that are so important in identification. Depending on verbal and non-verbal communication, these are probably the best argument one can find for the 'more-than-the-sum-of-the-parts'. Language itself is a good example. Competent language use doesn't require that one can explicate that language's working principles, nor does a competent individual speaker ever know a particular language's complete vocabulary. The definitive collectivity of language is further underlined in that we necessarily learn language from others, the primary context of language use is communication with others, and linguistic boundaries are typically indeterminate (with overlap and sharing between linguistic populations). Language is definitively 'more-than-the-sum-of-its-parts'.

Fourth, to return this time to Simmel's remarks about dyads and triads, the difference between two humans interacting and three humans interacting is qualitative: it is geometric, not arithmetic. Add a third participant and something different – not just *bigger* – emerges in terms of interactional possibilities: the spaces, inclusions and exclusions that become available. This is why we can talk about collectivities at all. The whole is 'more-than-the-sum-of-the-parts': one plus one plus one equals something other than three. This is one of the reasons why institutions and organisations are distinctive realities which are not reducible to their constituent individual parts.

Finally, there is time, and particularly something called 'the present'. Despite a well-established understanding of the present as a zone of transition between the future and the past, humans necessarily live in and establish a 'present' that is neither ephemeral nor fleeting. The tenses and turns of phrase of language, the apparent solidity of institutional continuity, the reality of a human-made physical environment, and the relative constancy of embodied, identified individuals, all constitute the present as a time-space which is sufficiently stable for human life to proceed (and without this working present, there would be neither future nor history). In Mead's words, the present is the 'locus of reality'; in mine, it is the locus of the human world. In either, it's 'more-than-the-sum-of-its-parts'.

The transcendence of the visible, the mutualities of group identi-fication, shared symbolism, relational form, and the stability of 'the present', can all be understood individually, interactionally, and institutionally. Taken together they suggest that collectivity is not so mysterious. There does seem to be such a thing as 'society', after all, and it isn't necessarily hard to find. Allowing that without them it would be nothing, the world of humans isn't only a world of indi-viduals. It is possible to separate the individual and the collective analytically, but *only* analytically. The observable and experiential realities of the human world insist that individuals and collectivities coexist in the same spaces: that in some sense, even if it may have so far proved sociologically elusive, they are inseparable.

This should not, however, lead us into the mistake of imagining that the individual and the collective are the same. That is not what inseparable means. As has already been said, it is immediately striking that individuals are obvious or visible in a way that collec-tivities aren't. Embodied humans are 'there', breathing, moving, and occupying a fairly definite space; collectivities are not always 'there'. Even when they do appear to be 'there', there's more to it than that. In the next section I will explore this in the context of a real world example.

The state of Denmark

The Kingdom of Denmark has been chosen as an example here because I have been doing research there for several years – and therefore can make some claim to know something about it (see Jenkins, 1997, pp. 142–163; 1999; 2000b) – and because, as an estab-lished nation state, it is as appropriate an example for the purposes of the argument as any other similar collectivity. It has a clearly defined territory – there are no disputed borders at the time of writing – and a secure seat at the United Nations and in similar inter-national bodies. Furthermore, as nations go, the Danes are, collectively, a fairly self-conscious group: they are a small nation, occupying a compact territory, who profess to a high degree of cultural homogeneity. They speak a distinct language, and they have all of the symbolic trappings of collectivity: in the monarch, a national flag, national songs, and so on. The Danes are, in every obvious sense, a group.

But will it still be the same group next year, after births, deaths, and naturalisations? And where does the group begin and end? Is membership dependent on Danish citizenship? What, for example, about the Danish-speaking minority in northern Germany? Are they members of the group? And the German speakers of southern Jutland, the *hjemmetysker* or 'home Germans'? Are they as Danish as someone from Hans Christian Andersen's native city of Odense? What about people from the Faeroes and Greenland, each of which is an integral part of the Kingdom of Denmark, but governed largely under home-rule frameworks, outside the European Union? What about *ny dansker*, the so-called 'new Danes'? What about, for example, children born in Copenhagen to Palestinian refugee parents, children who are entitled to a Danish passport? And does a Dane who emigrates to somewhere else and acquires another citizenship remain a Dane? And so on.

This is a simple example, but it underlines three of the points that I have been making. First, the boundary of membership of a collectivity is typically not clear. Who belongs is likely to be situational – for some purposes the Palestinian children will be 'in', for example, but not for others – and thus somewhat manipulable and prey to the rhetorical needs of the moment. Nor is the matter of who defines who is in or out consistent; it, too, is situational. Second, collectivities persist despite the coming and going of their individual members due to birth, volunteering, capture, resignation, expulsion, or death. This is because, third, there are aspects of any collectivity that exist and persist independently of its membership of the moment. In the case of Denmark, these include the following:

- *Territory and its associations*. Despite considerable change over the last several centuries – the country has effectively shrunk from a late medieval Nordic empire, which at its height included Iceland, Sweden, Norway and a large tract of what is now northern Germany, and the present Danish county of Southern Jutland was only regained, following the national disgrace of its annexation by the victorious Germans in 1864, after the First World War – the land matters. Try and imagine Denmark without Copenhagen, for example. It wouldn't work. However, even in this respect there is imprecision, as the ambiguous status of Greenland and the Faeroes – in the state but not fully of it – indicates.
- *National songs*. Denmark may be unique in having two recognised national anthems: one, 'King Christian', reserved for the ruling house and the state, the other, 'There is a Lovely

Land', for more popular national occasions, such as football matches. There are also many other national songs, such as Holger Drachmann's 'We Love Our Country', sung around the bonfires every Midsummer Eve and recently set to a new melody by the pop group Shu-Bi-Dua.

- *The national flag, Dannebrog.* Emphatically the flag of the state, and flown, in a formal calendar of observance, on all of the usual official ceremonial, ritual and commemorative occasions that one might imagine, *Dannebrog* is also extensively claimed by the Danish people as a popular symbol, and used to mark every kind of special occasion from baptism to funerals, taking in Christmas and special offers in the shops along the way. Many houses boast flagpoles, as do churches. The flag is very much a presence in everyday life.

- *The royal house.* Currently led by Queen Margrethe II, the House of Glücksborg, in claiming direct descent from Gorm the Old, in the tenth century, also claims to be the oldest royal house in Europe. A more defensible claim is that it is one of the most successful. Through a combination of astute modernisation, a sure populist touch, relative modesty, a preparedness to engage with the issues of a modern state, and a recognition of the continued importance of enchantment and ritual in the modern world, it has so far managed to avoid either irrelevance, or the scandalous entertainment value of, say, the Windsors.

- *The national Church.* Over 90 per cent of the Danish population are Church tax-paying members of the Lutheran *Folkekirke*, the 'People's Church' (a figure that has actually crept slowly upwards in recent years). Occupying a semi-detached position with respect to the state, it is the official registrar for all births (other than, for historical reasons, in Southern Jutland). It is a low-key background presence which visibly, through buildings, graveyards and key life-cycle rituals, symbolises an important sense of Danishness and belonging. The strength of Church membership, if not participation, raises questions – which are live questions in Denmark today – about whether someone can be Danish and non-Christian.

- *The political system.* Danish social democracy, in the non-party sense, rhetorically encompasses tolerance, consensus, co-operation, equality, welfare provision, and responsibility. It is enacted nationally in the legislature (*Folketing*) and locally in every municipality (*kommune*), and rooted, in part, in a nineteenth-century nationalism which galvanised rural Denmark and promoted notions of co-operative self-help as the road to modernisation. An important part of this complex of political values is decentralisation and autonomy, hence the apparent contradiction that all of this can go along with distrust of the state. Both left and right, at need, defend this perceived Danish political culture, and the welfare state which is its institutional manifestation.

- *The language.* Despite dialect differences – which are diminishing with the evolution of 'television Danish' – Denmark is characterised by one, shared, mutually intelligible language. As a small language it is sometimes, in the context, for example, of debates about Europe or globalisation, characterised as under threat. It is also a cornerstone of cultural and social integration policies applying to immigrants and refugees, and occupies a central place in the politics of the southern border region. Although it is popularly seen as a criterion of Danishness, not all 'Danes' have Danish as their first language. Nor is it unambiguously and only the language of the Danes: Norwegian, in many of its dialects, is sufficiently close to Danish to cast at least a reasonable doubt on their identities as separate languages.

- *Self-defined 'race'.* This, the 'whiteness' of being European – and Denmark is part of Europe – is not peculiar to Denmark. However, with the exception of Greenlanders, whose connection with Denmark provides, *inter alia*, a romantic narrative of the wilderness and savage nobility, outsiders of a perceived different 'race' lack the legitimacy offered by an imperial or colonial relationship. This sits uneasily alongside the political rhetoric of tolerance and equality, and raises sharp questions about membership and entitlement.

- *Myths, legends, stories and histories.* There are many of these: the genealogy of the oldest royal dynasty in Europe; *Dannebrog* coming down from Heaven during a thirteenth-century Crusade against the Baltic heathens; Hans Christian Andersen; the defeat by the Prussians at Dybbol in 1864; King Christian X riding on his white horse across the border to reclaim Southern Jutland in 1920; and again through Copenhagen during the Second World War; the evacuation of the Jews to

Sweden; and the defeat of Germany in the European Football Championship in 1992. These are just some that come to mind.

- *Relationships to other nations.* The external relationships which serve to define Denmark are: ambiguous sovereignty and inclusion with respect to Greenland and the Faeroe Islands; equality and political and cultural similarity with respect to Norway and Sweden (Scandinavia) and, to a lesser extent, the other Nordic countries of Iceland and Finland; difference, combined with a degree of popular hostility, with respect to Germany; conditional and ambiguous membership of the European Union; membership of the United Nations and the North Atlantic Treaty Organisation.

- *The constitution.* Since the first, of 1849, there have been three Danish Constitutions (*Grundlove*). Taken together with the current body of active law, the national accounts, bureaucratic regulations governing the conduct of public business, and so on, this body of precept and knowledge is fundamental to the existence of something called 'Denmark'. Quite literally it constitutes Denmark.

This does not claim to be an exhaustive catalogue, but it touches many of the important bases. Each of the above can be understood in terms of individuals, interaction, and institutions. Within the list, one can see the transcendence of the everyday (in religion, the sacredness of monarchy, and in legends), the mutual recognition of group identification, shared symbolism, institutional or relational form, and the stability of 'the present' (in repetitive and cyclical collective practices, in legal and institutional definition, and in a relationship to the past and the future).

What is more, symbolic as all the things itemised above are, they are not intangibles. Some of them are *very* tangible, indeed. They may be imagined – as products of the human imagination – but they are anything but imaginary. They are all the products of people, which continually need maintenance, and which have real consequences in everyday life. Thus they are not unchanging: it is one thing to persist, quite another to be set in concrete or immune from catastrophe. Nor are they necessarily congruent with each other: for example, the formal legal criteria of Danish citizenship do not specify 'race', other aspects of Danish law forbid the legitimacy of such a criterion, and the political tradition of tolerance has a history of rhetorical antiracism. Nor do they mean the same to all Danes, not all of whom acknowledge them all. Finally, nor are they all 'true' (or even believed to be true).

However, taken together, they do add up to something-more-than-the-sum-of-its-parts. Something of which only aspects are ever visible at any one time, or from any one point of view (although the totality can, perhaps, more easily be *felt*). They symbolise the nation. In an important sense they *are* the nation, in a way that its members at any one time are not.

This example will, I hope, illustrate the value of the simple model of the human world – as an individual order, an interaction order, and an institutional order – proposed earlier. Denmark exists in individuals, non-Danes as well as Danes, who know about it. It exists in interaction, in people doing things: being Danish and treating people as Danes. It exists institutionally, in established Danish ways of doing things. As an established way of doing things, Denmark, in fact, *is* an institution.

Not all institutions are groups, however. The collectivity of 'groupness' is achieved when the individual, the interactional, and the institutional come together under a symbolic umbrella that conjures them up as something other, something new: something sufficiently real to identify with, but sufficiently intangible to allow a diversity of members to do so – emotionally as well as cognitively – without the necessity for conformity or consensus. Something, in other words, more-than-the-sum-of-its-constituent-parts. Something even, perhaps, a little mysterious (and certainly enchanted).

The Danish example, and there is nothing exceptional about Denmark in this respect, suggests that, while human collectivities are *real*, we should only talk about 'societies' – and, indeed, 'cultures' – with a proper degree of caution. Territorially, Denmark's boundaries have throughout its history been fluid, coming and going. In anything other than the strictly formal sense – which, lest I be misunderstood, is not insignificant – they are not completely straightforward in the here and now: Greenland and the Faeroes complicate the matter, as, potentially at least, does the bogeyman of European unity. Nor is who counts as Danish a precise matter: around a core population for whom the matter appears to be clear at any given point in time, we find a less certain penumbra of Greenlanders, Faeroese, German-Danes, Danish-Germans, and 'new Danes'.

The symbolic universe that is Denmark is not fixed or definite either: the Constitution can be, and has been, rewritten; the current pattern of use of the flag is a recent thing; songs can change their tunes; not even the royal house is eternal; and so on. Finally, there is not even a clear-cut 'culture' that is Danish. Leaving aside generic Europeanness or Northern-Europeanness, there is a huge amount in common with Sweden and Norway and one of the probable reasons that so much Danish work goes in to the marking of differences between Germans and Danes is that they are, in so many senses, so similar: in what they eat, in what they drink, in their lifestyles in general. 'Cultural' boundaries are *very* fuzzy.

Beyond societies?

John Urry's recent *Sociology Beyond Societies* (2000b; see also 2000a) gives my argument in the rest of this chapter an extra fillip and a welcome new dimension. Urry argues that sociology has developed intellectually on the basis of a model of society which is rooted in the apparent certainties of the Western nation state and its citizenship. Essentially the 'normal social science' model identified earlier in this chapter, this depicts society as largely self-regulated, as possessing definite boundaries, as culturally unified if not homogeneous, as different in important respects from other societies, and as self-reproducing. Urry goes on to argue that, if this vision was ever accurate – and he repeatedly hints at his doubts about this – it fails the reality test of the twenty-first century. Extensive globalisation, in the shape of the increasing mobility and fluidity of people, social relations, artefacts, and communications, and the thoroughgoing internationalisation of politics, collective risk and business, means that sociologists must abandon their old model of society and societies. In its place at the conceptual centre of sociology we must set the study of 'mobilities' as constituting the definitive context and experience of human life.

Much of what Urry says is valuable, much resonates with my position in this chapter, and he is starting a debate that sociology needs to have. This chapter is a contribution to that debate. However, there are a number of serious problems with his argument. In the first place, I am definite about the utter implausibility of the bounded, static image of 'a society' (or 'a culture'). Human collectivities have *never* corresponded to the 'nation state model of society'; not even, as the Danish example suggests, conventional Western nation states. The boundaries and contents of human groups have always been – doubtless in different ways, in different contexts, at different times, but that is another matter – flexible, changeable, negotiable, anything but definite. Such is the nature of the human world. That humans may imagine and talk about collectivities *as if* they were definite, and the world as if it were tidy, is interesting, but it doesn't make it true.

This suggests either that the world may have perhaps have changed less – or in a different way – than Urry thinks it has, or that the implications of global changes for human collectivities are not what he thinks they are (i.e. that 'societies' have changed less than he thinks they have). Or both. For the purposes of this discussion I am agnostic on these issues, other than to observe that although globalisation is an observable reality, it may have been building longer than many of its analysts recognise.

The second major problem comes when Urry says that 'maybe Thatcher was oddly right when she said there is no such thing as society' (2000b, p. 6). This proposition is the crux of his argument with respect to the need to redirect our attention to 'mobilities'. As should be apparent from the rest of the argument so far, I think that he is wrong in this respect, too. There is something-more-than-the-sum-of-parts, from the smallest, most local sense of what that might mean, to the most extensive and societal, and that has not changed (although its local manifestations will, as they have always, vary enormously). This more-than-the-sum-of-parts has untidy, fluid boundaries, its membership is always at least potentially moot, and it is an imagined symbolic universe, but it is anything but imaginary.

The third problem is buried within his discussion, and has to do with boundaries. Something of which Urry may not fully appreciate the implications is that the definite boundedness of the sociological 'statist' model of 'society' is not, in fact, a product of a historical system of separate, individual 'societies', each nominally endogenously organised. Indeed, *individual* societies probably do not – cannot, in fact – have boundaries. What do I mean by this? Simply that boundaries are only meaningful in the context of relationships with whatever lies on their other side (for which, of course, *this* side must always be their *other* side). This is not only a theoretical point, in the best tradition of Fredrik Barth, it is also a historical observation. States have typically grown outwards until they butted up against their neighbours. In this process, 'here be dragons' becomes known wilderness, which becomes frontier country where the state's monopoly of violence is uncertain, which eventually becomes a demarcated – if not necessarily consensual, in the first instance – border, with civilisation on each side. Eventually, what was an ill-defined, fuzzy territorial entity, surrounded by the vague threat of The Wild, acquires firm – surveyed and mapped – boundaries. This happens across and on each side of the boundary, and doesn't make sense without both those sides. Boundedness is thus a product of increasing complexity and interconnectedness (which is probably why it shows no signs of going away, globalisation notwithstanding).

To conclude, there may well be reasons other than Urry's, and which there is no space to explore here (see Jenkins, 2002), for wanting to move away from words such as 'society' and 'culture'. There is certainly a need to attend to the varied portfolio of human activities that Urry glosses as 'mobilities'. However, neither of these propositions entails abandoning a sense of the existence of organised human groups, on either the small or the large scale. We can accept the messiness of the human world, and that the world is not, to hark back to Barth in 1969, an archipelago of different 'societies' in any clear-cut sense, without throwing the baby of human collectivity out with the bath water. It is to that task that sociological debate should now bend itself.

References

Anderson, B. (1983) *Imagined Communities: Reflections on the Origin and Spread of Nationalism* (London: Verso).

Barth, F. (1966) *Models of Social Organisation*, Occasional Paper No. 23 (London: Royal Anthropological Institute).

Barth, F. (1969) 'Introduction', in F. Barth (ed.) *Ethnic Groups and Boundaries: The Social Organisation of Culture Difference* (Oslo: Universitetsforlaget).

Berger, P. and Luckmann, T. (1967) *The Social Construction of Reality* (London: Allen Lane Press).

Cohen, A.P. (1985) *The Symbolic Construction of Community* (London: Ellis Harwood/Tavistock).

de Swaan, A. (2001) *Human Societies: An Introduction* (Cambridge: Polity Press).

Goffman, E. (1983) 'The Interaction Order', *American Sociological Review*, vol. 48, pp. 1–17.

Jenkins, R. (1996) *Social Identity* (London: Routledge).

Jenkins, R. (1997) *Rethinking Ethnicity: Arguments and Explorations* (London: Sage).

Jenkins, R. (1999) 'Why "Danish Identity" Doesn't Explain Much About Denmark's Rejection of the Maastricht Treaty in 1992', *Folk*, vol. 41, pp. 117–137.

Jenkins, R. (2000a) 'Categorization: Identity, Social Process and Epistemology', *Current Sociology*, vol. 48, no. 3, pp. 7–25.

Jenkins, R. (2000b) 'Not Simple At All: Danish Identity and the European Union', in Irene Bellier and Thomas M. Wilson (eds) *The Anthropology of the European Union: Building, Imagining and Experiencing the New Europe* (Oxford: Berg).

Jenkins, R. (2002) *Foundations of Sociology: Towards a Better Understanding of the Human World* (Basingstoke and New York: Palgrave).

Urry, J. (2000a) 'Mobile sociology', *British Journal of Sociology*, vol. 51, no. 1, pp. 185–203.

Urry, J. (2000b) *Sociology Beyond Societies: Mobilities for the Twenty-First Century* (London: Routledge).

2 The Construction of Collective Identities and the Continual Reconstruction of Primordiality

S.N. Eisenstadt

Part I – Analytical considerations

I

Collectivities, collective identities and boundaries – be they 'ethnic', 'national', religious, civilisational or under whatever name they are designated – are not, as has been often assumed in relevant literature, epiphenomenal or secondary to power and economic forces and relations constituting 'imagined' communities which in modern times developed in response to the expansion of capitalism, industrialism and imperialism, nor are they continual seminatural, primordial and ontologically independent entities, existing as it were almost in eternity.[1]

The construction of collective identities and boundaries – a construction which has been going on in all human societies throughout human history – constitutes, like the exercise and regulation of power, the production and distribution of economic resources and the structuring of economic relations with which it is indeed continually interwoven, a basic component of social life, of the construction of human societies. The central core of this analytical component is the cultural, 'symbolic' and social organisational or institutional, construction of boundaries of collectivities, and of trust and solidarity among the members of such collectivities.

The construction of boundaries of collectivities constitutes an aspect or component of the more general human tendency towards the construction of symbolic and organisational boundaries of social interaction. This general tendency is rooted in the openness of the human biological programme; in the concomitant development of basic indeterminacies in the structuring of any continual interaction between human beings and in the consciousness among them of such indeterminacies (Mayer, 1976; Wilson, 1980; Portman, 1944; Gehlen, 1971; Plessner, 1966; Diederichs, Plessner and Augen, 1982).

The most crucial such indeterminacies in any continual social interaction are: first, those among actors, whether individuals or collectivities; second, between actors and their goals; third, between actors and their goals, on the one hand, and the resources at their disposal, including the activities of other actors on the other hand. It is the first indeterminacy – that in the relations among actors interacting in any situation, each in continual interrelation with the others – that is of special interest from the point of view of our analysis. This indeterminacy is manifest in the fact that the range of actors who are, as it were, admitted to any such situation of continual interaction is not specified either by genetic programming or by some general rules or tendencies of the human mind; and that neither the boundaries of such interaction, nor the criteria determining who is entitled to participate, are automatically given by either of those determinants, and hence they necessarily constitute a focus of continuous change and of at least potential struggle.

The existence of some degree of such indeterminacy in patterns of behaviour and interaction is true of many other species, although in a more limited way than among humans. But human beings are also fully conscious of that indeterminacy and of the openness of their own biological programme. Such consciousness is closely related to the consciousness, manifest in the construction of burial places, of death and of human finitude, and it generates among human beings a core existential anxiety and a closely related fear of chaos. This anxiety is exacerbated by the human capacity for imagination, so brilliantly analysed by J.-P. Sartre, that is, by the ability to conceive of various possibilities beyond what is given here and now (Sartre, 1972), and in the closely related universal predisposition to play (Huizinga, 1970; Caillois, 1961; Brunner, Jully and Silva, 1979). All these lead human beings to problematise the givens of their own existence and to undertake a quest for the construction of meaningful order as an integral part of their self-interpretations and self-awareness, and of their self-reflexivity.

Such anxiety and fear of chaos and the quest for the constitution of a meaningful order through which such chaos can seemingly be overcome, generate among human beings a strong predisposition to construct a realm of the sacred, in which direct contact with the roots of cosmic or social order is established, and which serves as a focal point for the construction of symbolic and institutional boundaries inherent in the constitution of such order.

It is such construction of the realm of the sacred that constitutes the core of human charismatic activity. Such activity, oriented towards the construction of a meaningful order, does entail not only constructive but also destructive tendencies or potentialities. Such destructive potentialities are rooted in the fact that the constitution of such order cannot do away with either the indeterminacies inherent in any pattern of continual human interaction, with the awareness thereof or with the core existential anxiety. Indeed, the very construction of such an order generates a strong awareness of its arbitrariness and a strong ambivalence towards it in general and towards any concrete social and cultural order in particular. The construction of such order often gives rise to a dim, yet deep, awareness that any concrete answer to the problem of potential chaos imposes limitations on the range of possibilities open to human beings, giving rise in turn to a yearning to break through any such restrictions and actualise some different possibilities (Bateson, 1972; Taylor, 1985; van der Lieuw, 1957, pp. 324–353).

Hence the fervour attendant on many charismatic activities may also generate fear of the sacred and hence opposition to it, and contain a strong predisposition to sacrilege, manifest for instance in the close relation between the consciousness of death and the search for the sacred to be found in many sacrificial rituals; and it may breed opposition to any more attenuated and formalised forms of this order (Bateson, 1972; Taylor, 1985; Eisenstadt, 1995, pp. 167–201, 228–289, 378–380).

Needless to say, the awareness of the openness of human biological programmes, the fear of chaos and the concomitant search for a meaningful vision rooted in the realm of the sacred are not equally developed among different people, and are not structured or defined in the same mode among different societies and cultures. Nor are they necessarily central in most daily activities of most people. But the general propensity for such awareness and reflexivity and for the quest for the construction of a meaningful order is inherent in the human situation and is of far-reaching importance in the constitution of social life.

II

The constitution of collective identities and boundaries constitutes one of the most important manifestations of the search for the constitution of such order and of charismatic human activity. The central focus of the construction of collective identities is the combination of the definition of the distinctiveness of any collectivity, with the specification of criteria for membership of it; and of the attributes of similarity of the members of these collectivities. Or, in D.M. Schneider's terms (Schneider and Smith, 1973), it is the combination of 'identity' and membership in different collectivities; the definition of the attributes of similarity of members of a collectivity with the specification of the range of 'codes' available to those participating in such collectivities – delineating in this way the relations to other 'collectivities', to various 'others' – that constitutes the central focus of the construction of collective identities.

The construction of collectivities and collective identities entails the specification of the distinct attributes of such collectivities as related to basic cosmological and ontological conceptions and visions – i.e. to a specific cultural programme – and the concretisation thereof in a specific location in space and time (Eisenstadt, 1995, pp. 167–201, 378–380). The construction of collective identity or consciousness is also related to the distinction, recognised long ago by Durkheim, between the sacred and the profane, and to the different combinations of these two dimensions of social order.

The attributes of similarity of members of a collectivity are manifest in the formation of the human types and patterns of behaviour which seem to be appropriate for such members – be it the English gentleman; the 'good bourgeois', or, to follow Norbert Elias (1982), the civilised person; the good Confucian; and the like. The construction of 'similarity' of the members of any collectivity entails the emphasis on their contrast with strangeness, on the differences distinguishing them from another or others. It is such emphasis on the similarity of members of a collectivity that provides Durkheim's (1933) precontractual elements of social life, the bases of mechanical solidarity, and of solidarity and trust.

The definition of the 'other' or 'others' – and the relations to such others – poses the problem of crossing the boundaries of how a stranger can become a member; of how a member can become an outsider or a stranger. Religious conversion and excommunication represent obvious illustrations of the crossing of boundaries.

III

The construction of collective identities is influenced or shaped, as is that of most arenas of social activity, by distinct codes, schemata or themes, rooted in ontological or cosmological premises and conceptions of social order to be found in all societies.[2] The major codes or themata which shape the construction of collective identity are those of *primordiality*, *civility*, and *sacredness* (sacrality) or transcendence – each of which delineates distinct patterns of specification of the boundaries of collectivities, of the range of codes or patterns of behaviour, and of allocation of resources and regulation of power.

The theme or code of primordiality (Shils, 1975, pp. 111–126; Geertz, 1973, pp. 255–310) focuses on such components as gender and generation, kinship, territory, language, race, and the like for constructing and reinforcing the boundary between inside and outside. This boundary, though constructed, is perceived as naturally given. The second theme, that of civility or civic consciousness, the civic code, is constructed on the basis of familiarity with implicit and explicit rules of conduct, traditions, and social routines that define and demarcate the boundary of the collectivity (Durkheim, 1933). These rules are regarded as the core of the collective identity of the community.[3] The third theme – the sacral or transcendent – links the constituted boundary between 'us and them', not to natural conditions, but to a particular relation of the collective subject to the realm of the sacred and the sublime, be it defined as God or Reason, Progress or Rationality (Tenbruck, 1989). This code, just like the first two, can be found in all including preliterate and above all 'archaic' societies – in which it was usually embedded or interwoven in the two other types of codes – but the purest illustrations of such distinct sacred codes are the Axial age religions which will be discussed later on (Eisenstadt, 1983; 1987a).

These three codes or themes are of course ideal types. Within each there may develop many variations. Thus, to give only two illustrations, within the general framework of primordial orientation there may develop different emphases on territory, culture, language, or other components of primordiality, and on different conceptions of collective time. Similarly, the differences, to follow Weber's nomenclature, between this-worldly and other-worldly Axial religious ontological conceptions and orientations have been extensively analysed (Eisenstadt, 1983).

The construction of collective identities entails the concretisation of such codes or themes and the specification of their different contents and of different combinations thereof, and the designation of different institutional arenas as the bearers of such codes – as for instance the emphasis on primordiality in 'local' or 'ethnic' collectivities; on civil rules in the political collectivity or on banality in broad religious ones. The different combinations of such codes or themes and the specification of the institutional arenas in which they are implemented vary greatly between different societies and social settings – and it is the specific ways in which such themes are defined, combined and institutionalised that constitute the distinct characteristics of different collectivities. Whatever the concrete specification and combination of such themes in any collectivity, the construction of collective identity entails some – highly variable – combination of most – usually all – such codes or themes, and continual tension between them.

IV

The construction and reproduction of collective identity or consciousness is effected through the promulgation and institutionalisation of models of social and cultural order. Such models of cultural and social order – the Geertzian models 'of and for society' (Geertz, 1973, pp. 93–94) – represent and promulgate the unassailable assumptions about the nature of reality and social reality prevalent in a society, the core symbols of a society, the evaluation of different arenas of human activity, and the place of different symbolic ('cultural') activities as they bear on the basic predicaments and uncertainties of human experience.

The promulgation of models of social and cultural order and of the appropriate code orientations takes place above all in several types of situation – especially socialising and communicative ones; in different rituals and ceremonies, and through various agencies of socialisation and educational institutions, 'mass media', religious preachings and the like (Eisenstadt, 1995, pp. 55–70, 328–390). Among such situations, of special importance from the point of view of the construction of collective identities are the induction of members into the collectivity and various collective rituals – especially commemorative ones and public ceremonies in which the distinctive identity and cultural programme of the collectivity are portrayed.

In all such communicative, ritual, ceremonial and socialising situations, the 'natural' givens – sex, age, procreation, vitality, power, force – are presented, dramatised, often highly ritualised, and related to the organisational problems of the respective institutional arenas. In such situations, the distinctive attributes of any given collectivity and its relation to the cosmic order, to the cosmic attributes which it represents; its specific location in time and space; its relations to what is designated as its natural environment and to nature and to the sources of vitality; its collective memory and the perception of its continuity; are portrayed, articulated and promulgated in visual and narrative ways and in various combinations thereof. In these situations the distinctive attributes of the collectivities are endowed with some, often very strong, components or dimensions of sacrality and with very strong emphasis on the electivity or 'chosenness' of the collectivity in terms of such sacrality. Accordingly the designation of the distinctiveness of the collectivity is in these situations often portrayed in terms of inside and outside: of the purity of the inside as against the pollution of the outside.

Such sacrality and electivity can be expressed in terms of each of the major codes or themes of construction of collective identities – the primordial, civil or sacral – and in different combinations thereof, with different combinations shaping, among others, the relations to other collectivities.

It is in these situations that the attachment of members of a collectivity to its symbols and boundaries are inculcated; and that such orientation and attachment to collective identities become as it were components of one's personal identity. But needless to say, the extent to which such attachment to the different collectivities becomes an important component of a person's identity varies greatly between different individuals and different collectivities.

The construction of collective identity entails also usually very strong gender designations, manifest in such expressions as 'mother country' or 'father of the people', in which different vital forms are related to different codes, are attributed to different genders and are often defined in opposing yet complementary terms (Dragadze, 1996, pp. 341–351; Delany, 1995).

V

Given the inherent multiplicity of themes or codes of collective identity, the construction of a collectivity and the specification of attributes of similarity among its members is never, in any setting, homogeneous. Such construction always entails, in any concrete situation, some plurality of collective identities and of human types, as well as contestations between often competing construction and interpretations thereof. The nature of such plurality or heterogeneity varies greatly according to the constellations of codes and themes by which the different collectivities, above all the respective macro-collectivities, are constituted.

VI

The promulgation of the distinctiveness of any specific collectivity is closely related to, even if not identical with, major patterns of cultural creativity – such as art, literature, philosophy, architecture and drama – as well as in what has been sometimes designated as 'popular culture' in the great variety of their concrete manifestations.

The themes and problems depicted and elaborated in the great works of art, whether in literature, in philosophical discourse, in architecture, sculpture, and the like, as well as in popular culture, while each follows the 'internal' logic of its own field, are yet continually interwoven with the portrayal of the distinctiveness of the cultural programme of a given collectivity, and of the collectivity itself (Eisenstadt, 1988). Of special importance in this context are naturally those arenas of cultural creativity which focus on the depiction of the distinct memories of the different collectivities – genealogies, chronicles, and histories. Concomitantly the tension between the different components of collective identity often constitute – as for instance in *Antigone* – one of the major foci of great works of literature, or art.

VII

The construction of collective identities is effected by various social actors, especially various 'influentials' and elites in interaction with broader social sectors. The core of this interaction is the activation of the predispositions to and search for some such order which are inherent, even if not fully articulated, among all, or at least most, people. Such predispositions or propensities are activated by different influentials and actors who attempt to attain hegemony in various settings. Of special importance are those actors – like for instance the different promulgators of the visions of the Great Axial Civilisations or the bearers of the modern Great Revolutions, or of different conceptions of modern statehood and nationality – who attempt to promulgate distinct visions of collective identity, and/or distinct cultural programmes. In so far as such activists find resonance among wider sectors of the population, they are able to institutionalise the distinct symbols and boundaries promulgated by them, and crystallise different concrete collective identities and boundaries. Such actors often compete with each other, as was for instance the case with the competition between different religions in late antiquity (Brown, 1978; 1982; 1992; Burkert, 1987).

The competition between such activists is not purely 'symbolic'. The construction and promulgation of collective identities is not a purely 'symbolic' exercise – it is manifest not only in the 'symbolic' depiction of the boundaries of the collectivity, but also in the institutionalisation thereof. The institutionalisation of the boundaries of collectivities takes place through the interweaving of the promulgation of such models of cosmic and social order and of the visions of distinctiveness of any collectivity, and of the attributes of similarity of its members, appropriate to the members of these collectivities, with the control of the production and distribution of resources, with regulation of power and with access to such resources.

There exist certain affinities between the different codes or themes of collective identity and different criteria of allocation of resources (Eisenstadt and Giessen, 1995). To give a few very preliminary illustrations, primordial codes or themes tend to emphasise very strong egalitarian orientations and have a strong elective affinity with the institution of relatively wide 'package deals' of resources and access to public goods for all members of the community; and of the concomitant denial of any such access and entitlements to 'strangers', and of the constitution of relatively wide arenas of public goods. However, differences may arise between different primordial codes and communities – such as territorial, linguistic, or kin-based ones – regarding the relative emphasis on equality versus hierarchy.

Civil codes tend to restrict the egalitarian distribution of entitlements to particular spheres or social arenas and institute unequal distribution of such entitlements in other spheres. The range of public goods and entitlements distributed to all the members is smaller than in primordial communities and there has developed under these circumstances a distinction between private and public arenas. This has a certain affinity with the separation of the political from the economic sphere, with a sharp distinction between, on the one hand, the rights to entitlement and access to public goods, and on the other hand, access to various goods and commodities exchanged in economic markets. The former are restricted to members of the community, while access to the latter may also be permitted to strangers.

Sacral, especially transcendental code orientations emphasise the universal access of all 'believers' to those basic resources distributed and to the public goods constituted by the 'cultural' collectivity, but not necessarily by other 'civil' or 'primordial' collectivities.

Given the close relation between different codes and patterns of allocation of resources and regulation of power, the promulgation and institutionalisation of different patterns of collective identity and boundaries entails power struggles and struggles over resources – material and cultural or 'symbolic' alike. Such struggles are undertaken through the co-operation between different, often competing, bearers of collective identity and between other actors – influentials, political cultural elites, representatives of economic groups and social classes.

VIII

The construction of collective identities and boundaries – like that of any social order – bears within itself both constructive and destructive possibilities. The constructive dimension of such construction lies in the fact that it is such construction that generates trust without which no continuous human interaction can be assured and creativity take place (Eisenstadt, 1995), but at the same time by its very nature such construction entails exclusiveness and exacerbates the ambivalence to social order.

The destructive potentialities inherent in the construction of collective identities are inherent in the very structure of the situations in which the charismatic dimensions of human activity and interaction are promulgated. The promulgation in such situations of the models of cosmic and social order attempts to imbue the given order with charismatic dimension, to bring it into closer, often direct relation with the sacred, and concomitantly to 'convince' the members of a given society that the institutional order in general, and the concrete order of their society in particular, are the 'correct' ones. The symbols and images portrayed in these models extol the given order – the purity of the world inside the boundaries, and the danger of the world outside – or the need to remain within the boundaries despite the continuous attraction of the world outside, reinforcing, as it were, the existing ideologies or hegemonies (Eisenstadt, 1995, pp. 306–327). Yet at the same time paradoxically there develops in such situations an awareness of the arbitrariness of any social order and of the limitations on human activities which it imposes, as well as a growing awareness of the possibility of constructing new themes and models. Hence in such situations there tends also to develop a potentially strong ambivalence to any social order and especially to the given concrete social order, enhancing the attraction of stepping outside the boundaries thereof as well as the anxiety about doing so (Eisenstadt, 1995, pp. 167–201).

Such ambivalences and the consciousness of the arbitrariness of social order and of its fragility are intensified by the fact that the promulgation of such models is connected with the exercise and legitimation of power (Burkert, 1983; 1996; Vernant, 1991; Rappaport, 1999; Bloch, 1992). Consequently there may develop in such situations strong tendencies to sacrilege, transgression, violence and aggression – manifest amongst others things in the close relation between the consciousness of death and the search for the sacred which is apparent in many sacrificial rituals, and in the concomitant tendency towards the exclusion of others, making them the foci or targets of such ambivalence, depicting them not only as strange but also as evil.

IX

The construction of collective identities and boundaries as effected through the promulgation of different combinations and concrete specifications of the basic themes or codes and subcodes, as it is continuously interwoven with economic, political processes, has been going on throughout human history in all human societies and in different historical and international settings.

Of crucial importance in the construction of collective identities have been intersocietal and intercivilisational contacts. No 'society' exists as a single enclosed system. The populations which live within the confines of what has been designated as a 'society' or a macrosocietal order – and also of most other collectivities – are never organised into one 'system', but into a number of regimes, economic formations, different ascriptive collectivities, and civilisational frameworks. These different structures or frameworks evince different patterns of organisation, continuity and change. They may change within the 'same' society to different degrees and in different ways in various areas of social life. Moreover, it is only very rarely that members of such a population are confined to any single 'society' – even if one such 'society' seems to be the salient macroorder for them; usually they live in multiple settings or contexts.

The importance of such various 'international' forces or intersocietal interactions in the process of the construction of collective identities becomes visible already with the disintegration of relatively narrow tribal or territorial units, in connection with the crystallisation of the great archaic empires – ancient Egypt, Assyria, or the Meso-American ones – and later Axial age civilisations (Eisenstadt, 1983). These processes of disintegration and reconstruction of collective identities were in all cases connected with advances in agricultural and transport technology, with the growing mutual impingement of heterogeneous economic (nomadic, sedentary, etc.) and ethnic populations, with some degree of international political-ecological volatility in general, and with processes of immigration and/or conquest in particular. All these cases of growing internal structural differentiation involved the concomitant crystallisation of new broader collectivities, and new patterns of collective identity (Eisenstadt, Abitbol and Chazan, 1988a; 1988b; Bilde et al., 1990; Gledhill, Bender and Larsen, 1995).

The processes of the construction of collective identities within different broader societal settings entail also the crystallisation of a multiplicity or plurality of collectivities and collective identities. The broader international settings within which such collectivities develop, and the interaction between these settings and the various 'internal' groups and elites, does greatly influence the ways in which such multiplicity or plurality of collective identities and interpretations thereof develop both between different collectivities as well as *within* any relatively clearly defined macrocollectivity.

It is also in such situations that the continual reconstruction of the concrete specifications of the major themes of collective identity became most visible. One of the most interesting aspects of the processes of reconstruction of collective identities is the continual reconstruction of primordiality. Contrary to some of the recent studies on nationalism and ethnicity, which assume that the primordial components of collective identity are naturally and continually given, and on the whole unchanging, in fact those components have been continually reconstituted in different historical contexts and under the impact of intersocietal forces. Although primordiality is always presented by its promulgators as 'primordial', as naturally given, yet in fact it is also continually reconstructed under the impact of such forces – and in close relation to the promulgation and continual reconstruction of other – civil or sacred, above all universalistic – codes or orientations.

Part II – Comparative indications: The cultural programme and the construction of collective identities in pre-modern societies

Some comparative indications

X

The construction of collectivities and collective boundaries continuously interwoven with struggles for power and economic resources has been going on throughout human history, and it is possible to distinguish some broad types of such construction, but at the same time within each such type there have indeed developed great variations.

One convenient, and to some extent conventional way – rooted in evolutionary perspectives – to distinguish between such types is according to the extent to which there developed, in connection with the promulgation of different codes, distinctive collectivities, or whether these different codes or orientations were embedded together in common collective frameworks. The latter was in a very schematic way the case in 'tribal' societies, such as many different African, Polynesian or Meso-American 'preliterate' societies, or 'archaic' ones – like ancient Egypt or Assyria, the Maya and Aztec kingdoms and the like (Eisenstadt, 1983; Bilde et al., 1990; Gledhill, Bender and Larsen, 1995). In most of these societies there tended to develop a relatively close interweaving of the different codes or themes of collective identity within the frameworks of the same collectivities with some primordial criteria, often with strong sacral attributes being predominant. Such collectivities were constituted on different microlevels from local, family and kinship units – up to the broader 'macro' society of, for instance, the Great Egyptian Kingdom or Empire (Eisenstadt, Abitbol and Chazan, 1988a, pp. 1–27, 168–200; Moret, Davy and Childe, 1926).

In most of these societies there tended to develop a certain fluidity with respect to the categories 'race', 'language', 'kin' as specifications of membership of different collectivities, and a certain porousness of the boundaries between them (van Bakel, Hagestiejn and van de Velde, 1994) – with the partial exception of some caste-like arrangements for 'inferior' groups, especially certain professional occupations.

But even within this broad type, needless to say, there developed far-reaching differences with respect to the relative importance of the different themes or codes of collective identity; their concrete specifications, which were indeed wraught with much tension and contestation among their respective bearers. Given the relative neglect of the analytical distinction of the construction of collective identity as against the study of power and economic-class forces, there have been but few systematic analyses of these problems, and such systematic analysis is still very much a thing for future research.

At this point of our discussion, suffice it to point out, as the numerous studies of the early state in its great variety point out, that with growing structural differentiation, broadening of the scope of the 'macro'-societal communities (following Davy's and Moret's classical even if certainly rather simplified distinction, implied with respect to Ancient Egypt, in *From Tribe to Empire* (Moret, Davy and Childe, 1926)) and growing centralisation, there tended to develop both a growing distinction between different 'local' communities, and between them and the more central ones, as well as strong tendencies to fuller formalisation of criteria of membership thereof and to some closure of the boundaries between them.

The construction of collective identities in Axial age civilisations – general considerations

XI

One of the most important 'breakthroughs' with respect to the crystallisation of distinct collectivities combined with a distinct cultural programme, took place in the Axial civilisations (Eisenstadt, 1983).[4]

The Axial age civilisations brought about some of the greatest revolutionary breakthroughs in human history. The essence of these revolutionary breakthroughs was the development of revolutionary ontological visions, the central core of which was the emphasis on the chasm between a higher, transcendental order and the mundane given social one, and the call for the reconstruction of the latter according to the principles of the former. Such visions, which first developed among small groups of autonomous, relatively unattached 'intellectuals' (a new social element at the time), particularly among the carriers of models of cultural and social order, were ultimately transformed into the basic 'hegemonic' premises of their respective civilisations. In institutionalised forms they became the predominant orientations of both the ruling as well as of many secondary elites, fully embodied in the centres or subcentres of their respective societies. The hegemonic elites in all of these civilisations attempted to reconstruct the mundane world of human personality and the sociopolitical and economic orders according to the appropriate transcendental vision, the principles of the higher ontological or ethical order. At the same time, such institutionalisation gave rise to numerous heterodoxies and secondary interpretations of the hegemonic one.

The development and institutionalisation of the perception of basic tension between the transcendental and the mundane order in the Axial civilisations was closely connected with the emergence of a new social element, of a new type of elite, carriers of models of cultural and social order. These were often autonomous intellectuals, such as the ancient Israelite prophets and priests and later on the Jewish sages, the Greek philosophers and sophists, the Chinese literati, the Hindu Brahmins, the Buddhist Sangha, and the Islamic Ulema. Initial small nuclei of such groups of cultural elites or of intellectuals developed new ontologies, new transcendental visions and conceptions, and were of crucial importance in the construction of new 'civilisational' institutional formations in these societies and collectivities and in the concomitant patterns of collective identity.

Within these civilisations there developed strong tendencies to construct a societal centre or centres to serve as the major autonomous and symbolically distinct embodiments of the implementation of the transcendental visions; as the major loci of the charismatic dimension of human existence. The centre's symbolic distinctiveness from the periphery received a relatively strong emphasis; yet at the same time the centre tended to permeate the periphery and restructure it according to its own autonomous visions, conceptions and rules. Sometimes this tendency was accompanied by a parallel impingement by peripheries on the centre. Concomitantly, in close connection with the institutionalisation of Axial civilisations' cultural programmes, there developed a strong tendency to define certain collectivities and institutional arenas as the most appropriate ones to be the carriers of the distinct broader transcendental visions, and of new 'civilisational' – 'religious' – collectivities. While these collectivities were indeed distinct from political and from various 'primordial' 'ethnic' local or religious ones, yet they continually impinged on them, interacted with them, and challenged them, generating continual reconstruction of their respective identities. Such processes were effected by the continual interaction between the various autonomous cultural elites, the carriers of solidarity and the political elites of the different continually reconstructed 'local' and political communities.

XII

The construction of the Axial civilisations, with their distinctive cultural programmes and their continual confrontation between the civilisational and other collectivities, was also connected with the development of new patterns of cultural creativity.

On the purely 'intellectual' level it was theological or philosophical discourse above all that flourished and became constructed in much more elaborate and formalised ways, organised in different worlds of knowledge in manifold disciplines and generating continual developments within such frameworks (Eisenstadt and Friedrich-Silber, 1988). Within these discourses many problems attendant on the relations between the autonomous developments in different arenas of cultural creativity and some central aspects of the constitution of collectivities and of the relations between them – as for instance concern with the conception of cosmic time and its relationship to the mundane political reality, different conceptions of *historia sacra* in relation to the flow of mundane time and of sacred space in relation to the mundane one – became very central, giving rise to the construction of new types of collective memories and narratives thereof (Kedar and Werblowsky, 1988).

XIII

The very differentiation between different collectivities and themes of collective identity promulgated by them gave rise in the Axial civilisations to the emergence of open spaces in which different combinations and greater autonomy of primordial, 'ethnic', regional, as well as political, collectivities could develop. The relations between these different collectivities constituted a continual aspect of the dynamics of Axial civilisations – indeed of struggle and contestation within them.

Whatever the differences in this respect between different Axial civilisations, the very differentiation and distinction between different collectivities and themes of collective identity promulgated by them gave rise within the Axial civilisations to the development of continually reconstructed civil and primordial themes in relation to the sacral civilisational ones; to a multiplicity of combinations of primordial, civil and sacred themes on the local, regional and central levels, and to the concomitant potentiality of continual confrontation between them. No single locus, not even the centres of the most centralised European empires, could effectively monopolise the representation of all these themes on different levels of social organisation, and various collectivities – 'ethnic,' political, civic and religious – with relatively high levels of self-consciousness, each with different conceptions of time and space in relation to their collectivities.

Such continual opening up and potential reconstitution of conceptions of time and space in relation to the constitution of different collectivities was reinforced by the fact that with the institutionalisation of Axial civilisations, a new type of intersocietal and intercivilisational world history emerged. Within all these civilisations there developed, in close connection with the tendencies to reconstruct the world, a certain propensity to expansion, in which ideological, religious impulses were combined with political and to some extent economic ones. Although often radically divergent in terms of their concrete institutionalisation, the political formations which developed in these civilisations – which can be seen as 'ecumenical' – comprised representations and ideologies of quasi-global empire, and some, at moments in their history, even the facts of such empire.

To be sure, political and economic interconnections have existed between different societies throughout human history. Certain conceptions of a universal or world kingdom emerged in many pre-Axial civilisations, such as that of Genghis Khan, and many cultural interconnections developed between them, but only with the institutionalisation of Axial civilisations did a more distinctive ideological and reflexive mode of expansion develop. This mode of expansion also gave rise to an awareness of the possibility of creating 'world histories' encompassing many different societies. The impact of 'world histories' on the constitution of collective consciousness and the identities of the different societies became more clearly visible.

XIV

Tendencies towards such reconstruction developed in several, often overlapping but never fully identical directions. One such direction was generated by the development, inherent in civilisation, of heterodoxies and sectarian tendencies. Such development as seen for instance in the crystallisation of Jewish identity in the Second Temple and in exilic times (Cohen, 1990, pp. 204–224; Eisenstadt and

Giessen, 1995), in the case of the Iconoclasts in the Byzantine Empire (Eisenstadt, 1995, pp. 280–306), in the great divide between Sunni and Shiite Islam (Eisenstadt, 1998, pp. 15–33) and in Protestantism in Europe (Eisenstadt, 1968) also generates strong tendencies towards the redefinition of many of the components of the identities of their respective collectivities – and even gives rise to the construction of new, distinct ones – civilisational, political and ethnic alike.

Another direction of the reconstruction of collective identities inherent in the Axial civilisations was that generated by the development of autonomous political actors who attempted to redefine the scope of political communities in relation to the broader ecumenical ones. The third such direction, often connected with the former yet in principle distinct from it, was that of 'vernacularisation', which we shall discuss in greater detail below.

The directions of change and the concomitant construction of different types of collectivities and collective identities and of different relations between them – especially between the different 'local' 'civic,' ethnic and the civilisational sacral ones with their strong universalistic orientations – and the concomitant modes of reconstruction of primordiality developed in different ways in different Axial civilisations. These differences were shaped first by the basic premises and cultural programmes of these civilisations, especially by the ways in which the relations between attributes of the sacral, cosmic and social order and the basic attributes of the primordial ascriptive collectivities were perceived, in close relation to the distinct cultural programmes that crystallised within them, by the hegemonic elite in different Axial civilisations. Here three typical constellations can be distinguished. One, most fully illustrated by the Jewish case and, in a different way, in the Hindu one, has been characterised by the vesting of the sacral attributes within some such ascriptive collectivities. The second one, most fully illustrated in ideal typical way in Islam and Buddhism, occurs when there is a total disjunction between the two. The third possibility, most fully developed in different parts of Christianity and, in different ways, in Confucianism, arises when these attributes of the 'universalistic' and the primordial collectivities are conceived as mutually relevant and each serves as a referent of the other or a condition of being a member of the other without being totally embedded in it. Such a partial connection usually means that the attributes of the various ascriptive collectivities are seen as one component of the attributes of sacrality, and/or conversely, that the attributes of sacrality constitute one of the attributes of such collectivities.

Second, these directions of change were greatly influenced by the historical experiences and political ecological settings of these civilisations, especially if they were, as was the case in Europe and India, politically decentralised or, as was the case of China, the Byzantine Empire and the Islamic Empires, especially the later ones (the Ottoman and Safavid), more centralised.

XV

Thus to give only a few very preliminary indications, in Europe and India, throughout the Middle Ages, up to the early modern period, there crystallised in Europe different patterns of pluralism, of dispersed centres and collectivities, yet bound together by orientations towards the common civilisational framework (Eisenstadt, 1987b).

In India and Europe, major collectivities and central institutions were continually constituted in a variety of ways, all of which entailed different combinations of the basic terms and codes of collective identity: primordial attachments and traditions, and transcendental as well as traditional civic criteria. The continuous restructuring of centres and collectivities revolved in Europe around the oscillation and tension between the sacred, primordial, and civil dimensions. While, for instance, many collectivities were defined and legitimated mainly in primordial terms, they also attempted to arrogate sacred and civil symbols of legitimation and they all contained strong territorial and political orientations, and such orientations were also shared by many of the sectarian and heterodox groups that developed in Europe.

The relations between the broader civilisational and 'local' primordial collectivities developed in a different way in India, in close relation to its distinct cultural programme. The major difference was the weaker emphasis among them of territorial and political orientations. This was closely related to the fact that the political arena, the arena of rulership, did not constitute in 'historical' India – as it did in monotheistic civilisations or in Confucianism – a major arena of the implementation of the transcendental visions predominant in this civilisation. The conception of Indian civilisation as closely related to these visions and as promulgated by its bearers did not contain, as it did in Europe and in the other monotheistic religions (Judaism and Islam), and even more so in China, a strong political component. It is only lately that there have developed strong tendencies among some political groups to promulgate a specific Hindu political identity and to define Indian civilisation in political terms.

Concomitantly the sectarian movements which developed in the framework of Indian civilisation were not so strongly connected with reconstruction of the political realm as they were in Europe and, as we shall see later, the process of vernacularisation developed in India in a different direction than in Europe (Eisenstadt and Hartman, 1997, pp. 25–44; Dumont, 1970; Heesterman, 1985; Goodwin-Raheja, 1988).

XVI

Different patterns of relations between primordial and sacral themes developed, albeit in different modes, in the more centralised political systems which developed in Axial civilisations – in the different empires that developed in different Axial Civilisations, such as the Roman, Chinese and Byzantine ones (Eisenstadt, 1995) – in all of them strongly influenced by the respective cultural programmes of these civilisations and their distinct historical experience.

In these empires power was much more concentrated and centralised, and accordingly there developed in them, in contrast to the situation in India or Europe, a relatively strong tendency towards the regulation by the centre of the combination of different collective identities that developed in them. Such regulation did not usually entail, with the partial – but indeed only partial – exception of the Byzantine Empire, and of other Christian kingdoms (such as the Ethiopian one or the Armenian one), the appropriation by the centre of all the major – sacral, civil and primordial – themes on the macro-societal level; and certainly not on the local ones. Different 'ethnic' civil, local and even religious communities were allowed to maintain and develop quite far-reaching distinctiveness and autonomy and self-consciousness, which was indeed enhanced by the encounter with the broader civilisational ones in so far as their basic tenets did not negate the basic legitimacy of the Imperial order – as indeed they did in the Jewish case, in its relations to the Hellenistic and Roman Empire (Cohen, 1990; Eisenstadt and Giessen, 1995).

But the ways in which these centralistic tendencies were related to those towards local autonomous formations differed greatly between these empires – very much in line with the basic cultural programmes, the social *imaginaire*, promulgated within them and their distinct historical experience (the detailed analysis of which is beyond the scope of this chapter (Eisenstadt, 1995)).

The construction of collective identity in a non-Axial civilisation – Japan through the Tokugawa period

XVII

Japan provides a most instructive illustration of the crystallisation and continuity of a distinct type of collective identity of a non-Axial civilisation, which was successful in maintaining its distinct collective identity, in a continual confrontation with two Axial civilisations, Confucian and Buddhist, and later with the Western world's ideological, military, political and economic systems.[5]

Early in Japanese history there had already developed a very distinct type of collective consciousness or identity – a political and ethnic identity or collective consciousness, couched in sacral-primordial terms (Kitagawa, 1987; Rozman, 1991; Waida, 1980; Blacker, 1995; Werblowski, 1976). Unlike the collective identities that developed in Europe – or China, Korea or Vietnam – Japan's collective consciousness did not develop within the framework of a universalistic civilisation with strong transcendental orientations. Japan, to be sure, was greatly influenced by its encounter with Chinese Confucianism and Buddhist civilisation. However, in contrast to what happened in the realm of the Axial civilisations, Japan resolved its confrontation with universalistic ideologies by apparently denying them rather than attempting to relate them to its primordial symbols.

This collective consciousness was constructed around the idea of a sacred liturgical community and the uniqueness of the Japanese collectivity or nation. This conception of a divine nation – or, to follow Werblowski's felicitous expression, of sacred particularity – did not, however, entail its being uniquely 'chosen' in terms of a transcendental and universalistic mission. It did not entail the conception of responsibility to God in pursuing such a mission.

Japan's conception of sacred particularity usually held its own when confronted with successive waves of universalistic ideologies (Buddhist, Confucian, then liberal, constitutional, progressivist, or Marxist), all of which seemingly called for a redefinition of the symbols of collective identity. With the exception of small groups of intellectuals, redefinition in a universalist direction did not take hold in the Japanese collective consciousness. Instead the premises of these religions or ideologies were continually reconstructed in Japan and combined with sacral, primordial, and natural terms – indeed very often under the impact of the encounter with Buddhism and Confucianism, and later with Western civilisations.

Reformulations of the Japanese collective identity entailed very intensive orientations to 'others' – China, Asia, the West – and an awareness of other encompassing civilisations claiming some universal validity. But they did not entail the participation of the Japanese collectivity in such civilisations and its reconstruction according to these universalistic premises. The reformulations did not generate the perception of Japan becoming a part, whether central or peripheral, of such a universalistic system. In extreme form they asserted that the Japanese collectivity embodied the pristine values enunciated by the other civilisations and wrongfully appropriated by them. This yielded a very strong tendency – which played an important role in Japanese society from the Meiji up to the contemporary period – to define the Japanese collectivity in terms of 'incomparability', very often couched in racial, genetic terms, or in terms of some special spirituality. Such definitions of the Japanese collectivity made it impossible to become Japanese by conversion. The Buddhist sects or Confucian schools – the most natural channels of conversion – could not perform this function in Japan.

The ability of Japanese elites to promulgate and 'reproduce' such extreme denial of the universalistic components of the Axial age civilisations which were continually impinging on them was closely related to some of the basic characteristics of their elites, the most important of which, from the point of view of our analysis, is that these elites were not strong and autonomous. The common characteristic of these elites and their major coalitions was their embedment in groups and settings (contexts) that were mainly defined in primordial, ascriptive, sacral, and often hierarchical terms, and much less in terms of specialised functions or of universalistic criteria of social attributes (Eisenstadt, 1996a).

True, many cultural actors – priests, monks, scholars and the like – participated in such coalitions. But with very few exceptions, their participation was based on primordial and social attributes and on criteria of achievement and social obligations issuing from the different particular contexts shaping these coalitions, and not on any autonomous criteria rooted in or related to the arenas in which they were active. These arenas – cultural, religious or literary – were themselves ultimately defined in primordial-sacral terms, notwithstanding the fact that many specialised activities developed within them.

Such construction of the overall Japanese collective identity in particularistic primordial-sacral terms allowed, especially in the premodern period, the development of a wide scope for local and regional identities defined mostly also in particularistic primordial terms with lesser emphasis on sacral components – the latter being mostly vested in the centre, and thus enabling a relatively high degree of porousness of these respective boundaries.

Such porousness had already become weaker to some extent in the Tokugawa period when the first attempts on such rigid boundaries of the overall Japanese collectivity emerges, to become even stronger with the crystallisation of the Meiji state (Howell, 1988).

The reconstruction of primordiality in Axial civilisations – the process of vernacularisation

XVIII

One of the most interesting cases of the continual reconstitution of primordialities in relation to the 'broader' universal ecumenical frameworks attendant on the opening up of the spaces between the construction of different collectivities as bearers of different codes of collective identities was the development, in the frameworks of Axial civilisations, in conjunction with political and economic developments within them, of processes of 'vernacularisation' (Eisenstadt, Pollock, Schluchter and Wittrock, 1999).

'Vernacularisation' signifies first of all the challenge to and eventually the supersession of an ecumenical language through the upgrading of a local idiom. Such vernacularisation of ecumenical worlds occurred most visibly and richly, and perhaps earliest, in Southern Asia. Some examples (with dates necessarily simplifying complex matters) are Kannada and Telugu (ninth to eleventh century) in South India, Sinhala (tenth to eleventh century) in Sri Lanka, Java (tenth century) and Tai (fourteenth to fifteenth century) in South East Asia. In all these cases, courtly elites – the Rashtrakutas of Karnataka, the eastern Chalukyas of Andhra, the imperial Cholas in Tamil Nadu and Sri Lanka, in the emergent polities of Kadiri, Singhasari, Majapahit in Java, and Sukhotai and Ayudhya in Thailand – appropriated literary idioms and models from cosmopolitan Sanskrit for the creation of literatures in regional languages, while visibly reordering their notions of political space and their practices of governance.

Vernacularisation entails, on the most general level, a different way of being, articulated in language, from that made available in the great 'ecumenes' of the Axial civilisations. It entails a reconstitution of the relations and tensions between the 'primordial' and the broader civilisational ecumene from the pattern of such relations that developed in the 'classic' ecumene of the Axial age. It entails the confrontation of local languages with historically determinate and self-consciously theorised ecumenical forms – Sanskrit, Latin, Greek, Persian and, in a more complex way, Chinese – and the linkage of the new vernacular cultures thereby created with some political principles, the precise contours of which, it is crucial to realise, cannot be determined a priori. The bearers of vernacularisation are cultural and political elites typically associated with the courtly sphere. 'Vernacular' intellectuals define at once a literary and a political culture in conscious opposition to the larger ecumene; they speak locally and are fully aware that they are doing so, creating texts in local languages, languages that do not travel well, in conscious opposition to the ecumenical, well-travelled languages that had previously characterised text-production.

Vernacularisation comprises in the first instance the communicative enhancement of a language perceived to be local, for purposes of new text production – primarily literary but also documentary – and eventually political governance. This enhancement (or call it upgrading, elaboration, *Ausbau*) will show variation in different cases, but it often proceeds with the appropriation of the symbolic capital of styles and genres from the superposed ecumenical language.

The choice to become vernacular usually entails far-reaching changes in various domains of life. Such vernacularisation entails redefinition of collective identities, and a concomitant transformation of political order; and it is closely related to their changing modes of political self-understanding, of the production of territoriality and of the creation of new social collectivities.

In the political sphere, for example, the critical transformation appears to be a contraction of the domain of governance. This comprises a vision of a smaller world within which power is to be consolidated and exercised, a vision in some cases given shape by a new territorialisation of political space and a new construction of that community that inhabits it. In the sphere of literary culture, especially the creation of new belletristic texts and their grammatical and philological appurtenances, we can perceive the vernacular choice with special clarity.

Vernacularisation usually entails also some claims to a spatial reorganisation of the relevant frame of reference for the cultural practices. Previously undefined spaces are to some extent turned into places specific to the newly crystallising literary language. It entails a new component of 'placed' culture which conceives of itself in relation to the 'trans-area' culture of the cosmopolitan epoch, and to yet smaller zones incorporated in the new vernacular region.

The vernacularisation of literary language (and, possibly, of polity) is also connected with different forms of collective identity formation, with the construction of new genealogies, if any, and entails a new relation between local identities in relationship to earlier cosmopolitan or universalistic visions, as well as between such conceptions and notions of cultural or political authority, although here also a very great variation developed between different societies.

Such tendencies to vernacularisation, with all their institutional implications, especially the growing emphasis on some combination between territoriality and primordial dimensions of collective identity and the concomitant appropriation by them of some of the orientations to universal ecumene, developed in most Axial civilisations. But such parallel development did not necessarily mean, contrary to the assumption of many contemporary studies, that the pattern of relations between territorial boundaries and other components of collective identity (especially the primordial ones) and their relations to the centres of societies pointed in the same direction as in Europe. Indeed these tendencies developed in different Axial civilisations very much in line with some of the differences between them briefly outlined above.

Thus, in Europe, there was a slow but constant growth in the use of vernacular languages and a concomitant shift from imperial types of political order towards more nationally conceived ones. Indologists report a similar growth, in this instance complementing rather than replacing the sacred languages of Sanskrit and Pali in various parts of the Indian subcontinent, but there was no emergence of clearly defined, territorially bound political orders, at least not in the European sense of the term. In East Asia, on the other hand, both classical Chinese language and the imperial order (and the partial parallels in Japan) were maintained in spite of great turmoils during these centuries – thus minimising the possibility of the development of autonomous vernacular traditions and cultural creativities as a basis for new territorial collectivities.

Part III – The construction of collective identities and boundaries in modern societies: the cultural and political programme of modernity

XIX

With the emergence of modernity, of modern civilisation, in close relation to the distinct cultural programme of modernity and to the specific historical context of the development of the institutional contours of modernity, there emerged a new pattern of construction of collective identities. Such construction was characterised by some very specific characteristics, which have greatly influenced the entire modern historical, social science and general discourse about collective identity, especially of nationalism and ethnicity – often presenting them as if they were the natural attributes or forms of collective identities, but which have to be analysed in the broader comparative and analytical framework.

The modern project, the cultural and political programme of modernity as it developed first in the West, in Western and Central Europe, entailed distinct ideological as well as institutional premises. It entailed a very distinct shift in the conception of human agency, of its autonomy, and of its place in the flow of time. The core of this programme has been that the premises and legitimation of the social, ontological and political order were no longer taken for granted; and the concomitant development of a very intensive reflexivity about the basic ontological premises as well as around the bases of social and political order and authority – a reflexivity which was shared even by the most radical critics of this programme, who in principle denied the legitimacy of such reflexivity, and of a concomitant development of continual struggles and contestations about the construction of the major dimensions of social order, including the political order and that of collectivities and collective identities.

The central core of this cultural programme has been possibly most successfully formulated by Weber. To follow James D. Faubion's exposition of Weber's conception of modernity:

Weber finds the existential threshold of modernity in a certain deconstruction: of what he speaks of as the 'ethical postulate that the world is a God-ordained, and hence somehow meaningfully and ethically oriented cosmos.'

. . . What he asserts – what in any event might be extrapolated from his assertions – is that the threshold of modernity has its epiphany precisely as the legitimacy of the postulate of a divinely preordained and fated cosmos has its decline; that modernity emerges, that one or another modernity can emerge, only as the legitimacy of the postulated cosmos ceases to be taken for granted and beyond reproach. Countermoderns reject that reproach, believe in spite of it. . . .

. . . One can extract two theses: Whatever else they may be, modernities in all their variety are responses to the same existential problematic. The second: whatever else they may be, modernities in all their variety are precisely those responses that leave the problematic in question intact, that formulate visions of life and practice neither beyond nor in denial of it but rather within it, even in deference to it. . . . (Faubion, 1993, pp. 113–115)

It is because of the fact that all such responses leave the problematic intact that the reflexivity which developed in the programme of modernity went beyond that which crystallised in the Axial civilisations. The reflexivity that developed in the modern programme focused not only on the possibility of different interpretations of the transcendental visions and basic ontological conceptions prevalent in a society or societies, but came to question the very givenness of such visions and of the institutional patterns related to them. It gave rise to the awareness of the existence of a multiplicity of such visions and patterns and of the possibility that such visions and conceptions can indeed be contested (Eisenstadt, 1983). Concomitantly the programme entailed a conception of the future in which various possibilities which can be realised by autonomous human agency – or by the march of history – are open.

Such awareness was closely connected with two central components of the modern project, emphasised in the early studies of modernisation by Dan Lerner and later by Alex Inkeles. The first such component is the recognition, among those becoming and being modernised and modern – as illustrated by the famous story in Lerner's book about the grocer and the shepherd – of the possibility of undertaking a great variety of roles beyond any fixed or

ascriptive ones, and the concomitant receptivity to different communications and messages which promulgate such open possibilities
and visions. Second, there is the recognition of the possibility of
belonging to wider translocal, possibly also changing, orders and
communities (Lerner, 1958; Inkeles and Smith, 1974).

In parallel with this, this programme entailed a very strong
emphasis on the autonomous participation of members of society
in the constitution of social and political order and on the
autonomous access, indeed, of all members of society to these orders
and their centres. Out of the conjunction of these conceptions there
developed the belief in the possibility of the active formation of
society by conscious human activity.

The modern cultural programme also entailed a radical transformation of the conceptions and premises of the political order, of the
constitution of the political arena, and of the characteristics of the
political process and of the construction of collectivities – all of
which became foci of contestation and of struggle (Eisenstadt, 1999a;
1999b, pp. 51–75).

The core of the new conceptions was the breakdown of traditional
legitimation of the political order, the concomitant opening up of
different possibilities of construction of such order, and the
consequent contestation about the ways in which political order was
constructed by human actors, combining orientations of rebellion
and intellectual antinomianism, together with strong orientations
to centre-formation and institution-building, and giving rise to social
movements and movements of protest as a continual component of
the political process.

XX

This programme entailed also a very distinctive mode of construction of the boundaries of collectivities and collective identities. In
some, even if certainly not total, contrast to the situation in the Axial
civilisations, collective identities were not taken as given or as preordained by some transcendental vision and authority, or by
perennial customs.

At the same time the most distinct characteristic of the construction of modern collectivities, very much in line with the general core
characteristics of modernity, was that such construction was continually problematised in reflexive ways, and constituted a focus of
continual struggle and contestation.

Such continual contestation was borne by distinct social actors – whether they were political activists, politically active intellectuals, or distinct social movements, above all national or nationalistic movements – oriented to the construction of such new collectivities. Indeed one of the most distinctive characteristics of the continual process of reconstruction of modern collective identities was the centrality in this process of special social and political activists, and above all of organisations bearing distinct visions of collective identities and ideologies, and mobilising wide sectors of the population, the best illustrations of which are of course distinct social movements, especially the national or nationalistic ones, as well as the closely related promulgation of distinct ideologies, above all national and also modern ethnic ones, of collective identity.

It was these activists and movements that were the bearers of contestation and struggle, often couched in highly ideological terms, around the far-reaching transformation, in comparison with the preceding Axial periods, of the codes of collective identity and of the relation between them (Eisenstadt, 1999a; 1999b).

Among the most important such transformations of the codes of collective identity attendant on the development of modernity, and which first emerged in Europe, was the development of new, mainly secular definitions, yet couched in highly ideological and absolutised terms, of each of the components of collective identity – the civil, primordial and universalistic and transcendental 'sacred' ones; the growing importance of the civil and procedural components thereof, and of a continual tension among these components; and a very strong emphasis, in the construction and institutionalisation of the collective identities, on territorial boundaries.

Concomitantly there developed very intensive tendencies towards the establishment of a very strong connection between the construction of the political order and that of the major 'encompassing' collectivities, a connection that later became epitomised in the model of the modern nation state. The crystallisation of the modern nation state and its institutionalisation entailed the emphasis on congruence between the cultural and political identities of the territorial population; strong tendencies to attribute charismatic characteristics to the newly constructed collectivities and centres; the promulgation, by the centre, of strong symbolic and affective commitments of members of society to the centre and the collectivity; and a close relationship between the centre and the more primordial dimensions of human existence and social life, as well as the civil and sacred dimensions. Such relationships did not entail in most modern societies – with the partial exception as we shall see of Japan – the denial of the validity of the broader, civilisational orientations. Rather there developed strong tendencies of the new national collectivities to become also the repositories and regulators of these broader orientations – but at the same time there developed in them continual oscillation and tension between the national and the broader universalistic ones.

The central characteristic of the model of the modern state, especially the nation state, was the strong emphasis on cultural-political homogeneity of the population within the territorial boundaries. A central focus of such homogeneity, closely related to the basic premises of the cultural programme of modernity, was the image of the 'civilised man' as analysed by Norbert Elias and, if in a more highly exaggerated way, by Michel Foucault, and, in a more systematic way, by John Meyer, Ron Jepperson and others; and as presented above all both in the great works of modern literature, especially in the great novels, as well as in the more 'popular' literature which thrived in this period, in all of which the *mission civilisatrice* of modernity, of the modern period were promulgated (Meyer and Jepperson, 2000; Meyer, Boli and Thomas, 1987, pp. 12–38; Meyer, Boli, Thomas and Ramirez, 1997).

A very central component in the construction of collective identities was the self-perception of a society as 'modern', as bearer of the distinct cultural and political programme – and its relations from this point of view to other societies – be it those societies which claim to be – or are seen as – bearers of this programme, or various 'others'.

Concomitantly the images and attributes of such homogeneities and modernity have been promulgated, as John Meyer, Ron Jepperson and others have shown, through a series of very strong socialising agencies, such as schools, often the army, the major media and the like – all of them emphasising very strongly the idea or ideal of a politically and culturally homogeneous entity (Meyer and Jepperson, 2000; Meyer, Boli and Thomas, 1987, pp. 12–38; Meyer, Boli, Thomas and Ramirez, 1997).

A central aspect of such homogeneity was the conception of citizenship which entailed a direct relation of members of the collectivity to the state, unmediated by membership of any other collectivities, and the tendency to relegate the identities of other collectivities – religious, ethnic, regional and the like – to the private spheres as against the unitary public sphere which was seen as constituting the major arena in which the relations of citizens to the state and to the national collectivity were played out. The centres of these states become the regulators of the relations between the central identity and the various secondary, primordial or 'sacred' universalistic identities – religious, ethnic, regional and the like.

Concomitantly the distinctive visions of the new modern collectivities, above all, indeed, of the nation state, entailed the promulgation of distinctive collective memories in which the universal, often 'sacred' components, rooted in the universalistic components of the cultural programme of modernity, and the particularistic national ones, emphasising their territorial, historical and cultural specifities, came together – albeit in different ways in different societies, but constituting in all of them one of the major and continual foci of tension and contestation (Meyer and Jepperson, 2000; Meyer, Boli and Thomas, 1987, pp. 12–38; Meyer, Boli, Thomas and Ramirez, 1997).

These different orientations of overall collectivities were often symbolised or defined in distinctive gender terms – with the state, with its civic components as well as with the organisation of political force, often portrayed in masculine terms, and the nation, with strong primordial, nurturing and vitalistic components, in feminine ones. These two gendered symbols were usually brought together under the canopy of the overarching nation state, yet at the same time they constituted a focus of continual tension and of distinct, potentially competing identities.

Yet, despite the strong tendency to conflate, in the ideal model of the nation state, 'state' and 'nation' there developed within them strong tensions between on the one hand the 'state', with its emphasis on territoriality and the seeming potentially universalistic notions of citizenship; and on the other hand the 'nation' – with its more 'closed' definitions of membership with strong primordial components.

Thus, paradoxically, one central aspect of the constitution of modern collective identities, closely related to the tension between 'citizenship' and 'membership' of a primordial community, between state and nation, was also the construction of a growing tendency to a sharper delineation of the boundaries of different ethnic, regional and even religious communities, transforming the relative porousness of former semi-ethnic territorial, linguistic or kin boundaries into more formalised ones and with strong political orientations. Although in principle such different primordial communities were to be brought together under the overall canopy of the nation state, in fact there developed a potential for the continual development of a multiplicity of such distinct collectivities with strong potential political orientations – which needless to say varied greatly between different societies.

XXI

The promulgation and constitution of the model of the nation state entailed a very intensive construction of various commemorative artefacts, such as monuments, and special occasions in which collective memories were commemorated, such as national holidays, in which the sacral dimensions and the new electivity of 'chosenness' of the new collectivities were promulgated in various societies in different mixtures of revolutionary universalistic republican or 'romantic' primordial themes, and in which the centres of the nation states attempted to appropriate and monopolise all these themes, and at the same time to marginalise other – local, regional or ethnic – promulgations thereof (Spillman, 1997; Corse, 1997).

XXII

The model of the nation state, closely related to some of the basic ontological premises of the cultural programme of modernity, has become in many ways hegemonic in the modern international systems and frameworks that developed in conjunction with the crystallisation of the modern order (Meyer and Jepperson, 2000; Meyer, Boli and Thomas, 1987, pp. 12–38; Meyer, Boli, Thomas and Ramirez, 1997).

But despite its hegemonic standing, the model of the nation state was never homogeneous, internally within any single society or across different societies. Even in Europe there developed a great variety of nation states.

One of the most important aspects of such variety was the relative importance in them of the different codes or themes of collective identity, i.e. of the primordial and civil and sacral (religious or secular) and the different combinations thereof. The second aspect of such variety was the extent to which there developed totalistic as against multifaceted visions of those basic collective identities – i.e. the extent to which the basic codes and the ways in which primordial-national, civil and universalistic orientations were interwoven in them, and especially the extent to which in the historical experience of those societies none of these dimensions is totally absolutised or set up by their respective carriers against the other dimensions, or contrariwise, the extent to which there developed rather multifaceted patterns of collective identity.

In all modern European societies there developed a continual tension or confrontation between the primordial components of such identity, reconstructed in such modern terms as nationalism and ethnicity, and the modern, as well as more traditional religious, universalistic and civil components, as well as among the latter ones. The mode of interweaving of these different components of collective identity, which varied greatly among different European societies, greatly influenced the tension between pluralistic and totalistic tendencies of the cultural and political programme of modernity that developed in these societies.

Such different modes of construction of modern collective identities were promulgated by the many political activists and intellectuals, especially the major social movements in modern societies. It is such movements of protest that continually developed which promulgated the different antinomies and contradictions of the cultural programmes of modernity, selected and reinterpreted different themes thereof, and promulgated different programmes of modernity. Each of these movements promulgated a distinct interpretation of the cultural and political programme of modernity. The liberal and various reformist-socialist programmes of modernity constituted variants of the pluralistic renderings of the cultural and political programmes of modernity while the radical-socialist-communist and the fascist promulgated radical revision or reinterpretation.

Most of these movements were international even if their bases or roots were in specific countries and they constituted continual mutual reference points. The more successful among such movements have continually crystallised in distinct ideological and institutional patterns which often became identified with specific countries but whose reach went far beyond them.

It was indeed one of the most distinct characteristics of the modern scene that the construction of collective boundaries and consciousness could also become a focus of distinct social movements – the national or nationalistic ones; while in many modern societies, as for instance England, France and Sweden, the crystallisation of new national collectivities and identities, of different types of nation states, took place.

Without the national movements playing an important role, the potentiality of such movements existed in all modern societies. In some – in Central and Eastern Europe, and in some Asian and African, and to some extent Latin-American societies – they played a crucial role in the development of nation states.

XXIII

It was within the framework of these tensions, and above all those between pluralistic multifaceted and absolutising totalising visions, that there crystallised the specific modes of the destructive potentialities inherent in the modern cultural programme. These destructive potentialities became most fully manifest in the ideologisation and sanctification of violence, terror and wars which first became apparent in the French Revolution and later in the Romantic movements and in the combination of such ideologisation with the construction and institutionalisation of the nation states; in the fact that the nation states became the most important agent – and arena – of constitution of citizenship and of collective identity; in the crystallisation of the modern European state system and of European expansion beyond Europe, especially under the aegis of imperialism and of colonialism, which were very often legitimised in terms of some of the components of the cultural programmes of modernity – all of which became reinforced by technologies of war and communication.

These destructive forces, the 'traumas' of modernity which undermined its great promises, emerged clearly during and after the First World War in the Armenian genocide and became even more visible in the Second World War, above all in the Holocaust, all of them shaking the naive belief in the inevitability of progress and of the conflation of modernity with progress. These destructive forces of modernity were paradoxically ignored or bracketed out from the discourse of modernity in the first two or three decades after the Second World War. Lately they have re-emerged in a most frightening way on the contemporary scene in the new 'ethnic' conflicts in many of the former republics of Soviet Russia, in Sri Lanka, in Kosovo, and in a most terrible way in Cambodia and in African countries, such as Rwanda (Eisenstadt, 1996b).

It was insofar as the primordial components were relatively 'peacefully' interwoven, in the construction of their respective collective identities, with the civil and universalistic ones in multi-faceted ways, that the kernels of modern barbarism and the exclusivist tendencies inherent in them were minimised. In England, Holland, Switzerland and in the Scandinavian countries, the crystallisation of modern collective identity was characterised by a relatively close interweaving – even if never bereft of tensions – of the primordial and religious components with the civil and universalistic ones, without the former being denied, allowing a relatively wide scope for pluralistic arrangements. Concomitantly in these countries there developed also relatively weak confrontations between the secular orientations of the Enlightenment – which often contained strong deistic orientations – and the strong religious orientations of various Protestant sects.

As against the situations in these societies, in those societies (as was the case in Central Europe, above all in Germany and in most countries of Southern and Central Europe) in which the construction of the collective identities of the modern nation state was connected with continual confrontations between the primordial and the civil and universalistic, as well as between 'traditional' religious and modern universalistic components, there developed a stronger tendency towards crisis and the breakdown of the different types of constitutional arrangement. In the more authoritarian regimes, such primordial components were promulgated in 'traditional' authoritarian terms – in the more totalitarian fascist or national-socialist movements, in strongly racist ones – while the absolutised universalistic orientations were promulgated by various 'leftist' Jacobin movements.

France, especially modern republican France from the Third Republic on, but with strong roots in the preceding periods, constitutes a very important – probably the most important – illustration of the problems arising out of continual confrontations between Jacobin and traditional components in the legitimation of modern regimes – even within the framework of relatively continuous polity and collective identity and boundaries. The case of France illustrates that under such conditions, pluralistic tendencies and arrangements do not develop easily, giving rise to the consequent turbulence of the institutionalisation of a continual constitutional democratic regime (Eisenstadt, 1999a).

XXIV

The construction of different modes of collective identity has been connected in Europe – and beyond Europe – with specific institutional conditions; the most important among them being the flexibility of the centres, the mutual openness of elites, and their relations to broader social strata. There developed in Europe, and later in other societies, a close elective affinity between the absolutising types of collective identity and various types of absolutist regimes and rigid centres, and between the multifaceted pattern of collective identity in which the primordial, civil, and sacred components were continually interwoven with the development of relatively open and flexible centres and of mutual openings between various strata. It was the concomitant development of relatively strong but flexible and open centres, multifaceted modes of collective identity, and autonomous access of major strata to the centre that was of crucial importance in the development of a distinct type of civil society – a society that was to a large extent autonomous *from* the state but at the same time autonomous *in* the state, had autonomous access to the state and participated in formulating the rules of the political game; and it was such conditions that made possible the minimisation of the tendencies to barbarism and exclusion (Eisenstadt, 1999a).

XXV

In Europe these variations in the construction of collective identity were set within the frameworks of some of the basic parameters of European historical experience and of the civilisational premises thereof. The story was different in the countries beyond Europe, with the expansion of modernity beyond Europe. While the basic model of the nation state and its emphasis on territorial boundaries and cultural-political homogeneity has indeed become the predominant one throughout most parts of the world, the variations within it, and their differences from the European models, became even more pronounced.

This could already be seen in the Americas, where there crystallised in different American civilisations – especially in North America (the United States in particular) and the different Latin-American countries – distinctive patterns of collective identity. Despite the fact that there developed far-reaching differences between these different American civilisations, which constitute in some ways mirror images of one another, they shared also some common characteristics rooted in the processes of European settlement and colonisation and in the encounter with the various native populations and the populations of black slaves translocated from Africa.

One of the most important differences which distinguishes American civilisations from both European and Asian societies was the relative weakness of primordial criteria in the definition of their collective identities. In the initial phases of the crystallisation of American civilisation, the primordial attachments of the settlers were rooted in their European countries of origin and to a much lesser extent in the new environment. With the passing of time and the consolidation of the new colonies, strong attachments developed to the new territory, but these attachments were defined in different terms from those that had crystallised progressively in Europe. There developed a much weaker combination of territorial, historial and linguistic elements as components of collective identity. By sharing the respective languages with their countries of origin, the very definition of primordial distinctiveness was unrelated to common language in both North America and Spanish Latin America (less so in Brazil and Paraguay). A relative shift to administrative criteria of territoriality was thus effected from the beginning of colonisation, with important implications for the later development of 'natural' boundaries (Herzog, 1998).

The encounter with the native populations did also generate new possibilities and possible confrontations with the various 'primordial' components – traditions, languages, communities – but these created distinct problems of delimitation of the identity of the settlers in relation to the indigenous population, while at the same time there developed continual tensions between the English, French, Spanish or Portuguese born in the Americas and those who continued to 'represent' the mother country or came as the representatives of the respective crowns.

One of the most important differences between the various American civilisations and the Asian ones from the middle and end of the nineteenth century was that the confrontation with modernity, with 'the West', did not entail, for the settlers in the Americas, a confrontation with an alien culture imposed from the outside – but rather with their own other origins. Such encounters were often combined with a search to find their own distinct place within the broader framework of European, or Western, civilisation.

Concomitantly, the orientations to the 'mother' country, to the centres of Western culture, later to cultural centres in Europe – constituted continual models and reference points, to an extent probably unprecedented in any other society, including the Asian ones in their later encounter with the West (Eisenstadt, 2001; Roniger and Herzog, 2000). But beyond these common parameters of the construction of collective identity that developed on the American continent there developed great differences between the different Americas.

Although originally the Spanish (and Portuguese) empires aspired to establish a unified homogeneous Hispanic (or Portuguese) collective identity focused on the motherland, in fact, in Latin America, a much more diversified situation developed. From relatively early on there developed multiple components of collective consciousness and identity – an overall Spanish (or Portuguese) one, an overall Catholic one and various local Creole and 'native' ones.

Side by side with the formal hierarchical principles, there developed multiple continuously changing social spaces structured according to different principles and identities, with relatively shifting boundaries and with the possibility of the incorporation of many of these identities into the central arena.

To follow Herzog and Roniger:

The first theme is the malleability of collective identities in the region. Political and religious institutions introduced by the Spaniards in the sixteenth century were, by the eighteenth century, adopted by indigenous communities in order to forge a native identity. The characterization of people as belonging to a certain collectivity could be claimed if and when membership allowed access to resources and privileges. The nature of the community itself could change with changing circumstances and needs. Similarly, the emergence of states in Spanish America formed part of a greater liberal revolution. It embodied the will of social and political actors to assume the representation of the people, thus opening a process of multiple fragmentation. In this context, the creation of states and, once they existed, of nations is still an ongoing process, shaped by the international context – and to no less an extent by the experiences of mobilization during the independence wars, the civil wars and the political fighting that led to the state's consolidation. Although not analyzed in this volume, the contrasting experience of Brazil lends support to the importance of core centers and symbols of collective identity (primarily, the role of a legitimate imperial family and other factors, such as the shared education of regional elites) for maintaining the unity of a country of continental extension.

The second point on which the authors coincide is the prevalence of multiple patterns of identity construction at the communal levels, in ethnic terms, as local networks and coalitions and in terms of race and class. State formations in the region have been crucial for defining citizenship and establishing ground rules for participation in public spheres and access to institutional resources and recognition. However, state formations have been persistently contested. Different collective identities have developed that posed a serious challenge to the logic of the nation-state – for instance, the definition carried out by territorially concentrated minorities wishing to maintain a separate identity, such as the Miskitu Indians. Others have been submerged within the very institutional structures functioning at the level of state but also 'betwixt and between' them, such as coalitions and networks, associations and congregations. Thus, their intertwined presence is crucial for understanding the gaps between the ideal images and practices of public life throughout the region; in parallel, it is also important for tracing the various processes of politicization of identities and mobilization that challenge existing patterns of exclusion and institutional control. (Herzog and Roniger, 2000, pp. 303–304)

But the concrete ways in which such constellations of identities crystallised varied greatly between different Latin-American societies. To give only a few tentative illustrations: the Mexican Revolution was important in seeking to construct a collective identity that would embrace both the Creole/Mexican-Spanish and the Indians; as against this, in South America the Indians were marginalised much like the native American Indians. Brazil is a third type of collective identity, at least officially: native Indians were marginalised, but there crystallized a collective Brazilian identity allowing for racial intermixing between Europeans and Africans.[6]

XXVI

By contrast with Latin America, the pattern of collective identity that crystallised in the United States was eventually defined in inclusive ideological, universalistic, non-primordial and non-historical terms. It entailed the delineation of very sharp boundaries of the collectivity, informed by the basic premises of the American civil religion. This collective identity grew in part out of the transformation of the

'messianic' and millennial strands of the early American sociopolitical endeavour.

A crucial aspect of the new American civilisation was the construction of a mould based on a political ideology strongly rooted in
the Puritan religious conceptions, in a Lockean political orientation
and in the Enlightenment. The Puritan conceptions entailed a strong
emphasis on the special covenant between God and the chosen
people, a covenant oriented to the creation of a deeply religious polity
as it took shape in the late nineteenth century (Heimart, 1966; Becker,
1958; Haskins, 1960; Little, 1969; Hofstadter, 1972; Seligman, 1982).

The polity of the United States was characterised by a strongly
egalitarian, achievement-oriented individualism; republican
liberties, with the almost total denial of the symbolic validity of
hierarchy; disestablishment of official religion, beginning at the
federal level; basically antistatist premises; and a quasi-sanctification
of the economic sphere. Religious sentiment and religious values
imparted a strong 'messianic' and millennial dimension to the early
American sociopolitical endeavour, made both solidarity and individualism central components of collective identity, and together
with the antistatist orientation gave rise to a distinct new civil
religion (Bellah, 1970; 1975; Marty, 1987).

Primordial orientations or hierarchical principles could be
permitted in secondary informal locations, but not as components of
the central premises and symbols of society. Thus, the United States
civil religion could not easily accommodate 'native' Americans, with
their overwhelming primordial identity, completely unrelated to the
new ideological framework, and claiming a totality of their own.
Hence native Americans were virtually excluded from the new collectivity. While seemingly recognised as distinct nations, in reality
they were at least until recently relegated, in a highly repressive way,
to marginalised positions in the American collectivity.

At the same time a distinct attitude developed toward those –
especially ethnic – immigrant groups which were willing to accept
the basic terms of the American collective identity, and the basic
premises of American civilisation. Given the weakness of primordial
components in the construction of an American collective identity,
there was scope for tolerance, much greater than in Europe, not only
of religious diversity, but also of groups which defined their
secondary place in terms of primordial components. Such tolerance,
of course, was predicated on the acceptance of the basic ideological-
political premises of American civilisation. But the boundaries of the

social spaces of such groups were clearly delineated as secondary, even if such boundaries changed in different periods.

XXVII

Yet another distinct pattern of modern statehood closely connected with the model of the nation state was that of the revolutionary territorial state. Already in post-revolutionary France some components of such a state – especially the very strong emphasis on the universalistic mission thereof, embodied even to some extent in the *Code Napoléon* – were present. The specific characteristics of such models of the modern state became fully crystallised with the establishment of the Soviet and later the Chinese communist regimes. The basic legitimation of these regimes was radically transformed from a 'traditional' to a modern totalitarian one, with an even stronger emphasis on the territorial and on the homogenising tendencies thereof – with far-reaching impact on the construction of collective identities (Eisenstadt, 1992; Arnason, 1993).

The ultimate legitimation of the communist regimes and their elites was in their construal as the bearers of their respective salvationist vision and mission, which were presented as the ultimate pinnacle of the universalistic vision of the modern programme of the Enlightenment, with very strong revolutionary mobilisatory themes and policies. The communist regimes appropriated the major themes of this programme and presented their regimes as the ultimate bearers of the pristine vision of such instrumental vision, of progress, of technology, of the mastery of nature and of the rational, emancipatory restructuring of society.

These cultural-political visions and programmes promulgated in these revolutions and regimes – especially of the Soviet regime in Russia, and to a smaller extent in China – entailed also the construction of a specific pattern of cultural collective identity attendant on the encounter of non-Western European societies within the West and with modernity, and a very specific mode of selection, appropriation and reinterpretation of the major components of the cultural programme of modernity and of the antinomies inherent in it. In this respect the Soviet communist regime – to a much greater extent than the Chinese – promulgated a very far-reaching denial of the claims by the Slavophiles or of their parallels in Asian countries, which promulgated the total opposition to the Enlightenment and to instrumental reason, technology schemes and mastery of the environment, as against the authentic spirit or tradition of their respective societies.

The Soviet regime aimed at the total transformation of the symbols of collective identity and of the institutional structure of society and at the establishment of a new social order, based on the revolutionary universalistic ideological tenets, in principle transcending any primordial, national or ethnic units – even if not denying their partial legitimacy.

The collective identities promulgated by the communist regimes were in principle based on universalistic themes allowing for national identities as a secondary one; even if in fact the Russian (or the Han in China) components were predominant in the construction of their collective identities. On the one hand these regimes allowed for some expressions of distinct 'ethnic' or national themes, but in principle these components were subsumed under the universalistic salvationist ones – although they were indeed often conflated, and especially in situations of crisis, with particularistic ones. Moreover, these particular orientations were highly controlled, being defined by the authorities in the official census, but at the same time, by virtue of such control, generating stronger collective consciousness among their members. Such particularistic identities continued to be very strong in a secondary or subterranean way, and they were to acquire greater importance, in a highly restructured way, with the dismemberment of the Soviet regimes; but so long as the Soviet regime was intact they were secondary. In China, in the post-Mao period, these components acquired greater importance.

XXVIII

The patterns of modern collective identity that developed beyond the West and beyond the revolutionary states showed an ever greater variability, which it would be beyond the scope of this chapter to analyse in any detail. To give one very preliminary illustration, that of Japan, the first non-Western but also non-Axial society to become fully 'modernised' (Eisenstadt, 1994; 1996a). The collective identity and its institutional implications promulgated by the Meiji made Japan appear to be the most pristine nation state. Yet the construction of the collective identity of the Meiji state differed greatly from the European one, the core of this difference being that it was not based on a continual confrontation with a universal civilisation of which it considered itself to be a part. Unlike Europe, where the construction of national ideologies usually entailed strong tensions with universalistic religious orientations, no such tensions developed in principle in the ideology of *kokutai*. At most, this ideology emphasised that the Japanese nation, by virtue of its primordial and sacral qualities, epitomized to a much higher degree than any other civilisation those very virtues which were extolled by these other civilisations, the Chinese one earlier on, and the Western one in the modern era. Thus in sharp contrast to almost all the other, especially European, cases, tensions between the universalistic and the different primordial components inherent in the construction of the collective identity of the modern nation state were in Japan very muted.

A very interesting illustration of the persistence of the 'primordial' conceptions of the Japanese collectivity in modern times can be found in the attitude of some very distinguished Japanese leftist intellectuals in the twentieth century to Marxism. In common with many Chinese intellectuals of such disposition, these Japanese intellectuals, such as Kotuku or Kawakawi Hajime, attempted to de-emphasise the 'materialistic' dimensions of Marxism and infuse them with 'spiritual' values, with values of spiritualistic regeneration. But while most of the Chinese intellectuals tended to emphasise the transcendental and universalistic themes of 'classical' Confucianism, the Japanese ones emphasised the specifically Japanese spiritual essence (Hoston, 1989; 1990).

Very interesting and significant in this context are the ways in which modern Japanese historians, following the major tenets of modern Western historiography, attempted to place Japan within the context of world history. As Stefan Tanaka has recently shown in his incisive analysis, most of these historians, who naturally refused to accept the Western characterisation of the 'Orient', first redefined Japan as autonomous, equal to the West. Yet faced with the problem of their own relation to China and its disintegration, most of them ended by taking Japan out of the 'Orient', making its history distinct, separate and unique, and often portraying Japan as the bearer of the pristine values which other civilisations – Western or Chinese – claimed as their own (Tanaka, 1993) without on the whole attempting to proselytise the Japanese collective identity beyond its basic particularistic primordial bodies.

At the same time there developed in the Meiji state the appropriation by new centres of the major attributes of primordial solidary, combined with strong tendencies towards the national and civic homogenisation of both the central and local levels, giving rise to a greater formalisation of the defined initial collective identities and boundaries thereof (Howell, 1988).

Part IV – The contemporary scene – beyond the hegemony of the nation and revolutionary state model

XXIX

These multiple and divergent modernities of the 'classical' age of modernity crystallised during the nineteenth century, and above all the first six or seven decades of the twentieth century, in the different territorial national and revolutionary states and social movements that developed in Europe, in the Americas, and in Asian and African societies until after the Second World War. These contours – institutional and symbolic, ideological contours of the modern national and revolutionary states and movements which were seen as the epitome of modernity – have changed drastically in the contemporary scene with the intensification of tendencies towards globalisation, as manifest in the growing autonomy of world capitalist forces, in intensive international migration, and in the concomitant development on an international scale of social problems, such as prostitution and delinquency, all of which reduce the control of the nation state over its own economic and political affairs, despite the continual strengthening of the 'technocratic' rational secular policies in various arenas, such as education and family planning. At the same time the nation states lost some of their – always only partial – monopoly of internal and international violence to many local and international groups of separatists or terrorists, without any nation state or the concerted activities of nation states being able to control the continual recurrences of such violence.[7]

Above all, the ideological and symbolic centrality of the national and revolutionary state, its being perceived as the charismatic locus of the major components of the cultural programme of modernity and of collective identity and as the major regulator of the various secondary identities, became weakened, and new political and social and civilisational visions and visions of collective identity developed. These new visions and identities were promulgated by several types of new social movements. Such 'new' social movements, which developed in most Western countries, such as the women's and ecological movements, all closely related to or rooted in the student and anti-Vietnam War movements of the late 1960s and 1970s, were indicative of a more general shift in many countries in the world, 'capitalist' and communist (such as China): a shift from movements oriented towards the state to more local ones. The fundamentalist movements which developed in Muslim, Protestant and Jewish communities, and the communal religious movements which developed for instance in the Hinduist and Buddhist ones, and the various particularistic 'ethnic' movements and identities which constituted deformations of the classical model of national or revolutionary states gathered momentum, especially in the last two decades of the twentieth century in the former republics of the Soviet Union, but also in most terrifying ways in Africa and in part of the Balkans, especially in the former Yugoslavia.

One of the most significant manifestations of such transformation of the model of the nation state on the contemporary scene is the resurrection, or rather radical transformation (as it were) of hitherto 'subdued' identities – ethnic, local, regional, and transnational – and their movement into the centres of their respective societies, as well as often also into the international arena. Concomitantly there have developed new types of social settings or sectors – important examples of there being new diasporas and minorities. The common denominator of many of these new movements and minorities is that they do not see themselves as bound by the strong homogenising cultural premises of the classical model of the nation state – especially by the places allotted to them in the public spheres of such states. It is not that they do not want to be 'domiciled' in their respective countries. Indeed part of their struggle is to become so domiciled, but on new terms – as compared to classical models of assimilation. Moreover while the identities are often very local and particularistic, they tend also to be strongly transnational, often rooted in the great religions – Islam, Buddhism, and different branches of Christianity, which are reconstructed in modern ways (Eickelman, 1993; Piscatori, 1987). In a parallel manner, separatist, local or regional settings, develop direct connections with transnational frameworks and organisations such as the European Union.

Thus in these, and in many other settings, there crystallised new types of collective identities often promulgated by some of the movements mentioned above, which went beyond the models of the nation state and which were no longer focused on it. Many of these hitherto seemingly 'subdued' identities – ethnic, regional, local and transnational alike – moved, albeit naturally in a highly reconstructed way, into the centres of their respective societies and also often into the international arena. They contested the hegemony of the older homogenising programmes, claiming their own autonomous places in central institutional arenas – whether in educational programmes or in public communications and the media – and very often they also made far-reaching claims with respect to the redefinition of citizenship and of the rights and entitlements connected with it – as illustrated, for instance, in the recent debate about *laïcité* in France – both for the construction of new public spaces and for the reconstruction of the symbols of collective identity (Eisenstadt, 1999b). In these settings local dimensions were often brought together in new ways beyond the model of the classical nation state, with transnational ones such as for instance the European Union; or with broad religious identities – many of them rooted in the great religions such as Islam, or Buddhism, or different branches of Christianity, but reformulated in new modern ways.

In parallel there took place continuous shifts in the relative hegemony of different centres of modernity – first in Europe and the United States, moving to East Asia – shifts which became continually connected with concomitant growing contestation between such centres about their presumed hegemonic standing (Eisenstadt, 1999b).

The contours and impact of these changes differ between different societies – even between European ones. These differences are influenced, *inter alia*, by the extent of the homogeneity in particular European countries, from a high degree of homogeneity as in France, to a more multifaceted society as in the United Kingdom and the Netherlands; by the place of religious symbols and traditions in the construction of nations' identities; by different ways in which State–Church–religion relations have been worked out in these societies. These differences can be seen also in the ways in which such different minority groups are designated in different European societies, 'strangers' in Germany, 'racial minorities' in England, 'immigrants' in France, 'ethnic and cultural minorities' in the Netherlands, and so on.

XXX

One of the major bearers of such transformation of the discourse of modernity in relation to the construction of collective identities has been the numerous fundamentalist movements and the communal religious movements which have been portrayed – and in many ways have also presented themselves – as *diametrically* opposed to the modern programme. But a closer examination of these movements presents a much more complex picture. First is the fact that the extreme fundamentalist movements evince distinct modern Jacobin characteristics which paradoxically have much in common – sometimes in a sort of mirror image way – with the communist ones, albeit combined with very strong anti-Western and anti-Enlightenment ideologies. Both these movements promulgate distinct visions formulated in the terms of the discourse of modernity, and attempt to appropriate modernity on their own terms; and they advocate the total reconstruction of personality and of individual and collective identities by conscious human, above all political, action, and the construction of new personal and collective identities entailing the total submergence of the individual in the totalistic community.

There were, of course, radical differences in the respective visions of the two types of Jacobin – the communist and the fundamentalist – movements and regimes, above all in their attitudes to modernity, and in their criticism thereof, in their attitudes to the basic antinomies of modernity and in the concomitant rejection and interpretation by them of different components of the cultural and political programmes of modernity – or, in other words, in their interpretations of modernity and their attempts to appropriate it. But they all evince a strong preoccupation with modernity as their major reference frameworks.

Second, these attempts to appropriate and interpret modernity in close relation to the construction of new ideals in their own terms were not confined to the fundamentalist movements. They constitute part of a set of much wider developments which have been taking place throughout the world, seemingly continuing the contestation between different earlier reformist and traditional religious movements that developed in different societies and religious frameworks throughout non-Western societies. But at the same time all entailed an important, even radical, shift in the discourse about the confrontation with modernity and in the conceptualisation of the relation between Western and non-Western civilisations, religions or societies (Eisenstadt, 1999b).

Third, one can identify some very significant parallels between these various religious, including fundamentalist, movements and their seemingly extreme opposites – the different postmodern ones with which they often engage in contestation about hegemony among different sectors of society. While within these movements there develop similar combinations of different cultural tropes and patterns, they compete among themselves about who presents the proper 'answer' to the ambivalences towards processes of cultural globalisation. All these movements shared the concern which has constituted indeed a basic component in the discourse of modernity from its beginning in Europe, namely the concern about the relations between their identities and the universal themes promulgated by the respective hegemonic programmes of modernity; and above all the concern about the relation between such authentic identities and the presumed hegemony, on the contemporary scene, of a globalising American culture in particular. At the same time, in most of these movements, this fear of the erosion of local cultures and of the impact of globalisation and its centres was also continuously connected with an ambivalence towards these centres giving rise to a continuous oscillation between this cosmopolitanism and various 'particularistic' tendencies.

At the same time these movements have reconstituted the problematic of modernity in new historical contexts, in new arenas, in new ways. First among these new ways is the worldwide reach and diffusion (especially through the various media) of such movements and of the confrontations they entail; second, their politicisation, their continual interweaving with fierce contestation formulated in highly political ideologies and terms; and third, a crucial component of these reinterpretations and appropriations of modernity is the continual reconstruction of collective identities with reference to the new global context and contestations between them. Such contestations may indeed be couched in 'civilisational' terms – but these very terms are already couched in terms of the discourse of modernity, defined in totalistic and absolutising terms derived from the basic premises of the discourse of modernity, even if it can often draw on older religious animosities. When such clashes or contestations are combined with political, military or economic struggles and conflicts they can indeed become very violent.

Fourth, the reconstructions of the various political and cultural visions and such collective identities on the contemporary scene entail a very important shift in this discourse with respect to the confrontation between the Western and non-Western civilisations or religions or societies and the relations of these confrontations to the Western cultural programme of modernity. As against the seeming, even if highly ambivalent, acceptance of these premises, combined with their continual reinterpretation, which was characteristic of the earlier reformist religious and national movements, most of the contemporary religious movements – including the fundamentalist and most communal religious movements – as well as the more general discourse of modernity which developed within these societies, promulgate a seeming negation of at least some of these premises. They promulgate a markedly confrontational attitude to the West, to what is conceived as Western, and attempt to appropriate modernity and the global system on their own modern, but non-Western, often anti-Western, terms. The confrontation with the West does not with them take the form of seeking to become incorporated into the new hegemonic civilisation on its own terms, but rather of seeking to appropriate the new international global scene and the modernity for themselves, for their traditions or 'civilisations' – as they were continually promulgated and reconstructed under the impact of their continual encounter with the West. These movements attempt to dissociate Westernisation completely from modernity and they deny the monopoly or hegemony of Western modernity, and the acceptance of the Western cultural programme as the epitome of modernity. Significantly enough, many of these themes are espoused also, even if naturally in different idioms, by many of the 'postmodern' movements.

All these developments and trends constitute aspects of the continual reinterpretation and reconstruction of the cultural programme of modernity; of the construction of multiple modernities; of attempts by various groups and movements to reappropriate modernity and to redefine the discourse of modernity in their own new terms. At the same time they entail a shift of the major arenas of contestation and of the crystallisation of multiple modernities, of modern political programmes of modernity and of the construction of modern collective identities, from the arenas of the nation state to new areas in which different movements and societies continually interact and cross each other.

While the common starting point of many of these developments was indeed the cultural programme of modernity as it developed in the West, more recent developments gave rise to a multiplicity of cultural and social formations which goes far beyond the very homogenising and hegemonising aspects of this original version. All these developments do indeed attest to the continual development of multiple modernities, or of multiple interpretations of modernity – and above all to the de-Westernisation of the decoupling of modernity from its 'Western' pattern, of depriving, as it were, the West from a monopoly of modernity. It is in this broad context that European or Western modernity (or modernities) has to be seen not as *the* only real modernity but as one of multiple modernities – even if, of course, it has played a special role not only in the origins of modernity but also in the continual expansion and reinterpretation of modernities. But at the same time these developments constitute illustrations of the different potentialities inherent in the Axial, especially global Axialities, as they unfold at the beginning of the twenty-first century.

Notes

1. This part of the discussion is based on Eisenstadt and Giessen (1995) and on an extension of some of the arguments presented there.
2. Such codes are somewhat akin to what Max Weber called '*Wirtschafts-ethik*'. Unlike contemporary structuralists, Weber did not consider such an ethos, like the economic one, to be a purely formal aspect of the human mind, which generates only a set of abstract, symbolic categories. He saw such an ethos as given in the nature of man, in his social existence, and as carrying a direct implication for the order of society. Weber conceived of such codes as variant expressions of the symbolic orienta-tion of human beings towards the facts of their existence in general and towards the problems of social interaction in particular. Thus, a '*Wirtschaftsethik*' does not connote specific religious injunctions about proper behaviour in any given sphere; nor is it merely a logical derivative of the intellectual contents of the theology or philosophy predominant in a given religion. Rather, a '*Wirtschaftsethik*', or a status or political ethos, connotes a general mode of 'religious' or 'ethical' orientation, focused on the evaluation of a specific institutional arena, and with broad implica-tions for behaviour and for the distribution of resources in such an arena. The orientation is rooted in premises about the cosmic order, about the nature of ontological reality and its relation to human and social existence. (For greater detail, see Eisenstadt, 1995, chapters 1 and 13.)
3. This of course is due to the fact that tacit and formal knowledge are not of the same order. (See Polanyi, 1962, pp. 87ff.)
4. By Axial age civilisations (in Karl Jasper's nomenclature) we mean those civilisations that crystallised during the centuries from 500 BCE to the first century CE, within which new types of ontological visions, of con-ceptions of a basic tension between the transcendental and mundane orders, emerged and were institutionalised in many parts of the world – in ancient Israel, later in Second-Commonwealth Judaism and Christian-ity; Ancient Greece; Zoroastrian Iran; early Imperial China; Hinduism and Buddhism; and, beyond the Axial age proper, Islam.
5. This analysis is based on Eisenstadt (1996a).
6. I owe these illustrations to E. Tiryakian.
7. This analysis is based on Eisenstadt (2000).

References

Arnason, J.P. (1993) *The Future that Failed: Origins and Destinies of the Soviet Union* (London: Routledge).

Bateson, G. (1972) *Steps to an Ecology of Mind* (New York: Ballantine Books).

Becker, C. (1958) *The Declaration of Independence* (New York: Vintage Press).

Bellah, R.N. (1970) *Beyond Belief* (New York: Harper and Row).

Bellah, R.N. (1975) *The Broken Covenant* (New York: Seabury Press).

Bilde, P., Engberg-Pedersen, T., Hannestad, L. and Zahle, J. (eds) (1990) *Religion and Religious Practice in the Seleucid Kingdom* (Aarhus: Aarhus University Press).

Blacker, C. (1995) 'Two Shinto Myths: The Golden Age and the Chosen People', in C. Henny and J.-P. Lehman (eds), *Themes and Theories in Modern Japanese History* (Atlantic Highlands, N.J.: Athlone Press).

Bloch, M. (1992) *Prey into Hunter: The Politics of Religious Experience* (Cambridge: Cambridge University Press).

Brown, P. (1978) *The Making of Late Antiquity* (Cambridge, Mass.: Harvard University Press).

Brown, P. (1982) *Society and the Holy in Late Antiquity* (London: Faber and Faber).

Brown, P. (1992) *Power and Persuasion in Late Antiquity: Toward a Christian Empire* (Madison, Wisc.: University of Wisconsin).

Brunner, J.S., Jully, S.A. and Silva, K. (eds) (1979) *Play: Its Role in Development and Evolution* (Harmondsworth: Penguin Books).

Burkert, W. (1983) *Homo Necans: The Anthropology of Ancient Greek Sacrificial Ritual and Myth* (Westport, Conn.: Greenwood Press).

Burkert, W. (1987) *Ancient Mystery Cults* (Cambridge, Mass.: Harvard University Press).

Burkert, W. (1996) *Creation of the Sacred: Tracks of Biology in Early Religions* (Cambridge, Mass.: Harvard University Press).

Caillois, R. (1961) *Man, Play, and Games* (New York: The Free Press).

Cohen, S.J.D. (1990) 'Religion, Ethnicity and "Hellenism" in the Emergence of Jewish Identity in Maccabean Palestine', in P. Bilde et al. (eds), *Religion and Religious Practice in the Seleucid Kingdom* (Aarhus: Aarhus University Press), pp. 204–224.

Corse, S.M. (1997) *Nationalism and Literature: The Politics of Culture in Canada and the United States* (Cambridge: Cambridge University Press).

Delany, C. (1995) 'Father State, Motherland and the Birth of Modern Turkey', in C. Delany and S. Yanagisako (eds) *Naturalizing Power: Essays in Feminist Cultural Analysis* (London: Routledge).

Diederichs, E., Plessner, H. and Augen, A. (1982) *Aspekte einer Philosophischen Anthropologie* (Stuttgart: Ph. Reclam).

Dragadze, T. (1996) 'Self Determination and the Politics of Exclusion', *Ethnic and Racial Studies*, vol. 19, no. 2, pp. 341–351.

Dumont, L. (1970) *Homo Hierarchicus* (Chicago: The University of Chicago Press).

Durkheim, N. (1933) *The Division of Labor in Society* (New York: Free Press).

Eickelman, D.F. (ed.) (1993) *Russia's Muslim Frontiers: New Directions in Cross-Cultural Analysis* (Bloomington: Indiana University Press)

Eisenstadt, S.N. (1968) *The Protestant Ethic and Modernization: A Comparative View* (New York: Basic Books).

Eisenstadt, S.N. (ed.) (1983) *The Origins and Diversity of Axial Civilizations* (Albany, N.Y.: SUNY Press).

Eisenstadt, S.N. (1987a) *Kulturen der Achsenzeit: Ihre Institutionelle und Kulturelle Dyanamik*, 2 vols (Frankfurt am Main).

Eisenstadt, S.N. (1987b) *European Civilization in Comparative Perspective* (Oslo: Norwegian University Press).

Eisenstadt, S.N. (1988) 'Explorations in the Sociology of Knowledge: The Steriological Axis in the Domains of Knowledge', in S.N. Eisenstadt and I. Friedrich-Silber (eds) *Cultural Traditions and Worlds of Knowledge: Explorations in the Sociology of Knowledge* (Greenwich, Conn.: JAI Press), pp. 1–71.

Eisenstadt, S.N. (1992) 'Center and Periphery Relations in the Soviet Empire: Some Interpretative Observations', in A.J. Motyl (ed.) *Thinking Theoretically about Soviet Nationalities* (New York: Columbia University Press), pp. 205–223.

Eisenstadt, S.N. (1994) 'Japan: Non-Axial Modernity and the Multiplicity of Cultural and Institutional Programmes of Modernity', in J. Kreiner (ed.) *Japan in Global Context* (Munich: Ludicium Verlag), pp. 63–95.

Eisenstadt, S.N. (1995) *Power, Trust and Meaning: Essays in Sociological Theory and Analysis* (Chicago: The University of Chicago Press).

Eisenstadt, S.N. (1996a) *Japanese Civilization: A Comparative View* (Chicago: University of Chicago Press).

Eisenstadt, S.N. (1996b) 'Barbarism and Modernity', *Transactions*, vol. 33 (May-June).

Eisenstadt, S.N. (1998) 'Sectarianism and the Dynamics of Islamic Civilization', in G. Stauth (ed.) *Islam – Motor or Challenge to Modernity* (Frankfurt: Yearbook of the Sociology of Islam), pp. 15–33.

Eisenstadt, S.N. (1999a) *Paradoxes of Democracy: Fragility, Continuity and Change* (Baltimore: The Johns Hopkins University Press).

Eisenstadt, S.N. (1999b) *Fundamentalism, Sectarianism and Revolution: The Jacobin Dimension of Modernity* (Cambridge: Cambridge University Press).

Eisenstadt, S.N. (2000) 'The Reconstruction of Religious Arenas in the Framework of "Multiple Modernities"', *Millennium: Journal of International Studies*, vol. 29, pp. 591–611.

Eisenstadt, S.N. (2001) 'The First Multiple Modernities: Collective Identity, Public Spheres and Political Order in the Americas', in L. Roniger and C.H. Waisman (eds) *Globality and Multiple Modernities: Comparative North American and Latin American Perspectives* (Brighton: Sussex Academic Press).

Eisenstadt, S.N., Abitbol, M. and Chazan, N. (1988a) 'The Origins of the State Reconsidered', in S.N. Eisenstadt, M. Abitbol and N. Chazan (eds) *The Early State in African Perspective: Culture, Power and Division of Labor* (Leiden: E.J. Brill), pp. 1–27.

Eisenstadt, S.N., Abitbol, M. and Chazan, N. (1988b) 'State Formation in Africa: Conclusions', in S.N. Eisenstadt, M. Abitbol and N. Chazan (eds) *The Early State in African Perspective: Culture, Power and Division of Labor* (Leiden: E.J. Brill), pp. 168–200.

Eisenstadt, S.N. and Friedrich-Silber, I. (1988) *Cultural Traditions and Worlds of Knowledge: Explorations in the Sociology of Knowledge* (Greenwich, Conn.: JAI Press).

Eisenstadt, S.N. and Giessen, B. (1995) 'Construction of Collective Identities', *European Journal of Sociology*, vol. 36, pp. 72–102.

Eisenstadt, S.N. and Hartman, H. (1997) 'Historical Experience, Cultural Traditions, State Formation and Political Dynamics in India and Europe', in M. Doornbos and S. Kaviraj (eds) *Dynamics of State Formations: India and Europe Compared* (New Delhi: Sage Publications), pp. 25–44.

Eisenstadt, S.N., Pollock, S., Schluchter, W. and Wittrock, B. (1999) 'Ecumenical Worlds, Regional Worlds, and the Problem of Vernacularization', (working paper).

Elias, N. (1982) *The Civilizing Process*, 2 vols (Oxford: Basil Blackwell).

Faubion, J.D. (1993) *Modern Greek Lessons: A Primer in Historical Constructivism* (Princeton, N.J.: Princeton University Press).

Geertz, C. (1973) 'The Integrative Revolution: Primordial Sentiment and Civil Politics in the New States', in C. Geertz (ed.) *The Interpretation of Cultures* (New York: Basic Books), pp. 255–310.

Gehlen, A. (1971) *Studien zur Anthropologie und Soziologie* (Berlin: Luchterhard).

Gledhill, J., Bender, J.B. and Larsen, M.T. (eds) (1995) *State and Society: The Emergence and Development of Social Hierarchy and Political Centralization* (London: Routledge).

Goodwin-Raheja, G. (1988) 'India: Caste, Kingship and Dominance Reconsidered', *Annual Review of Anthropology*, vol. 17, pp. 497–522.

Haskins, G. (1960) *Law and Authority in Early Massachusetts* (Lanham, Md.: University Press of America).

Heesterman, J.C. (1985) *The Inner Conflict of Tradition: Essays in Indian Ritual, Kingship and Society* (Chicago: The University of Chicago Press).

Heimart, A. (1966) *Religion and the American Mind* (Cambridge, Mass.: Harvard University Press).

Herzog, T. (1998) 'A Stranger in a Strange Land: The Conversion of Foreigners into Members in Colonial Latin America', in L. Roniger and M. Sznajder (eds), *Constructing Collective Identities and Shaping Public Spheres: Latin American Paths* (Brighton: Sussex Academic Press), pp. 46–64.

Herzog, T. and Roniger, L. (2000) 'Conclusion: Collective Identities and Public Spheres in Latin America', in L. Roniger and T. Herzog (eds), *The Collective and the Public in Latin America: Cultural Identities and Political Order* (Brighton: Sussex Academic Press), pp. 303–304.

Hofstadter, R. (1972) *The United States* (Englewood Cliffs, N.J.: Prentice Hall).

Hoston, G. (1989) *Marxism and the Crisis of Development in Pre-War Japan* (Princeton, N.J.: Princeton University Press).

Hoston, G. (1990) 'IKKOKU Shakai-shugi: Sano Manabu and the Limits of Marxism as Cultural Criticism', in T. Rimer (ed.) *Culture and Identity* (Princeton, N.J.: Princeton University Press), pp. 168–186.

Howell, D.L. (1988) 'Territoriality and Collective Identity in Tokugawa Japan', *Daedalus*, vol. 127, no. 3, pp. 105–132.

Huizinga, J. (1970) *Homo Ludens: A Study of Play Elements in Culture* (London: Paladin).

Inkeles, A. and Smith, D.H. (1974) *Becoming Modern: Individual Change in Six Developing Countries* (Cambridge, Mass.: Harvard University Press).

Kedar, B.Z. and Werblowsky, Z.R.J. (eds) (1988) *Sacred Space: Shrine, City, Land* (New York: The Israel Academy of Sciences and Humanities/ New York University Press).

Kitagawa, J.M. (1987) *On Understanding Japanese Religion* (Princeton, N.J.: Princeton University Press).

Lerner, D. (1958) *The Passing of Traditional Society: Modernizing the Middle East* (Glencoe, Ill.: Free Press).

Little, A. (1969) *Religion, Order and Law* (New York: Harper & Row).

Marty, M. (1987) *Religion and Republic: The American Circumstance* (Boston: Beacon Press).

Mayer, E. (1976) *Evolution and the Diversity of Life* (Cambridge, Mass.: Harvard University Press).

Meyer, J.W., Boli, J. and Thomas, G.M. (1987) 'Ontology and Rationalization in the Western Cultural Account', in G.M. Thomas, J.W. Mayer, F.O. Ramirez and J. Boli (eds) *Institutional Structure: Constituting State, Society and the Individual* (Newbury Park: Sage), pp. 12–38.

Meyer, J.W., Boli, J., Thomas, G.M. and Ramirez, F.O. (1997) 'World Society and the Nation State', *American Journal of Sociology*, vol. 103, pp. 144–182.

Meyer, J.W. and Jepperson, R.L. (2000) 'The "Actors" of Modern Society: The Cultural Construction of Social Agency', *Sociological Theory*, vol. 18, pp. 100–120.

Moret, A., Davy, G. and Childe, G. (1926) *From Tribe to Empire: Social Organization among Primitives and in the Ancient East* (London: Kegan Paul, Trench, Trubner & Co.).

Piscatori, J.P. (1987) 'Asian Islam: International Linkage and their Impact on International Relations', in J. Esposito (ed.) *Islam in Asia: Religion, Politics and Society* (New York: Oxford University Press), pp. 230–261.

Plessner, H. (1966) *Diesseits der Utopie: Ausgewahlte Beitrage zur Kultursoziologie* (Dusseldorf).

Polanyi, M. (1962) *Personal Knowledge: Towards a Post-Critical Philosophy* (Chicago: University of Chicago Press)

Portman, A. (1944) *Biologische Fragmente zu einer Lehre von Menschen* (Basel).

Rappaport, R.A. (1999) *Ritual and Religion in the Making of Humanity* (Cambridge: Cambridge University Press).

Roniger, L. and Herzog, T. (eds) (2000) *The Collective and the Public in Latin America: Cultural Identities and Political Order* (Brighton: Sussex Academic Press).

Rozman, G. (1991) *The East Asian Religion, Confucian Heritage and Its Modern Adoption* (Princeton, N.J.: Princeton University Press).

Sartre, J.-P. (1972) *Imagination: A Psychological Critique* (Ann Arbor: The University of Michigan Press).

Schneider, D.M. and Smith, R.T. (1973) *Class Differences and Sex Roles in American Kinship and Family Structure* (Englewood Cliffs, N.J.: Prentice Hall).

Seligman, A. (1982) 'The Failure of Socialism in the United States: A Reconsideration', in S.N. Eisenstadt, A. Seligman and L. Roniger (eds) *Centre*

Formation, Protest Movements and Class Structure in Europe and the United States (London: Frances Printer), pp. 24–56.

Shils, E. (1975) 'Primordial, Personal, Sacred and Civil Ties', in E. Shils (ed.) *Center and Periphery: Essays in Macrosociology* (Chicago: The University of Chicago Press), pp. 111–126.

Spillman, L. (1997) *Nation and Commemoration: Creating National Identities in the United States and Australia* (Cambridge: Cambridge University Press).

Tanaka, S. (1993) *Japan's Orient: Rendering Past into History* (Los Angeles: University of California Press).

Taylor, C. (1985) *Human Agency and Language* (Cambridge: Cambridge University Press).

Tenbruck, F.H. (1989) *Die kulturellen Grundlagen der Gesellschaft* (Opladen: Westdeutscher Verlag).

van Bakel, M., Hagestiejn, R. and van de Velde, P. (eds) (1994) *Pivot Politics: Changing Cultural Identities in Early State Formation Processes* (Amsterdam: Het Spinhuis Publishers).

van der Lieuw, G. (1957) 'Primordial Time and Final Time', in J. Campbell (ed.) *Man and Time* (New York: Bollinger Foundation), pp. 324–353.

Vernant, J.P. (1991) *Mortals and Immortals: Collected Essays* (Princeton, N.J.: Princeton University Press).

Waida, M. (1980) 'Buddhism and the National Community', in Reynolds, F.E. and Ludwig, T.M. (eds) *Transactions and Transformations in the History of Religions* (London: E.J. Bailly).

Werblowski, J.R. (1976) *Beyond Tradition and Modernity* (Atlantic Highlands, N.J.: Athlone Press).

Wilson, P.J. (1980) *Man, The Promising Primate* (New Haven: Yale University Press).

3   The Fundamentals of the Theory of Ethnicity[1]

John Rex

The study of ethnic relations has in recent years come to play a central role in the social sciences, to a large extent replacing class structure and class conflict as a central focus of attention. This has occurred on an interdisciplinary basis involving sociology, political theory, political philosophy, social anthropology and history. It has dealt with the theory of nationalism and the theory of transnational migrant communities and the problem of incorporating them into modernising national societies. Each of these foci of study has developed its own separate theory but, what is worse, has sometimes claimed that it incorporates all the others. Thus, for example, the theory of nationalism has claimed to be a general theory of ethnicity, not recognising the difference between national groups and transnational systems of social relations and culture which bind together the members of migrating groups. Again, those who work within the discipline of social anthropology may feel that the field is exhaustively dealt with within its own problematic and limited range of interests.

The object of this chapter is not simply to substitute a new general theory for these specialised theories but, while trying to do justice to their insights, to demonstrate the major points of theoretical connection between them by a careful process of conceptual analysis. I shall deal successively with the theoretical concepts involved as follows: the notion of primordiality and small-scale community; the notion of 'ethnies' and ethnic nationalism; the concept of the modern nation state and related forms of nationalism; the analysis of the structure of empires and colonial societies; that of the reconstitution of post-imperial societies; the concepts of economic and political migration and migrant ethnic mobilisation; what is involved in national policy responses to migration; and, finally, with the notion of multicultural societies. I believe that an analysis of the concepts used at these various levels can point the way to an overall systematic theory.

A fully comprehensive review of the literature on ethnicity and nationalism would include many detailed empirical and historical studies of particular cases. The theories mentioned above take one step beyond this, attempting to analyse the concepts which are implicit in such studies. A further step, however, is that of discovering the common elements in all of these theories. It draws upon classical sociological theories dealing with forms of social relations, social structures and social systems at the more abstract level found in the work of Tönnies, Weber, Marx, Durkheim and Parsons, and seeks to place the theories focused on particular problems within this framework. It is only at this level that a general theory of ethnic relations can be formulated. The object of the sections which follow is to look in each case at the general sociological problems involved in the structure of the theories which have been developed to deal with them.

The theoretical problems of community and primordial relations

One of the most fundamental problems in theoretical sociology is that of the distinction between 'community' (*Gemeinschaft*) and 'association' (*Gesellschaft*) posed originally as the basis for his sociology by Tönnies (1963). Tönnies based this on what is really a metaphysical distinction between the real and the artificial wills. The same distinction, however, is used by Max Weber when he seeks to distinguish between different types of 'solidary social relationships' (Weber, 1968).

As he puts it,

A social relationship will be called communal if and insofar as the orientation of social action … is based upon a subjective feeling of the parties that they belong together. A social relationship will on the other hand be called associative if and insofar as the orientation of social action within it rests on a rationally motivated adjustment of interests or a similarly motivated agreement. (Weber, 1968, p. 54)

This much clearer definition rests upon Weber's reduction of all social relations, not to varieties of the will as in Tönnies, but rather to actors taking account of each other's behaviour in the course of planning their own actions.

The discussion of the nature of ethnicity in sociological and anthropological literature is very reminiscent of this debate about these concepts of community and association. This is particularly true of the distinction made by Geertz between primordial and other social bonds. In a famous paragraph Geertz writes,

> By primordial attachment is meant one that stems from the 'givens' of existence or more precisely, as culture is inevitably involved in such matters, the assumed givens of social existence; immediate contiguity and live connection mainly, but beyond them the givenness that stems from being born into a particular religious community, speaking a particular language, or even a dialect of a language, and following particular social practices. These continuities of blood, speech, custom and so on are seen to have an ineffable, and at times overpowering coerciveness in and of themselves. One is bound to one's kinsman, one's neighbour, one's fellow believer *ipso facto* as the result not merely of personal attraction, tactical necessity, common interest or incurred moral obligation, but at least in great part by virtue of some unaccountable absolute import attributed to the very tie itself. (Geertz, 1963, p. 109)

There are serious problems involved in Geertz's notion that some attachments are 'unaccountable'. Such notions can have no place in social science. Geertz, however, suggests something else, namely that the attachments are 'given' in the very nature of social existence. Such attachments are contrasted with those which are a matter of choice. Apart from the few reported cases of individuals brought up by animals, so-called 'feral' individuals, it would seem to be the lot of human beings that they are caught up in a network of interlocking social and cultural constraints. It is worth considering in some detail the nature of these constraints, not with the suggestion that they are ever to be found in a pure form in any actual small-scale community, but in order to establish a basic theoretical point of reference.

Primordial relations and community

The distinction made by Geertz between primordial and other social relations approaches that between community and association as in Tönnies and Weber. Attachments which are not primordial, at least those based on 'common interest' or 'tactical necessity', seem to suggest Tönnies' *Gesellschaft* or Weber's associative relations. This leads one to ask whether there is not also an equivalence between social attachments which follow from the very nature of social existence and *Gemeinschaft* or communal social relations.

In fact these two ideas do not imply one another. What Geertz's discussion does, however, is to add to the notion of 'belonging together' the notion that this feeling arises when individuals are bound together by the necessities of social existence.

Geertz further develops the notion of community by suggesting that it involves a number of different yet mutually supportive and perhaps functionally interrelated types of attachment. The ones he lists are kinship, neighbourhood or territory, shared language, shared religion, and shared customs. He might also have added the social division of labour and a shared history or myth of origin.

Types of primordial attachment

Social anthropology has traditionally been based upon the analysis of kinship terminology. It is one of the 'givens' of social existence that every individual entering the world finds that there is a set of terms which have the effect of defining his/her rights and duties vis-à-vis specific other persons or groups of persons. The fact that such terms can refer to groups as well as individuals means that such terms can be quite extensive. This is quite clear in classical anthropology,[2] for example in the work of Spencer and Gillen (1968), whose study of classificatory kinship became the basis of Durkheim's *Elementary Forms of Religious Life* and indeed of his whole theoretical sociology (Durkheim, 1915). Such studies were also undertaken in the classical period by the leading social anthropologists like Radcliffe Brown (1922; 1931; 1950; 1952).

Anthropologists studying small-scale primitive communities, however, were always aware of the fact that not all those who lived together were kin. Some were merely neighbours. But neighbours were inevitably involved in working together with kin groups in dealing with the problems of a shared immediate environment. This was also made clear in classical anthropology, particularly in the work of Raymond Firth (Firth, 1929; 1936; 1958).

The third primordial factor is religion. In the small-scale community this is primarily a matter of belief in the supernatural. This includes, firstly, an extension of kinship to include the dead as well as the living so that ancestors play a continuing role in social organisation; secondly, a set of beliefs relating to the natural world which are superadded to those of common sense; thirdly, an account of origins going beyond those given in ordinary history, the Australian tribes, for example, believing in a 'dream time' in which human history was merged with that of the animal kingdom.

Of course religion is not merely a matter of belief, and Durkheim, for instance, argued that there was 'no religion without a church' (Durkheim, 1915). What is the case in the small-scale community, however, is that there is no specialised 'church'. The collective practices of the general kinship system constitute the only church, and Durkheim went so far as to argue that 'worship' which purported to be worship of the divine was in fact worship of society itself.

Finally under the heading of religion we should note that in the theoretical primordial community it does not include many other elements which we take for granted as being part of religion. It does not provide a general philosophy of existence, does not deal with the problem of the disparity between an ideal divinely governed world and the institutions of the secular world, does not address what Weber called the problem of unmerited suffering, and does not offer some kind of moral code (Weber, 1968, Vol. II) These are all factors which have to be discussed in dealing with the role of religion in larger collectivities.

The fourth primordial form of attachment is that based upon shared language. Any individual born into the community clearly has a special relationship with others who speak the same language. Language is a means first of all for an agreed naming of objects, but it also involves evaluation of those objects, having a built-in set of moral and aesthetic standards.

The fifth primordial form of attachment, and one which Geertz's paragraph does not mention, is the social division of labour. It is true, of course, that he does see the kinship system as involving a distribution of rights and duties but, additionally to this, there is a system of co-operation in work and practical matters, a simple economy, which is one of the 'givens' of existence at this level. It is something which is taken for granted as being in the nature of things.

Finally there is the question of a shared history. Although this may be supplemented by a supernatural account of origins, as we have seen above, there is also usually some shared account of secular history, albeit an orally transmitted one.

The relative closure of the small-scale community

The notion of a closed small-scale community involves some difficulties. Even in a small community of a few thousand people the various forms of attachment may attach others from outside the community. This is particularly true in the case of religious and linguistic attachments, because the religion may be believed in or practised by, and the language spoken by, a wider group. This is even more likely in the case of religion if the religion itself becomes more complex than the elementary form which we have discussed. Moreover it is possible that the boundaries created by one of these forms of attachment may not coincide with that created by others.

Thus even the notion of a small community appears to be fuzzy at the edges and indeed this may sometimes be the case. But one may also expect mechanisms to arise which lead to the religion practised or the language spoken by the local group being made subtly different from that which exists more widely. This may be facilitated if there are those in the community capable of exercising leadership, but, even where no such leadership exists, the force of community itself may serve to counteract the fuzziness at the edges.

The existence of communities with their own individual membership logically must imply the possibility simply of individuals, or groups of individuals, who have the negative characteristic of being non-members or of belonging to other groups which are out-groups from the point of view of the group from which we started. The existence of such groups does not *necessarily* imply hostility and conflict. We may find that there are simply a number of coexisting groups or even communities which co-operate with one another. It is, however, commonly the case that such conflict does occur, and that the feeling of belonging within a community may be enhanced by hostility to out-groups.

Community and ethnicity

So far we have confined ourselves to the discussion of community as such. We should now notice that, when such a community exists based upon mutually supportive forms of attachment, the community is thought of as having an additional characteristic over and above that represented by any of the groups created by the various forms of attachment. Ethnicity is a term which is used to describe this additional characteristic.

The communities which will be of concern to us in this chapter are therefore to be thought of as ethnic communities. The tradition of functionalist analysis in social anthropology might lead to the various forms of attachment being seen as functionally interrelated. At a theoretically simple level, however, it is perhaps best to describe them as mutually supportive. Attachment to an ethnic group involves not merely a sense of psychological belonging but also a sense of sacredness. This is of course embodied above all in religion but the various specific forms of attachment, kinship itself, sense of territory, language customs and myths of origin are all imbued with it. When we speak of ethnicity we are not dealing with what Durkheim saw as the 'profane' world.

The primordial community in a wider context

Self-chosen and other attributed ethnicity

All that we have said so far refers to the way in which a community or ethnic community sees itself. But it may also have a view of the nature of other ethnic communities and may itself be the object of an attributed ethnicity. One of the things of which we have continually to be aware in the study of ethnicity and ethnic relations is that all ethnic situations have this duality. On the one hand there is a feeling of belonging, of primordial attachments of various kinds and an overall sense of ethnicity felt by group members; on the other the nature of their community may be described differently by outsiders. In more complex modern situations what is accepted as a group's ethnicity or ethnic community structure is often simply the ethnicity which government or those who exercise power attribute to it.

The attribution of ethnicity to outsiders is something that applies not only to groups physically located outside the boundaries of a community. It may also occur in relation to groups who live within the same territory but who do not participate in the community's system of primordial attachments. Such groups are commonly referred to as minorities, a term which does not have a merely numerical connotation but refers to non-participation in social networks. The group concerned may even be a numerical majority.

The effect of the existence of an out-group on a group's own self-image

A further and more complex problem is the effect on a group's self-image of the existence of out-groups. A recent paper by Zolberg and

Woon (1999) indeed appears to go further than this, implicitly arguing that the self-concept of an ethnic community depends above all upon its having an out-group in relation to which it defines itself. Thus instead of dealing with self-chosen community and ethnicity or ethnicity attributed by other groups it refers to the complex matter of what might be called reflexive ethnicity or perhaps reflexive identity.[3] It is within this context that it argues that specific out-groups might play this role in different nations. Islam is seen as playing this role for West European nations, Spanish-speaking communities for Americans.

Questions of this kind may certainly be asked. It should however be recognised that this reflexive identity has to be set alongside the less complex cases of self-chosen and attributed ethnicity and ethnic identity. It would be quite wrong to assume that the study of such reflexive ethnicity represented a complete study of ethnicity or ethnic relations.

The instrumentalist or situational view of ethnicity

What we have discussed above is a theoretically small enclosed community with definite boundaries, although we did suggest that there was a certain fuzziness at the edges where those bound together by the different forms of primordial attachment were also bound together with others beyond those boundaries. A different issue, however, is raised by Fredrik Barth in his study of the North West Frontier Province in Pakistan (1959) and in his later work on *Ethnic Groups and Boundaries* (1969). He suggests that the question of who is and is not a member of a community (in his study, who is and who is not a Pathan) depends not upon the content of the culture but upon the purpose for which the community acts together. This is the basis of the instrumentalist as opposed to the primordialist view of community. Taken to its extreme this would suggest that the ethnic group should be regarded not as a community at all but as a rational and purposive association. A more moderate view is that there is indeed a cultural content in an ethnic community but that the boundaries of the group which has that culture depend upon the purpose in hand.

The expansion of small-scale ethnic communities and the formation of 'ethnies'

The problem of instrumentally or situationally determined boundaries is not one which occurs in the sort of small-scale community we have been discussing. By definition, such a community is a primordial group. The possibility of instrumentally determined boundaries is, rather, something which occurs when the small-scale community is thought of as expanding to become what we shall call an *ethny*. This is one of a number of features of the increasing structural complexity of larger groups. We must now proceed, therefore, to consider the nature of ethnies and ethnic nations. In doing this we have to embark upon the second part of our discussion suggested above.

The institutional structure of ethnies

It may be argued that very few small-scale local communities of the kind which we have been discussing exist in the contemporary world. To some extent the very notion is an analytic abstraction, but the usefulness of such an abstraction is that, having made it, we may bracket it away, or use it as a basis for comparison with the structure of the larger collectivities which we do encounter. We shall therefore now look at the way in which the various forms of attachment operate in these larger groups, what such groups actually do, and the ways in which they operate.

While classificatory kinship makes it possible for fairly large kinship groups to be constituted, the idea of kinship can also be extended to take the form of fictive kinship. Thus the notion of brotherhood, sisterhood or parentage is extended as these terms are used to refer to many others with whom no biological link exists. In territorially based groups, moreover, there are likely to be references to the mother- or fatherland.

Similarly the notion of territory is extended to refer not simply to groups of neighbours but to the inhabitants of large geographical areas who are thought to share an emotional attachment to such areas.

The content of religious belief and practice becomes more complex in these larger groups. A specialised priesthood may emerge; the religion might come to include a philosophy of existence, possibly involving the idea of a divine creator; the notion might arise that there is a disparity between an ideal world and the institutions of 'this world' from which people must be saved; pain and suffering have to be explained; and the religion may come to be supportive of a moral code, as is the case with the so-called 'religions of the book', Judaism, Christianity and Islam.

Of course all these elements are to be found in the world religions in different combinations and with different emphases, and the larger group or ethny still faces the problem that its religious beliefs and practices are shared with many outsiders. Here again, however, the ethny usually succeeds in adopting a distinctive form of the more widespread religion which belongs especially to its members.

Similar processes occur with regard to language. A language like Arabic is spoken by hundreds of thousands of people across many countries but it is spoken in each ethny with a distinct dialect. A larger unity of language may be preserved in a sacred form used for religious purposes (e.g. Koranic Arabic or Church Latin) and there are dialect continua which connect one dialect community with another in a kind of chain, but this does not mean that any particular dialect community does not contribute to the solidarity of the ethny. Very similar relationships to these exist with regard to customs. Archaic versions of the customs may be ritually preserved and there may be customs continua across the boundaries of the ethny, but the distinctive version of the customs within the ethny contribute to its solidarity.

The division of labour in the larger ethny may well be based far more on economic specialisation than is the case with the small-scale local community. Furthermore it might very well come to involve social stratification of the population. Such differentiation in terms of prestige will also be coupled with the existence of political power and authority.

Finally there is the question of history. This will no longer be based upon a myth of origin and still less upon some notion of dream time. Rather it will be based upon actual political events involving the group's relation to its territory and its neighbours.

Shared symbols and the imagined community

In the primordial community it was suggested that the mutually supporting system of attachments came to be thought of as sacred. In the larger ethny this sense of sacredness is attached to symbols such as flags and anthems, which is a common topic of research amongst Anthony Smith's students.

Another aspect of the unity of this community is that which is suggested by the title of Benedict Anderson's influential book (Anderson, 1991). It should be pointed out that Anderson's whole thesis is a very complex one, focusing especially on the interactions made possible by print capitalism, but the implication of his title is important in earlier situations. In the ethny the interrelated set of institutions is understood as a community in the imagination of its members.

Functional and dysfunctional relations between institutions in the ethny

In the case of small-scale communities we spoke of the various forms of attachment as mutually supportive or perhaps as functionally related. In the ethny functional relationships may be more important. In speaking of functional relationships one implies that any one set of structures (kin, territorial, religious, linguistic, political and so on) may be thought of as rationally contributing to the effective working of the whole.[4] Such functional relationships, however, do not necessarily come smoothly into being. There is always the possibility of dysfunction or system contradiction between the different structures of attachment or what we should now call institutions as well as conflict between the participating social actors.

Of major importance in the development of an ethny is the conflict between religious and political leaders. In some cases the ethny will simply be led by the religious authorities, but it is in the nature of expanding ethnies that secular political authorities emerge as well. This is a conflict which goes on in all the great civilisations and not least in Europe, where the conflict was between the authority of the Pope and the Emperor.

So far as language is concerned there are not usually separate linguistic authorities asserting a lead role for the institutions of language. Rather such authorities are concerned with establishing one single language for the ethny and suppressing local dialects without their playing a lead role in the complex of institutions.

Another theme in the development of the ethny is that of control of a territory. Such control is dependent upon soldiers and their weapons and one type of authority is military authority. If this development is closely associated with kinship the system of authority will be what Weber calls 'patrimonial' (Weber, 1968, Vol. I) but there is also the alternative of feudalism in which the ruler offers military protection in return for economic tribute.

The ethnic nation

In this complex system of overlapping ties and institutions the boundaries of the ethny will no longer be of the closed kind as in a simple small-scale ethnic community. Which institutions play a lead role and which individuals exercise authority may be very much dependent on the purpose in hand. One such purpose will be the control of territory and insofar as this is the case we should speak not simply of ethnies but of ethnic nations. The system of authority in such ethnic nations becomes more sharply organised but it still remains embedded in the various institutional orders of kin, religion, language, and so on. This embeddedness is what is challenged by the emergence of the modernising nation state, which will be discussed in the next section.

Looked at from an instrumentalist point of view the ethny may have as its purpose the creation of a nation with its own state. This is what I would call the first project of ethnicity. But this is not the only purpose which the ethny might have. One other important purpose which I shall discuss below is migration. I call this the second project of ethnicity (Rex, 1996, Chapter 5; Guibernau and Rex, 1997) (see p. 101 below). In this case the ethnic group is not tied to a particular territory and does not seek to establish its own state. There may also be national non-migrant communities which do not seek to establish a state. Guibernau (1999) speaks of 'nations without states'. She refers to situations like that of Catalonia where the Catalan nation has no state of its own but aspires to achieving autonomy within a larger national state. A more radical distinction would be that which distinguished the pure ethny from the ethnic nation, which is what most sociologists would regard as a nation without a state.

Before we go on to discuss the difference between the ethnically embedded nation and the modernising nation state there is one other point which we should remember. This is the fact that along with the question of the self-chosen definition of the boundaries of ethnicity and that of which of the various institutions plays a lead role, there is always the fact that members of other groups may see the original one differently from the way it sees itself. Whichever institution

100 Making Sense of Collectivity

members of the original group see as dominant, other groups may see them as defined by and led by a different institution. Thus while they may see themselves as a national political group, outsiders may see them as defined by, say, their religion or their language.

The social anthropology of ethnicity

It is convenient here to note that the range of problems discussed under the heading of ethnicity differs in different disciplines. In the influential work of Thomas Hylland Eriksen, for example, there is little discussion of the more political aspect of social relations (Eriksen, 1993). Jenkins (1997), however, combines an anthropological perspective with an interest, shared with other students of ethnies, in national symbols, while Fenton (1999) discusses the relation between ethnicity and class. In all of these cases, while the narrower focus of social anthropology does draw attention to some important aspects of social interaction in ethnic groups, there does seem to be a need to place this within a more comprehensive sociological context. It might also be asked whether Barthian-inspired sociology of ethnicity does not require some supplementation by a consideration of primordial elements. While I have concentrated my attention on the work of Eriksen, Jenkins and Fenton there is now a considerable literature dealing with the questions of ethnicity and ethnic identity, including the work of Banks, writing from a specifically anthropological perspective (Banks, 1996), while writers like Oommen (1997) deal with these questions from the point of view of political sociology.[5]

Intellectuals and ethnic consciousness

A last point to be made here concerns the role of intellectuals in the development of ethnic consciousness. Intellectuals do help to formulate the notion of ethnic solidarity and, as a consequence, it is necessary to recognise that a distinction may usefully be made between the solidarity which they perceive and that which is felt and imagined by common people. On the one hand, one may have the work of poets, dramatists, musicians, artists and architects at a high level. On the other, one may have folk art, folk music, folklore and folk culture. This is a point of wider relevance however. It deserves mention here, however, because it does emerge at the level of the ethnic nation.

Ethnic nations and the modernising nation state

In his extensive writings on nationalism, Anthony Smith (1981; 1989) has emphasised the ethnic origins of nationalism.[6] An ethnic community may become an ethnic nation when its prime purpose is to lay claim to a territory, but such an ethnic nation remains embedded in a network of ethnic institutions. Very different is the notion of the modernising nation state described by Weber (1968, Vol. I, Chapter 1) and Gellner (1983). Weber defines the state as 'a compulsory political association with continuous operations' whose 'administrative staff successfully upholds the claim to the monopoly of the legitimate use of physical force in the enforcement of its order' (p. 54).

Defining the modern nation state

Gellner, whose writings have been central to the theorisation of the modernising state and its accompanying types of nationalism, emphasises the needs of the economy which brings the modernising state into being and which is corrosive of all pre-existing forms of social bonding.

As he puts it,

> The economy needs both the new type of central culture and the central state; the culture needs the state and the state probably needs the homogeneous cultural branding of its flock, in a situation in which it cannot rely on largely eroded sub-groups either to police its citizens, or to inspire them with that minimum of moral zeal and social identification without which social life becomes very difficult. ... [T]he mutual relationship of a modern culture and state is something quite new and springs inevitably from the requirements of the modern economy. (1983, p. 140)

It is not clear who or what group directs the new nation state in Gellner's conception. The emphasis is more on the method which any group might use to govern. It seems to be based upon the idea of the new nation state which emerged from the French Revolution, but which has been used by a variety of different groups seeking to modernise their societies.

In this new nation all institutions must ideally be subordinated to central control. The economy must be centrally directed even if it allows freedom within this to individual entrepreneurs; any priesthood must be subject to state control; there must be an official language; and there must be a national education system so that individuals, instead of being trained only for specialised roles, receive the sort of education which enables them to be moved flexibly from one position to another.

The central nation state seeks to erode all previous forms of solidarity, particularly those based upon class, status or ethnicity. What an ethnic community might expect, however, is that if it is territorially concentrated it might be given some degree of autonomy. There will be a debate about devolution, the community concerned being allowed to make decisions for itself so long as they do not run counter to the purposes of the centre. Yet even within this, the devolved community will itself be partially transformed so that it has more rational forms of government and authority. These questions have all arisen in cases like those of Catalonia within the Spanish state and Scotland within the United Kingdom. Their devolved authority is quite compatible with the existence of a modern nation state.

The national state has also to control not only internal sources of division but also any relationships which its institutions have beyond its borders. It has to retain control of its own economy where this is threatened by the operation of an international system of entrepreneurship. It has to resist the attempts of international religious bodies to control its priests by creating a national church within the larger international church and it has to keep control of the national language.

Gellner and Marxism

Gellner's account of the modern nation state accepts the Marxist notion of economic determinism. It is the transition from an agricultural society to an industrial one which requires the new type of political order. His approach is also functionalist in that changes in any one of its institutions require appropriate changes in others. His position is, however, clearly non-Marxist in other respects. As he puts it, 'The socio-economic base is decisive. That much is true in Marxism, even if its more specific propositions are false' (1983). These 'more specific propositions' relate to the expected role of the working class. It is the nation rather than the working class which carries through what the change in the economic base demands.

Traditional loyalties and the invention of new traditions

A further implication of Gellner's notion of the new unitary culture is that the state must indoctrinate all of its members with it and it must displace any pre-existing ethnic cultures. The state needs its own culture as a means of winning the loyalty of its citizens. They have to feel identified with it. Hobsbawm, however, sees that the state appeals to a false kind of ethnic nationalism. It purports to be basing itself upon tradition, but it invents its own version of that tradition invoking many practices as traditional which are actually of relatively recent origin (Hobsbawm and Ranger, 1983). Hobsbawm sees this as happening in revolutionary France. Eugene Roosens sees a similar process as occurring amongst the Huron in Canada, whose present leaders present a particular version of Huron ethnicity based on those elements which are useful in their present political projects rather than being part of a true ethnic tradition (Roosens, 1989).

Other forms of the modernising state

Gellner sees the modernising nation state as being exemplified above all by the French Revolution. Others, however, reject the notion that the political arrangements which Gellner describes are the product of either the French or the Industrial Revolution. Thus Liah Greenfeld argues that they were in place in fifteenth and sixteenth century England (Greenfeld, 1993). Moreover Gellner's theory is stated in abstract terms and does not deal with individual cases in any detail. One particularly interesting case is that of the Kemalite revolution in Turkey, which attempted to establish a modern nation state within part of the Ottoman Empire.

None of what has been said above, however, detracts from the importance of the central distinction which Gellner is making between the modernising nation state and its attendant forms of nationalism and any form of ethnic nation.

Nations and empires

The age of empires

During the past five hundred years most people have been conscious of living, not simply in ethnic nations or modern nation states, but in empires. In the earliest part of this period this took the form of the establishment of the rule by one dominant nation over its neighbours, as was the case in Britain, where the English attempted to establish their rule over Wales, Scotland and Ireland. In other cases what came to be thought of as nations were also based upon the rule of one nation over another. Much more far reaching, however, were the longer distance empires. Europe and a large part of the Middle East and Asia were divided up between the Austro-Hungarian or Hapsburg, the Tsarist (later the Soviet) and the Ottoman empires. Large parts of North and South America, Africa and Asia were ruled by the British, French, Portuguese, Spanish, Dutch and Belgians. Within these longer distance empires the subordinated nations had differing degrees of autonomy. In the French model all of the subordinated peoples were regarded as overseas French. The Portuguese distinguished between some of the colonial native people who were regarded as *évolués* who were entitled to be treated as Portuguese, while others were not. The British model, by way of contrast, is usually thought to be one of indirect rule in which traditional rulers continued to govern. Normally, however, these powers were restricted to certain areas so that the continued existence of the traditional systems did not conflict with the purposes and interests of the imperial power. In all cases of empire it was the imperial government which ruled overall.

The establishment of empires

In the ideal and extreme form of empire the imperial power simply extends its rule through establishing its institutions amongst the subordinate people as though they were the subjects of the metropolitan nation state. Such unified control however is not usually possible. The actual actors who carry out the transformation of the subordinate nations are the soldiers, the bureaucrats, the economic entrepreneurs, the settlers and the missionaries. These various groups become participant actors in the newly created society and are sometimes in conflict with one another. This was clearly true in the overseas empires of the European powers; the imperial civil service, the military, the plantocracy and other business interests, the settlers and the missionaries were often in conflict with one another and the art of the imperial government often lay in balancing their various interests against each other. It was probably also true in the case of the Central and Eastern European empires whose rule was over neighbouring territories.

This situation of imperial control is never complete and will clearly encounter resistance from the conquered nation, be it an ethnic or itself a modernised nation. Here, as in dealing with internal ethnic nations, the imperial power may resort to indirect rule or to granting a limited autonomy under which traditional institutions continue to exist insofar as they do not conflict with the purposes of the imperial nation. It is important to recognise that there is always a potentiality for resistance here by the subordinated peoples. The art of the imperial government therefore lies not only in balancing the interests of the different sections of its own people in the conquered territories, as has been said above, but also in dealing with this potential resistance.

A different approach to the study of imperial/colonial societies in the longer distance empires is suggested by the theorists of the so-called plural colonial society of whom the leading representatives are J.S. Furnivall (1939; 1948) and M.G. Smith (1965).

Furnivall describes colonial society in Indonesia in the following way: on the one hand one sees a plurality of tightly bonded ethnic groups; on the other one has a marketplace in which individuals from these groups encounter individuals from other groups. Social and cultural bonding within the different groups is intense and emotional. In the marketplace by contrast one has only what Marx and Engels in *The Communist Manifesto* called the 'callous cash nexus'. Furnivall does not refer to Marx but points out that, whereas for Durkheim a market-based society in Europe was bound together by a common will, no such common will existed in the colonial marketplace.

M.G. Smith sees the nature of the separate groups and what binds them together in a larger society somewhat differently. Each of the ethnic groups who have been brought together in a colony, including both the native people and various groups of migrants, has its own nearly complete set of institutions. This set of institutions is only nearly complete because they do not each have their own political institution. The political institution is controlled by the imperial power.

Smith does not discuss Furnivall's marketplace but he does have to look at other forms of tie than those simply imposed by the imperial government. He is concerned with such forms of organisation as the plantation, and this does seem to be an economic as well as a political institution.[7]

Attempting to apply this notion to more complex societies like the United States, which combines some of the institutions and structures which succeeded the plantation system in the South with those of the North in which free migrants from several European societies are united by the adoption of English as a language, involves the notion's elaboration and modification. Such societies are not homogeneous as functionalist sociology suggests, but neither are they plural. Smith describes them as heterogeneous. There is more than merely a political bond between the groups. They share a common culture ranging over many areas of life. Within this, however, the various groups, and particularly Black Americans, retain their own culture in relation to limited areas of life. Some of Smith's associates, such as Leo Kuper and Pierre van den Berghe (Smith and Kuper, 1969), have sought to develop these notions, particularly as they seek to apply them in South Africa.[8]

The breakdown of empire and the post-imperial situation

Whereas the world of the nineteenth and early twentieth century was a world organised and controlled by empires (the Ottoman, Austro-Hungarian, Tsarist and Soviet Communist empires in East Europe and Asia and the overseas empires of Spain, Portugal, Britain, France, Holland and Belgium), the world of the late twentieth century was one in which the old imperial systems had been overthrown, either because of their own economic and political weakness, or through the resistance of subject peoples. At this point the question arises of what types of social bond and what types of institution were likely to arise in the formerly subject areas.

Post-imperial nationalism

Sometimes what has happened is that there has been a simultaneous overthrow of imperial power and of modernising tendencies within these areas. In these circumstances one might well see a return to the ethnic nation. More commonly however some form of the modern nation state survives and this may even be governed by those who had served the imperial power but now seek to represent themselves as the new nationalists. In these cases what we may have is a halfway house which will be further challenged by ethnic nationalism. In these circumstances the various groups who had constituted the imperial/colonial order find their situation fundamentally altered. This is particularly true of settler groups from the metropolitan centre. They may find that they have difficulty in returning to the metropolis, partly because they are not wanted there, but also because they have developed their own communities with a settler culture different from that of the metropolitan centre.

Intergroup relations in post-colonial plural societies

M.G. Smith, in discussing what happens in former colonial territories after independence, suggests that there are a number of possible situations. One is that the society will simply break up. A second is that in which one of the ethnic segments takes over the state and governs the others. A third is a differentiation of function, in which one will take over government while another pursues an economic role – an alternative which is evident in Malaysia after independence, where the Malays control the government and the Chinese control the economy.[9] This, however, oversimplifies the actual empirical situations which occur. There are class differences within the different groups and there may also be some interpenetration between them so that, for instance, some members of a group which performs an economic function actually enter the government, or members of the governing group engage in business.[10]

Migrant ethnic communities

The discussion in the previous section dealt with situations in which the purpose of nationalism has been control of a territory. We must now turn, however, to what I have called 'The Second Project of Ethnicity' (Rex and Drury, 1994). Much of the sociological literature, deriving from the work of Anthony Smith and Gellner, purports to deal with ethnicity in general terms but actually addresses itself to the problem of nationalism. If we look at this in terms of instrumentalist theory, what we have been discussing are situations in which ethnicity serves national purposes in ethnic nations or modernising nation states. What it does not deal with is the ethnic mobilisation of migrant communities, where the purpose of such communities is precisely movement from one territory to another. The theory of nationalism seeks to deal with this by referring to migrant communities as forms of 'diasporic' nationalism. This is misleading because the concept of diaspora involves the notion of return to an original homeland whereas in point of fact many migrant communities have no such intention to return. What we have to do therefore is to give an account of ethnic mobilisation in migrant communities to supplement that given for nationalist communities.[11]

The study of ethnic organisation and mobilisation in transnational migrant communities has to be set within the framework of migration theory. Existing theories on an interdisciplinary basis have been usefully reviewed by Douglas Massey and his colleagues. (Massey et al., 1993). I have sought to place my own account of ethnic mobilisation within the framework which they suggest, looking particularly at the new economic theory which sees migration as a group decision.[12]

I suggest that migration is normally organised by an extended family seeking to improve its estate. When such a family is in migration it has three points of reference. These are the society and culture of the homeland, the society and culture of the land of first migration and then thirdly that of any country of possible onward migration. Each of these has to be analysed in a way parallel to that which we employed in looking at the structure of ethnies and ethnic nations.

It is, however, important in making this analysis to avoid what is called an essentialist approach, in which the various societies and cultures are thought of as closed and unchanging systems. Rather, each of them is to be seen as changing and developing in complex ways. The society of the homeland changes when it sends migrants abroad, when those migrants exercise their influence on its social relations and institutions and when they sometimes return; the structure of the community in the land of first settlement results from its encounter with the host culture and, usually, with a modern type of society; similarly the community in any country of onward migration involves the relationship between 'twice migrants' and the institutions of the new land of settlement.

The changing homeland society

There are, of course, traditional authorities and there is a surviving traditional culture in the homeland. This, however, is something which is challenged by the influences of emigrant culture. The emigrants send back remittances which can be used to buy land and houses which increase their economic power and their social status. They offer opportunities for spouses from the homeland to enter countries of settlement. They also send their children to the homeland for an education complementary to that in the land of settlement. Finally, political groups which may be suppressed in the homeland may have bases for political action in these countries.

Thus, far from the homeland community being closed and stable in a traditional way, it is in fact based upon a struggle between the traditional authorities and the way of life they represent and the sort of society which emigrants work to create. Of course this is not to say that this struggle is not sometimes muted because there are those who remain traditional despite emigration, both while abroad and on returning home.

The immigrant community in the land of first settlement

Going to live abroad means that migrants must also orient their behaviour to a society different from that of the homeland. The key unit in the migrant community is, of course, the extended family, which will seek to gain maximum advantage from migration by fighting for equality with host society individuals and families. In this fight for equality they share the universal values of a modern society and this would seem to be a central feature of migrant culture. But families compete both individually and collectively together with their ethnic peers. Clearly there is a sense that those who share the same language, religion and customs can be relied upon in a way which distinguishes them from families drawn from the host society. The boundaries of the community that can be relied upon in this way are often strengthened by religious organisation. Thus the life crises of birth, death and marriage are attended to through religious services in religious buildings like churches, mosques, synagogues and temples.

Immigrant culture is, therefore, a complex entity evolving from the simultaneous participation of immigrants in the culture of a modern democracy and in a continuing element of ethnic culture. The continuing ethnic culture helps to provide the immigrants with an emotional and moral home which protects them from a situation of anomie while at the same time giving them the organisational means for collective action in support of their rights.

As the children and grandchildren of the original immigrants become more secure they may find other ways of gaining communal protection from anomie, and other means of collective action. Inevitably therefore there will be some who will abandon their ethnic culture altogether. The loss of these descendants is a price which most immigrants are prepared to pay. It is part of the overall cost of migration, which brings other advantages. The experience is not in fact unlike that of the working class in industrial society in the past. Working-class parents fight for equality including the right to social mobility through education. Where this is achieved there is always the chance that the children will develop interests which conflict with those of their parents. What is interesting, however, is the way in which both working-class children and the children of migrants do retain some links with the class or ethnicity of their parents. All sorts of hybrid balance are possible in individual cases.

It could be that the need to maintain a separate immigrant culture will disappear and that what we are dealing with is simply a two or three generation problem which will be ended by the assimilation of the third generation. Where migration from a particular point of origin continues, however, a further nuance of the situation will be that of the relationship between earlier settlers, more or less assimilated, and new arrivals, amongst whom an ethnic culture is still strong. But even amongst the earlier arrivals there are examples which suggest that the experience of discrimination and failure to gain equality could lead to the reassertion of ethnic culture, including its religious expressions. This has been particularly true amongst Muslim immigrants in Europe.

In the next section we shall be dealing with different policies towards migrants and towards cultural pluralism and we shall argue that it is actually in the interest of host societies to encourage assimilation as well as protecting the communal cultures of immigrant ethnic minorities. In that way they will not lose valuable recruits to onward migration or to rebellion.

Communities of onward migration

Since the dynamic of migration lies in extended families trying to improve their estate, it will always be the case that, rather than envisaging a return to the homeland or being assimilated in the society of first settlements, many migrants will seize any better economic opportunities which occur through onward migration. In this second migration many of the problems experienced in the land of first settlement will recur and will serve to produce a similar migrant culture for several generations.

The transnational migrant community and the extended family

If we ask the question, 'To what society do migrants belong?' the answer may not be the homeland, the society of first settlement or that of onward migration. In fact they belong to all of these simultaneously and the most important binding factor is kinship.

The migrant is first of all a member of a kin group and that kin group stretches across all three societies. A migrant from the Punjab living in Britain, for example, might have relatives in the Punjab itself, in various parts of Britain and Europe and in North America. What he belongs to perhaps primarily is this transnational community of kinship.

Religion and language as unifying factors amongst migrant groups

The self-chosen ethnicity of migrant groups may unite several such groups. This will be the case particularly if several groups speak the same language or practise the same religion. Thus several groups may speak Arabic or a South Asian language in European countries or Spanish in the United States, and different groups may be able to act together because they share the same religion (e.g. Islam). This tendency toward joint action will be even more likely if the groups concerned are classified and stereotyped in terms of language or religion by the host society.[13]

Cross-border migrants

In the account of economic migration given above it has been assumed that the migrants, are long distance migrants both geographically and culturally. Connections with the homeland are greatly facilitated, however, if the migrants come to settle from adjacent countries. The extreme case is that of seasonal labour, in which case the migrants remain primarily as members of the sending society. Less extreme but also important to distinguish from longer distance migration is the case of cross-border migrants who actually commit themselves to longer term settlement but are able to maintain lively contact through visits and other forms of direct communication.

Economic and political migrants

Not all migrants move for economic reasons. In Western Europe for example there was an immigration stop in the early 1970s, and, since then, asylum seekers, refugees and, more generally, those migrating for political reasons have been more important numerically (see Joly and Cohen, 1989; Joly, 1996).

It is necessary here to include more than those migrants who are able to make a case for asylum. Under the Geneva Convention such a claim rests upon the ability of the claimant to show that he/she would be in personal danger at home. Only a small proportion of political migrants, however, can make this claim. They are not in *personal* danger but simply come from situations of political conflict or sometimes, ecological disaster. Often their home societies will be in a process of breaking up and in a state of civil war, or a group (like the Roma of Slovakia) may suffer such sustained oppression and discrimination that the only society to which they could return would be one in which the whole political order in their homelands had been radically changed.

In extreme cases the political migrant will have no kin because they have been killed or have disappeared, but usually there is a strong remaining tie to those who are missing, and reunion with them may be a primary goal for those who have escaped. There will also be strong political links, and for the community of political migrants the political project of altering the situation back home may be a central theme.

For many of these migrants there is a strong 'myth of return'. As a result their view of their situation in the land of refuge is that it is temporary. What they need is temporary housing accommodation, the possibility of paid employment, education for their children and medical and other minimal social services. If, however, the prospect of return fades, or if there is a chance of complete integration into the society in which they have taken refuge, they may see themselves as in a similar position to economic migrants. With these two alternative possibilities existing, the life of these migrants may well be one of uncertainty and ambiguity.

As we shall see, the response of the society that is a reluctant host to these migrants is that they are 'bogus asylum seekers', and this response will be made because these hosts are reluctant to fulfil their obligations. There is, however, some truth concealed in this notion, in that the political migrants are not sure themselves what their aims are. Probably they simply want to keep their options open: to return if the situation at home can be changed so as to offer better economic opportunities, as well as a sense of belonging, than are available in the land of refuge, but to stay and seek assimilation if that gives greater economic security and better prospects for their children.

The use of the term 'diaspora' in the study of migrant communities

I have suggested above that there are those who seek to absorb all studies of ethnicity under the heading of nationalism and that they believe that they have accomplished this by the use of the term 'diasporic' nationalism. Separately from this there are others who do recognise the distinction between the study of nations and migrant communities, but use the term 'diaspora' to cover the latter. My main objection to this is that it is a loosely used term which fails to capture the detailed structural complexity of migrant communities as we have been discussing it above. It also carries the overtones of a more specific use of the concept, namely that deriving particularly from Jewish history, which refers to communities which have suffered a traumatic political experience, have been dispersed and envisage a return to 'Zion'.[14] One of the better attempts to deal with this question is that of the American anthropologist James Clifford in his article simply entitled 'Diasporas' (Clifford, 1994). In this article Clifford distinguishes a large number of structurally different situations in relation to which the term might be used. Another contributor to the debate is Paul Gilroy (whom Clifford does discuss) (Gilroy, 1993). In Gilroy's case the term is stretched to, and probably beyond, its limits, seeing it as involving not the hankering after an old lost culture and society but the creation of a wholly new one. On this basis he rejects the Africanist notion of a return to Africa by the descendants of those who were forcibly transported across the Atlantic, and suggests that there is a new consciousness which is based both upon the culture developed in the Americas and upon that which arises for migrants who move from colonial to metropolitan societies.

There are real insights which can be derived from the work of writers like Clifford and Gilroy, but it would be better if they did not attach themselves to the concept of diaspora. In fact many of these insights might very well fit in with some of the distinctions made above. If there is to be a general term which covers this whole area it might be better to speak not of diasporas but simply of 'transnational communities'.

Policy responses and host society attitudes to immigration

The range of responses to the presence of immigrants

There are four main policy responses by modern governments to the arrival of immigrants. These are the response which simply demands that they should be excluded, expelled, persecuted or exterminated, and the three alternatives represented by the use of immigrants as labour without allowing them rights of citizenship, the assimilationist approach which accepts their settlement provided that they give up their culture and separate social organisation, and that of multiculturalism. No government deliberately adopts the first of these policies in Europe today although there is a substantial minority representation in the politics of parties which advocate exclusion and expulsion in France, Austria, Belgium and Switzerland. The second policy is that adopted in the German-speaking countries and very widely in Africa and Asia, which, in its German version, is euphemistically called the *Gästarbeiter* policy. German policy even denies that the *Gästarbeiter* is an immigrant, since the notion of an immigrant suggests someone who will stay in the long term and even be assimilated. The third policy, assimilationism, is commonly regarded as the characteristic French policy. This offers immigrants relatively easy access to citizenship but has no place for the encouragement of minority cultures or separate political organisation. Finally there is the policy of multiculturalism, usually said to be the policy of the Netherlands, Britain and Sweden.

Forms of multiculturalism

The most radical version of multiculturalism is the Netherlands' policy of 'pillarisation'. This evolved as a means of securing religious tolerance by allowing for a separate education system, separate social services, separate media and separate trades unions to the Catholic, Protestant and secular communities. There is now some argument as to whether Muslims constitute a separate pillar, but it is not surprising that the Netherlands has been more willing to allow separate Muslim schools than any other country. The British government accepts the coexistence of diverse ethnic communities without setting up separate institutions, or denying a common and equal citizenship to all individuals.[15] Eventually this allowed for state financial support for Muslim schools along with the Catholic, Protestant and Jewish schools which had enjoyed it for more than a century. In Sweden there was considerable willingness to consult with those whom the government deemed to be the representatives of ethnic minority communities.

In my book *Ethnic Minorities in the Modern Nation State* (Rex, 1996) I have shown at length how in practice all countries deviate from the policy towards minorities which they proclaim an ideological level, and I have noted the very considerable literature which claims that even the high-sounding policy of multiculturalism can conceal unequal treatment of minorities or their manipulation for its own purposes by governments.[16] Nonetheless it is still possible to set out the different policy options of exclusion, assimilation, the denial of full citizenship and multiculturalism and, within this, the different forms of multiculturalism which have occurred in Europe and America.

The position of political migrants in a multicultural society

The settlement of political migrants raises separate policy problems. The Western European countries have dealt with this question by making it difficult for asylum seekers to arrive by imposing visa requirements, by sending them back to their first country of refuge, and by punishing the carriers of claimants. This has also made the status of a Geneva Convention refugee difficult to achieve, and life is made difficult for those awaiting decisions and those whose claims are rejected but who are given some kind of 'exceptional leave to remain'. Foreign policy is also directed towards creating 'safe havens' for potential refugees in their own countries so that they have no need to seek asylum. All in all what prevails is a reluctant acceptance of some international obligations which allow relatively small numbers to succeed with their applications. Countries outside Europe differ in their degree of generosity, but it is noteworthy that the Organisation of African States, which has to deal with a far greater refugee problem than Europe, shows a greater willingness to accept them. A satisfactory analysis of contemporary multicultural societies has to deal with these political migrants as well as with those who immigrate for economic reasons.

Multiculturalism in the United States

Turning to the United States, on the question of multiculturalism it has adopted the distinctively assimilationist policy represented by the notion of the 'melting pot'. Although this is a country of immigrants, the institutions and language of the first immigrants, White Anglo-Saxon Protestants, has provided the framework within which later immigrants must work. Arthur Schlesinger Jr. in his book *The Disuniting of America* (1992) has forcefully defended this position which sees American society as threatened both by black separatism and by the spreading of the Spanish language.[17]

On immigration policy as distinct from policy on multiculturalism American policy has been more generous than its European equivalent, particularly since the removal of many of the restrictions which had stood in the way of immigrants from Asia, Africa and Latin America. This is still true today so far as legal immigration is concerned, but there is a considerable problem of illegal arrival and settlement by immigrants, particularly from across the Mexican border, and refugees arriving from all parts of the world. Since employers need the labour of such immigrants, the flow of illegals cannot be stopped, but there is pressure to prevent their receiving many of the social rights of citizens, such as the attempt in California to deny them education.

Official and popular responses to the arrival of immigrants

All the above discussion has been about policies of governments which on the whole are benign and progressive. We should also note here, however, that such benign and progressive policies are not shared by the population at large. Overwhelmingly, the citizens of European countries fail to distinguish different classes of immigrants and would be opposed to them indiscriminately. This is why politicians discussing almost any immigrant or refugee situation will set their public statements in a context which suggests that they are fighting to stave off a potentially overwhelming immigrant flood. In Britain, Margaret Thatcher famously declared that the British were afraid of being 'swamped'.

Not surprisingly, this fear of being swamped by a tide of immigrants and asylum seekers has been expressed in a number of European countries in the adoption of anti-immigrant policies by parties of the extreme right, most notably by Haider's Peoples Party in Austria, by the National Front of Le Pen in France and by the Vlaamse Blok in Belgium. Such parties seem able to command about 20 per cent of the vote in elections, but are more influential than that, because the parties of the centre usually move towards adopting their anti-immigrant policies in order to win back the vote, even if they don't actually enter into coalition with them, as has happened in Austria. It is against this background that the attempts by governments to introduce their official policies of assimilation or multiculturalism have to be seen.

Conclusion

One aim of this chapter has simply been that of recording the different types of study which have been concerned with the questions of nationalism and ethnicity, working from the simplest to the more complex (e.g. from discussions of primordial relations through to those concerned with nationalism and ethnicity in an increasingly globalised world) or in the order in which they have been thought to succeed each other historically. These, however, may be looked at at a higher level of abstraction. Looking at the matter in this way, the basic issues which are raised by the specific theories of nationalism and ethnicity are the following: the types of social relations involved and whether these involve instrumental or affective ties; more complex structures of social relations; institutions and functional and dysfunctional relations between them; groups and collectivities such as ethnies and ethnic nations; affective ties, symbolic unity and group consciousness; rationalisation of national structures; relation between rationalising agents and affectively bonded groups; interaction and conflict between collectivities within larger groups such as nations; relations of conflict and subordination between nations; transnational structures of affectively bonded groups; the internal structure of transnational groups; the relation between modern nation states and transnational groups; supranational societies.

My argument is that the problems which have been discussed in specific theories are ones which recur at different levels of scale and complexity. It is for this reason that it is possible to envisage an overall general theory of nationalism and ethnicity transcending the more specific theories which have been used in understanding small-scale communities, nations and transnational communities. Such a theory is not simply another new one competing with those which have been developed by theorists like Geertz and Barth, Anthony Smith and Gellner, or Furnivall and M.G. Smith. Rather it provides the context in which their theories may be better understood.

Notes

1. The earlier version of this chapter has been published in *Sociological Research Online* (2001, vol. 6, no.1) under the title 'The Basic Elements of a Systematic Theory of Ethnic Relations'. I am grateful for the permission to republish this paper in this volume.

2. I refer here to the classical period of social anthropology, in which the study of kinship played a central role in the study of social structure. Naturally I am not attempting to review all contributions by social anthropologists who study kinship as one specialised aspect of social structure.

3. I shall in general avoid using the concept of identity, because it is often introduced as a kind of joker in the pack to cover all sorts of situations, sometimes referring to the subject in a cognitive mapping of the world, sometimes referring to social position, sometimes to social characteristics, sometimes to the personality system. It also has something of the same mysteriousness which seems to follow from Geertz's definitions of primordiality. I use the term here only to refer to a sense of belonging. The notion of reflexive identity refers to the particular sense of belonging which arises from relations to out-groups.

4. It would be inappropriate here to go into the whole argument about 'functionalism' in sociology. My own position is made clear in my book *Key Problems of Sociological Theory* in which I reject the use of the organic analogy in Radcliffe Brown's work and offer my own account based upon the Weberian concept of social action.

5. There are also now a number of edited collections, such as those of Romanucci and de Vos (1995) and Sollors (1989), which include articles written from the perspective of anthropology and of a political sociology which deals with conflict as well as intergroup accommodation.

6. In my discussion of the work of Smith and Gellner I have not sought to follow the exact distinctions which they make, but starting from their basic ideas I have sought to develop the implications of these ideas in a logical way.

7. I have set out my own account of the relation between forms of economic exploitation on the one hand and the political order on the other. I do think it important to strengthen Smith's pluralist theory with a recognition of the forms of economic exploitation. This, however, can be combined with a recognition of the importance of political relations. The concept of estates rather than classes is a necessary one in the study of colonial societies as it is in the study of medieval Europe (Rex, 1981; 1983). I also draw upon the work of Max Weber in the analysis of the various forms of economic exploitation (Weber, 1961).

8. Actually there is more theoretical complexity than this represented in the volume edited by Smith and Kuper (1969), but the main lines of the distinction between homogeneous, heterogeneous and plural societies remain at the centre of the argument.

9. I have discussed some of the changes which occur after the end of empire for the colonial people, which include the development of a purer market-based economy than that which existed in colonial times,

the marginalisation of some groups on the edges of this economy and the development of new nationalist forms of revolution (Rex, 1981; 1983).

10. My aim here is to provide a theoretical starting point from which it should be possible to go on to look at the complicating details of actual political history.

11. I have in mind here the work of the Association for the Study of Ethnicity and Nationalism at the London School of Economics, which has never addressed the question of transnational communities except under the heading of diasporas.

12. Another account of this process is that given by Castles and Miller (1998), while Robin Cohen, who had previously discussed the term diaspora in relation to the Jews, Armenians and Africans across the Atlantic, in his more recent work seeks to set the concept of diaspora within the overall framework of globalisation (Cohen, 1997).

13. There are a number of studies of groups united by language or religion in Britain. Floya Anthias has looked at the question of the Greek Cypriot community united by language if divided internally by social class (Anthias, 1992) while Modood has discussed the ways in which the Asian and the Muslim populations of Great Britain can act together (Modood, 1994 ; Modood et al., 1997).

14. Apart from the Jewish case, the term was at one time used for the dispersal of Armenians and the forced migration of Africans to the Americas and their ambitions to return.

15. The official policy of the British government was described as one of 'integration', defined by the Home Secretary, Roy Jenkins, in 1966 as 'cultural diversity, coupled with equal opportunity in an atmosphere of mutual tolerance' (Rex and Tomlinson, 1979).

16. I would draw attention particularly to the criticisms of multicultural policy by Wieviorka, Radtke, Rath and Schierup and Alund set out in my book *Ethnic Minorities in the Modern Nation State* (1996) and the volume edited by Beatrice Drury and myself (Rex and Drury, 1994).

17. In saying this I would also note that there are features of Schlesinger's argument which are less acceptable, notably his claim that American institutions are essentially European rather than American, and his representation of much black culture as being akin to that of General Idi Amin.

Referencess

Anderson, B. (1991) *Imagined Communities: Reflections on the Origin and Spread of Nationalism* (London: Verso).

Anthias, F. (1992) *Ethnicity, Class, Gender and Migration* (Aldershot: Avebury).

Banks, M. (1996) *Ethnicity: Anthropological Perspectives* (London: Routledge).

Barth, F. (1959) *Political Leadership amongst the Swot Pathans* (London: London School of Economics).

Barth, F. (1969) *Ethnic Groups and Boundaries* (London: Allen & Unwin).

Castles, S. and Miller, M. (1998) *The Age of Migration: International Population Movements in the Modern World* (Basingstoke: Macmillan).

Clifford, J. (1994) 'Diasporas', *Cultural Anthropology*, vol. 9, no. 3, pp. 302–338.

Cohen, R. (1997) *Global Diasporas* (London: University College London).

Durkheim, E. (1915) *The Elementary Forms of Religious Life* (Glencoe, Ill.: Free Press).

Eriksen, T. (1993) *Ethnicity and Nationalism: Anthropological Perspectives* (London: Pluto Press).

Fenton, S. (1999) *Ethnicity: Racism, Class and Culture* (Basingstoke: Macmillan).

Firth, R. (1929) *Primitive Economics amongst the New Zealand Maori* (London: Routledge).

Firth, R. (1936) *We the Tikopia* (London: Allen & Unwin).

Firth, R. (1958) *Human Types* (London: Nelson).

Furnivall, J. (1939) *Netherlands India* (Cambridge: Cambridge University Press).

Furnivall, J. (1948) *Colonial Policy and Practice* (Cambridge: Cambridge University Press).

Geertz, C. (1963) *Old Societies and New States: The Quest for Modernity in Asia and Africa* (Glencoe, Ill.: Free Press).

Gellner, E. (1983) *Nations and Nationalism* (Oxford: Blackwell).

Gilroy, P. (1993) *The Black Atlantic* (London: Verso).

Greenfeld, L. (1993) *Nationalism: Five Roads to Modernity* (Cambridge, Mass.: Harvard University Press).

Guibernau, M. (1999) *Nations without States* (Cambridge: Polity Press).

Guibernau, M. and Rex, J. (eds) (1997) *The Ethnicity Reader* (Cambridge: Polity Press).

Hobsbawm, E. and Ranger, T. (eds) (1983) *The Invention of Tradition* (Cambridge: Cambridge University Press).

Jenkins, R. (1997) *Rethinking Ethnicity: Arguments and Explorations* (London: Sage).

Joly, D. (1996) *Haven or Hell: Asylum Policies and Refugees in Europe* (Basingstoke: Macmillan).

Joly, D. and Cohen, R. (1989) *Reluctant Hosts, Europe and its Refugees* (Aldershot: Gower).

Lockwood, D. (1964) 'Social Integration and System Integration', in G. Zollschan and W. Hirsch, *Explorations in Social Change* (London: Routledge & Kegan Paul).

Massey, D., Arango, J., Hugo, G., Kouaouci, A., Pellegrino, A. and Taylor, J. (1993) 'Theories of International Migration: A Review and Appraisal', *Population and Development Review*, vol. 19, no. 3, pp. 431–466.

Modood, T. (1994) 'The End of a Hegemony: The Concept of "Black" and British Asians', in J. Rex and B. Drury (eds) *Ethnic Mobilisation in a Multicultural Europe* (Aldershot: Avebury).

Modood, T., Berthoud, R., Lakey, J., Nazroo, J., Smith, P., Virdee, S. and Beishon, S. (1997) *Ethnic Minorities in Britain* (London: Policy Studies Institute).

Oommen, T. (1997) *Citzenship, Nationality and Ethnicity* (Cambridge: Polity Press).

Radcliffe Brown, A. (1922) *The Andaman Islanders* (Cambridge: Cambridge University Press).

Radcliffe Brown, A. (1931) *The Social Organisation of Australian Tribes* (Melbourne: Oceania Monographs).

Radcliffe Brown, A. (1950) *African Systems of Kinship and Marriage* (Oxford: Oxford University Press).

Radcliffe Brown, A. (1952) *Structure and Function in Primitive Society* (London: Cohen & West).

Rex, J. (1961) *Key Problems of Sociological Theory* (London: Routledge & Kegan Paul).

Rex, J. (1981) 'A Working Paradigm for Race Relations Research', *Ethnic and Racial Studies*, vol. 4, no. 1, pp. 1–25.

Rex, J. (1983) *Race Relations in Sociological Theory* (London: Routledge & Kegan Paul).

Rex, J. (1996) *Ethnic Minorities in the Modern Nation State* (Basingstoke: Macmillan).

Rex, J. and Drury B. (eds) (1994) *Ethnic Mobilisation in a Multicultural Europe* (Aldershot: Avebury).

Rex, J. and Tomlinson, S. (1979) *Colonial Immigrants in a British City: A Class Analysis* (London: Routledge & Kegan Paul).

Romanucci-Ross, L. and de Vos, G. (eds) (1995) *Ethnic Identity: Creation, Conflict and Accommodation* (London: Altamira Press).

Roosens, E. (1989) *Creating Ethnicity: The Process of Ethnogenesis* (London: Sage Publications).

Schlesinger, A., Jr. (1992) *The Disuniting of America* (New York: Norton).

Smith, A. (1981) *The Ethnic Revival in the Modern World* (Cambridge: Cambridge University Press).

Smith, A. (1989) *The Ethnic Origins of Nations* (Oxford: Blackwell).

Smith, M. (1965) *The Plural Society in the British West Indies* (Berkeley: University of California Press).

Smith, M. and Kuper, L. (1969) *Pluralism in Africa* (Berkeley: University of California Press).

Sollors, W. (ed.) (1989) *The Invention of Ethnicity* (Oxford: Oxford University Press).

Spencer, B. and Gillen, F. (1968) *The Native Tribes of Central Australia* (New York: Dover Books).

Tönnies, F. (1963) *Community and Association* (New York: Harper & Row).

Weber, M. (1961) *General Economic History* (New York: Collier Books).

Weber, M. (1968) *Economy and Society* (2 volumes) (New York: Bedmister Press).

Zolberg, A. and Woon, L. (1999) 'Why Islam is like Spanish: Cultural Incorporation in Europe and the United States', *Politics and Society*, vol. 27, no. 1, pp. 5–38.

4   Nationalism and Modernity

Mark Haugaard

In the Introduction it was argued that collectivities are social systems with a sense of membership. Because of the contemporary tendency of assuming that nation state is the only really significant form of collectivity, it was pointed out that there are many other forms of collectivity. That it was necessary to point this out reflects the huge success of nationalism in the modern world. Marx assumed that as capitalism advanced class consciousness would become the dominant basis of collectivity formation. The First World War was the first of a number of falsifications of Marx's hypothesis – the working classes of the part of the world where capitalism was most developed at that time did not form an international collectivity but instead fought and died for nation states (King and Kaiser in many instances!). Durkheim thought that the increasing mutual dependence brought about by the expanding division of labour associated with modernity would provide the basis for collectivity formation. In many respects Durkheim's analysis is a paradigmatic instance of the failure of liberals to predict the success of nationalism. Neither socialists nor liberals predicted the success of nationalism; an observation which brings us to the topic of this chapter and the intellectual problem that inspired most of Gellner's analysis: why is nationalism associated with modernity?

  Given the essentialist logic of nationalism and the instrumental logic of modernity, it is a surprising fact that nationalism is associated with modernity. Gellner goes part of the way towards explaining the nature of the affinity between the two. He demonstrates how nationalism is functional to the creation of a modern society whereby the state and culture are fused through the establishment of a state monopoly of education; which is a prerequisite for creating the type of accreditalised society presupposed by industrial production. With regard to breakaway nationalism, in the entertaining parable of Ruritania and Megalomania, Gellner shows us how the fusion of state and culture in Megalomania gives Ruritanians an instrumental interest in their own Ruritanian nationalism because hierarchy has become legitimated through egalitarian meritocratic accredentialised principles.

Important though these contributions may be, he offers only a partial explanation of the success of nationalism. Stating that it is an ideology which is functional to particular relations of domination and that individuals may have an instrumental interest in subscribing to that ideology is not the same as explaining why people actually subscribe to it. To take a parallel: using the Nietzschean/Marxist argument, it can be argued that Christianity is functional to certain social systems and that elites benefit from subservience of the Christian poor, but this does not tell why so many people converted to the religion. Gellner's thesis explains in what way states and elites have a vested interest in exploiting nationalism, but this still does not tell us why this ideology should appeal to so many people. That is, unless it is argued that nationalism is a Pareto-style rationalisation which is used to dupe the masses. Something like this is suggested by Gellner when he states that nationalism is a *Gesellschaft* using the idiom of a *Gemeinschaft* (Gellner, 1997, p. 74). However, I have never been convinced of the plausibility of convincing the general populace of the 'myth of metals' in Plato's *Republic* and, with regard to three-dimensional power, while it is the case that the formation of consciousness is important to understanding relations of domination, it is a theoretical error to theorise this as *false* consciousness. As a social theorist, I would concur with Durkheim's sentiments when he stated that religion is never wrong. Consequently, in order to understand nationalism, we have to take it seriously. Nationalism is a genuine *Gemeinschaft* which, for reasons that need to be explained, has a genuine appeal to many within the modern world. Our question, irrespective of the functional consequences to either elites or systems, is why is it the case that many modern individuals are nationalists? This is an ontological question concerning the being-in-the-world that characterises modernity and, in particular, what beings so constituted consider legitimate. Not only does the understanding of the synergy between nationalism and modernity tell us something about nationalism but, because its success has been so unpredicted, it is a key to understanding modernity – one of the key elements of hermeneutic phenomenological understanding is analysing that which does not make sense rather than that which does.

What are the essential ontological transformations which characterise the move from traditional to modern society? As Gellner argues, one of the key transformations is a move away from an ontology based upon essential essences. The feudal order was considered legitimate because it was taken as given that each member of the hierarchy was considered to embody a certain essence which gave them a *telos* that was actualised by doing 'one's duty' within the Great Chain of Being. The principle of legitimacy underpinning Plato's *Republic* is a paradigm example of this kind of world view. The Republic is a utopia by virtue of the fact that it is based upon a division of labour that mirrors to perfection the essential essences of each person. Each individual realises their particular good by doing their duty. Similarly, Aristotle justified slavery by arguing that the *telos* of slaves lies external to themselves in realising the wishes of their masters. Extending Dworkin's argument (1977) concerning the ubiquity of equality as a normative basis for modern political theory, it could be the case throughout the ages, not just in the modern world, that political legitimacy is based upon equality. What changes is not the principle of equality but ontologies. Be that as it may, the European feudal order embodied an egalitarian logic once the implied ontologies of the Great Chain of Being are factored into the equation.

This essentialist, teleological and discontinuous view of social order was inconsistent with the idea of the continuous world of Newtonian physics and the Enlightenment call to understanding without authority. If plants and planets do not move because of their *telos* and the authority of the word of God or the sanctity of tradition can be questioned, then the hierarchy of the Great Chain of Being comes tumbling down. If planets and stars no longer stay in the heavens because of particular physics derived from essential essences, then it is inconsistent for humans to obey others because it is in their particular teleologically constituted nature to do so. If authority is no longer the source of truth, then everything is open to question. From the perspective of social hierarchy, the result is that the only forms of class and status which are legitimate are those which are based upon provable differences between people. We enter a meritocratic society where accreditation, qualifications and effort are considered the legitimate basis for domination. The state controls education and qualifications which are dispensed not upon arbitrary favour but through rigorous examinations that are considered objective. Of course, in reality the actual distribution of privilege is a very poor reflection of this ideal, but the existence of this perception of legitimacy is proved by the fact that the failure of society to live up to these meritocratic principles is continually considered grounds for social critique. If particular ethnic groups, particular classes or women are shown to be intrinsically disadvantaged by the system by virtue of who they are, this is considered illegitimate, unless there is some essential difference which can be proved. 'Proved' in this case does not mean by appeal to authority but by scientific truth and bureaucratically administered qualifications. The former is the normative basis of the type of scientific race theory that was so popular in the nineteenth century but which has largely been discredited by the horrors of Nazism. Except for this type of argument, those who defend the inequalities of the modern world rarely resort to the type of teleological essentialist claims which sustained feudalism but, rather, are forced to argue that the equality in question is, in some sense, earned. In this context, I would concur with Ulrich Beck's observation that the intrinsic disadvantages which used to be (or are) suffered by women are a hangover from a feudal world view (1992, pp. 103–127). While individuals may be different from each other and, as a consequence, can reap different rewards, modernity allows for no groups for whom a discontinuous essentialist logic applies. It is for this reason that one of the first tasks of early feminists was to argue that the differences in power resources between men and women did not reflect innate biological qualities.

In political philosophy one of the overall effects of this ontological change is a search for normative grounding without metaphysics. Liberalism based upon utility and Marxism based upon the labour theory of value are typical in this regard. Both these ideologies make sense within the logic of early modernity: but where does nationalism come from? 'Norwegianness' and 'Irishness' smack precisely of the metaphysical essences of the feudal age. There are two types of answer to this question, one in terms of normative political theory and the other sociological. While the sociological answer is the one we are going to pursue, I will briefly allude to the former because the normative claims of nationalists are usually trivialised. This is exemplified by Anderson's interrelated claims that there are no great nationalist thinkers and that nationalism should not be classified as an ideology due to the fact that it has no theoretical grounding (1983, p. 5). If this is the case, it impacts upon our sociological analysis because it necessitates an explanation of the fact that a theoretically irrational belief should be so powerful. If nationalism has no normative justification, then it would appear that all nationalists lack a critical faculty. We are back to 'false consciousness', which presupposes a theorisation of agency whereby populations do whatever is functional to the system (cultural dopes) or to elites (simple-minded victims of rationalisations) – sociologically a highly unsatisfactory state of affairs. There are plenty of beliefs which may be functional or beneficial in certain situations, but no one holds them because they are obviously philosophically, or otherwise, flawed. Consequently, it is sociologically necessary to show that nationalism is not normatively irrational.

The normatively logical basis of nationalism is implicitly found (this is a reconstruction) in two insights of early nationalism. Against Enlightenment rationalism, Romantic nationalists argued that the essence of the individual was not simply reducible to either utility or abstract reason. Culture and aesthetics presuppose life-giving forces which are beyond these elements. Contrary to simple utility/felicity calculus or, in a modern context, economic modelling and rational choice theory, the human spirit contains metaphysical forces which give meaning to life and creativity – there is a parallel here with John Stuart Mill's breakdown at the discovery of the soul-lessness of the utilitarian principles which he had learned from James Mill and Bentham. According to nationalists, these life forces have their origin externally in the culture of a nation. The unen-cumbered self of liberalism and the labouring man of Marxism are spiritless things whereas, in contrast, a creative soul goes beyond the economic self by internalising the collective memories of a national consciousness and reconstituting them through life-giving social practices. A person becomes a true self by uniting with a specific culture. From there, it is not a very large to step to arguing that the power of the state should be used to promote the culture of a nation – nationalism.

The second normatively perceptive insight of nationalists is what can be termed the hermeneutic insight. As has been argued by Isaiah Berlin (1992; 1981), many early nationalists, most notably Herder and Fichte, shared with Vico the philosophical insight that knowledge is grounded in meaning. While they accepted Kant's claim that knowledge of the world was constituted through the ability of humans to impose order upon the world, they did not believe that such ordering was a priori. Kant believed that the nature of the faculty of reason was universal, which was a premise which enabled him to conclude that it is possible to derive universal laws of justice. However, if it is the case that our ability to reason is not an empty abstract one but presupposes reasoning through language, this universal aspiration runs into difficulty. If reasoning without meaning is a theoretical impossibility and languages reflect culture, then language is the only basis of a political order using 'local' justice. If language reflects a way of life and, for instance, Germans actually make sense of the world differently from French speakers, then there are good normative grounds for a thinker like Fichte (1968) to argue that all Germans should have one government embodying their particular system of justice which reflected 'their' mode of thought – even if it is unjustifiably chauvinistic for him to argue that the German way of seeing the world is better than the French. While German nationalism is linguistically based, if it happens to be the case that a nation seeking independence does not have a distinctive language of its own, the hermeneutic argument can be extended to embrace other semiotic signifiers (customs and practices) constituting the interpretative horizon of a nation. However, it has to be acknowledged that language is the most complete system of meaning for interpreting the world, and it is for this reason that, where necessary, nationalists devote considerable energy to linguistic revival (Irish and Basque) and/or creating/ emphasising linguistic differences (between Norwegian and Danish; or between Serbo-Croat and Croatian, Serbian and Bosnian).

This normative argument is not presented as an incontestable defence of nationalism. If I were to put on the hat of political philosopher, there are flaws in it, but, from a sociological point of view, it makes the point that nationalism is not normatively unreasonable. However, while this gets us off the sociological hook of theorising nationalism in terms of 'false consciousness' and irrationality embraced by 'cultural dopes', it does not explain the appeal of nationalism. Ideologies do not simply gain adherents because of normative rationality – it is a necessary but not sufficient condition. There are many normatively coherent political philosophies which have few, if any, adherents.

In order to understand the success of nationalism we must revert to the ontology presupposed by our previous account of the transition to modernity. The ontology presupposed by Enlightenment logic is of agents who do not accept teleological, essentialist metaphysical accounts of reality and who question all authority. As modernity advances, this leads to the type of reflexive agency which many have argued characterises modernity. As argued by Giddens (1990) and Berger et al. (1973), modern people are agents who are confronted with the task of constituting themselves. You are no longer the type of person you are because of some essence conferred upon you by birth but, rather, you are who you are because of choices upon which you have reflected. Such a proposition is entirely consonant with the meritocratic principles of legitimacy. In such a theorisation, the overcoming of tradition means the replacement of habitual routines derived from the past by reflectively constituted choices. It is because of the absence of reflectivity that tradition was perceived of by Weber as a form of irrationality. In this theorisation an essential element is the idea that modernity is characterised by a displacement of meaningless routines by creative self-reflection (Mouzelis, 1999, p. 83). This is to be found not only in theorists of modernity, such as Giddens, Berger and Beck (to mention but a few), but also in the Foucauldian postmodern concept of the 'care of the self'. In the latter, identity in all its facets, including the body and gender, become like living art – an aesthetics of existence, a form of self-fashioning.

While it is undoubtedly the case that the spirit of the Enlightenment has problematised identity and, as a consequence, contributed to pressure towards self-reflexive constitution of identity there is good reason to believe that this has created new ontological insecurities which in turn have led to a desire for ideologies and modes of behaviour which counteract this drive toward reflexivity.

Let me also add that there is a sense in which the idea of increased reflexivity has an unfortunate affinity with the Hegelian idea of increased rationality. People are not more rational, they are differently rational and the nature of reflexivity has changed, not simply increased. To take a parallel, in *The Civilizing Process* (1978) Elias argues that modernity entails increased civilisation – interpreted as internalisation of constraint. Many sociologists have a resistance to Elias' hypothesis partly because they, mistakenly, believe that he uses the concept of civilisation as a term of commendation, but also because they sense that it is not the case that constraints have increased but, rather, that they have changed (Giddens, 1984, pp. 240–241). Elias' hypothesis would have been better put if he had argued that people have become differently civilised rather than more civilised. A similar point is made by Foucault, when he argues that different systems of knowledge entail different constraints, not simply a progression of constraints. In the realm of punishment, torture may appear to us as unstructured savagery, but this is only because the constraints of the sovereign mode of punishment are not completely obvious to us. In fact there were exact rules concerning the types of weights which could be used and in what way (Foucault, 1979, p. 40). Order does not replace disorder but, rather, different order. While this is not essential to our argument, I would suggest that we change our interpretation of modernity from more reflexive to differently reflexive.

How does the changed reflexivity of modernity have an elective affinity with nationalism? We are very much in the territory of Weber. At the time he was writing it appeared counterintuitive that there is an elective affinity between other-worldly Calvinism and capitalism. Similarly it is counterintuitive that modern reflexivity, which entails a questioning of essential essences, produces actors who are attracted to the essentialist and metaphysical idea of nations.

Modern reflexivity is tied to democratisation, emancipation and consequent changes in legitimacy. The former concepts are central to the idea of undermining three-dimensional power and what I term the fourth dimension of power as derived from Foucault. In order to understand how these aspects of power relate to reflexivity we need to analyse agency.

Agents are essentially interpretative beings who impose order upon the world through meaning. This meaning is largely at the level of tacit knowledge. Following Giddens' terminology, we will call this tacit knowledge practical consciousness knowledge – Elias and Bourdieu called it 'habitus' (the choice of terminology is irrelevant). The social actor also has a discursive consciousness, which is made up of knowledge that actors can put into words. Practical consciousness knowledge is tacit knowledge, which actors use in order to 'go on' in social life. Separate from discursive and practical consciousness knowledge, there is the unconscious (the conceptual equivalent of the id), which contains a number of drives which have to be repressed if ontological security is to be maintained.

Right at this moment I am discursively explaining a particular theory by using my ability to 'go on' derived from a practical consciousness knowledge of the norms of the English language and rules of interaction. Discursive consciousness presupposes practical consciousness knowledge. While the unconscious is generally kept repressed, there are continual transfers of knowledge between practical and discursive consciousness knowledge. When adults learn a language or custom they may learn it discursively but, when they speak the language fluently, or when acculturation has taken place, they have converted discursive consciousness knowledge into practical consciousness knowledge. Since everyday life is so complex, successful agency presupposes that most of the social knowledge used in social action is practical consciousness knowledge. This is an explanation for the familiar experience of learning the rules of a foreign language in school, demonstrating this in an an examination and, yet, being unable to speak it when visiting the country where the language is spoken. It would not be possible to get out of bed in the morning, never mind speak a language, if all meaning were interpreted discursively.

Knowledge also frequently moves from practical consciousness to discursive consciousness – for instance, when a foreigner asks a 'local' concerning social norms or when an actor moves into unfamiliar social environments. A similar form of transfer of knowledge is central to reflexivity. The act of converting tacit knowledge into discursive consiousness is the method by which tacit assumptions and taken-for-granted ways of life becomes interrogated. Once practical consciousness knowledge becomes converted into discursive consciousness knowledge it can become subjected to tests of legitimacy. Actors can confront social structures and ask themselves why things are done this way.

As I have argued before, it is a mistake to consider structures as reproduced singly. Actors do not simply structure their actions but they also have to find others who impose more or less the same meanings upon these actions as they do. This is precisely why Garfinkel's breaching experiments elicited the reaction that they did. In those experiments the students were being asked to structure in ways that were at variance with established patterns of structural reproduction and, as a consequence, those with whom they interacted rejected the meaning/orderedness of their actions. In Goffman's analysis, the creation of a performance is not dependent solely upon the intentions of the performer, but upon the audience. A dramaturgical performance fails if misinterpreted by others. To be successful, every act of structuration must elicit an act of confirming structuration. The generalised other, toward whom actors orient themselves, is a potential confirm-structuring other. Interacting others who reject a particular act of structuration engage in non-confirming structuration.

Order is meaning. What makes the one act the same as another act, done in a different place and time, is the fact that the same meaning is created again and again. This applies not only to meanings in language but also to the meaning of self. When a self-identity is created it entails the creation of a self as a carrier of meaning. The self becomes a carrier of meaning in much the same way as sounds or emblems are carriers of meaning. Because the reproduction of structure is not a solipsistic event, confirm-structuring others have to be found. Establishing a self-identity which is considered valid by others is an act of structuring the self in a manner which will elicit confirm-structuring others. This should not be considered a form of determinacy but, rather, a constraint which is not binding. Individuals can, if they so wish, insist on a meaning of self which does not receive confirming structuration from others. This is what the eccentric, the 'madman', those who are victims of labelling but refuse to accept their ascribed self, and those whom Foucault describes as resisting systems of meaning, all do.

As has been argued by Jenkins (1996, p. 20), the understanding of self is a complex and ongoing synthesis of internal self-definition and external definitions offered by others. In this language, identity is a complex and ongoing synthesis of structuration with regard to self and either confirming- or nonconfirming-structuration practices from others.

The fact that structural reproduction involves both structuration and confirming structuration entails that structural reproduction is essentially a collaborative affair. If structures are not considered legitimate in the eyes of one participant in an interaction, they may refuse to participate. Once practical consciousness knowledge of structural reproduction becomes discursively based the potential for noncollaboration increases. Structures of domination are frequently sustained by the fact that they are routinely co-reproduced by individuals acting purely out of practical consciousness knowledge (Haugaard, 1997, pp. 136–162).

Emancipatory politics does not entail an enlightened elite telling others what their true interests are but, rather, in destabilising relations of domination by facilitating in the conversion of practical consciousness knowledge into discursive consciousness knowledge (Haugaard, 1997, p. 141; Haugaard, 1992, pp. 220–237). Reflexivity is essentially a process whereby practical consciousness knowledge is reflected against the discursive self. The overcoming of three-dimensional power does not entail a privileged insight into true interests but an ability to critically examine practical consciousness knowledge. Based upon such self-reflection, the self as defined by other is not necessarily confirm-structured if, in the light of discursive consciousness knowledge, such an act is shown to entail the reproduction of structures of domination.

Once social knowledge becomes discursive and it becomes apparent that particular modes of collaborative structural reproduction contribute to the relative powerlessness of one of the necessary co-reproducers of structure, nonconfirming structuration may take place. However, the interrogation of practical against discursive consciousness knowledge does not necessarily entail rejection. It may be the case that structures are considered legitimate even if they entail relative powerlessness for some. There can be no hard and fast rule as to what people consider legitimate, but, at the most general level, once knowledge is discursive the most significant source of legitimation is the belief that the structures in question exist for a reason. The perception of legitimacy entails the type of situation described by Habermas as an ideal speech situation, in which convergence is established when the best reason wins. Contrary to Habermas, I would argue that this applies not only to modernity but also to feudalism. If the feudal serf is to contribute to the reproduction of the feudal structures of domination because of a belief in legitimacy, this entails that when they discursively interrogate the construction of serfness as an identity it is considered reasonable – the Great Chain of Being and essential essences make it so. In modernity this particular mode of legitimation is ineffective and, as a consequence, once the practical consciousness knowledge of structural reproduction is shown to reflect this type of reason, structures are challenged – which is why Beck argues that because inequalities between the sexes are remnants of essentialist feudal logic they are incompatible with the logic of high modernity.

With regard to social order, the conversion of practical consciousness knowledge into discursive consciousness knowledge is an ever-present potential source of social disintegration. If social actors find there is no reason for a particular structural practice, they may no longer collaborate willingly in structural reproduction. Of course, coercion can be used and, in that event, structures are held in place through the use of potential sanctions. In this case, power becomes obvious and violence is either just beneath the surface or continually in use. Here physical power takes the place of social power. Others are controlled by fear for their body rather than by the desire to contribute a collaborative construction of power structures. However, this is not what is at issue with regard to nationalism as a popular ideology.

The fact that structures have to be interactively reproduced is a continual potential source of social disintegration which is exacerbated by the fact that meaning is essentially arbitrary. Why should actors co-reproduce social structures which are 'mere convention' if they do not derive direct instrumental benefits from those structures? As I have argued in Chapter 2 of *Power in Contemporary Politics* (Haugaard, 2000), an important source of legitimacy is derived from the belief that structures are not arbitrary. Through reification, actors believe that meanings could not be different than they are. Meanings are the way they are because this is the only way in which they could be – a reaction which is a flight from ambivalence. In a Habermas ideal speech situation convergence will take place (contrary to what Habermas appears to assume) only if some kind of foundation is reached. If all that is found is pure conventionality, regress will be endless. This point is made by Wittgenstein in an imaginary conversation between someone who does not accept convention as a good reason and another who can offer only conventions. In the end, the latter's powers of persuasion are useless (Wittgenstein, 1967, p. 24).

How does one make meanings nonarbitrary? One of the most significant ways is a process of reification whereby structures are grounded outside social order. The meanings which sustain a particular social order are made to appear noncultural. There are many ways of doing this. The Great Chain of Being is one and tradition is another. In the modern world these will not suffice and other foundations take their place. Scientific truth is one such foundation. When Foucault practised his critique of the present through archaeology and genealogy, his stated goal was to show that things need not be as they are (Foucault, 1988, pp. 36–37). He unmasks the idea that the meaning of the present is an inevitability driven by truth. Rather, truth performs a reifying function which makes the conventionality of our interpretative horizons, the systems of meaning by which we make sense of the world, appear as outside the conventionality of meaning. Truth performs this function admirably because it is regarded as a view from nowhere. Nature can perform precisely the same function. Aristotle accepted that slavery was unjust if it existed by convention only, but not if it reflected nature. In Bourdieu's description of the fine taste of the bourgeoisie, he makes the point that for their local culture to be cultural capital it has to appear more than simply the arbitrary quaint taste of a particular group. Counterintuitive though it might be, their cultural practices are portrayed as natural. As one of the great aesthetes of the culinary art observed with regard to taste (a form of cultural capital): '... *taste* is a natural gift of recognizing and loving perfection ... There is such a thing as bad taste ... and persons of *refinement* know this *instinctively*' (quoted in Bourdieu, 1986, p. 68; italic original).

This need for reification is essential to our understanding of the ideological appeal of nationalism. As described by Gellner, nationalism sees

> ... itself as a universal, perennial and inherently – self-evidently – valid principle. It is, on this view, simply 'natural' that people should wish to live with their own kind, that they should be averse to living with people of a different culture and, above all, that they should resent being governed by them. (Gellner, 1997, p. 7)

In other words, nationalism is legitimate because it provides a foundation outside culture. Just like the truth constructed surrounding the science of delinquency, as described by Foucault, or the divine right of Kings, as portrayed in the Great Chain of Being, the naturalness of nations is a moment of closure. It is not arbitrary that people organise themselves into nations, it is a primordial urge which just is. It is a naturalness which transcends all mere convention. The metaphysical essentialist element of nationalism is an anchor against social disorder; it is what makes a particular social order legitimate.

Nationalism may provide legitimacy, but why is this form of legitimacy appealing to reflexive social actors? Social order is held in check by reifying factors. Let us imagine a reflexive actor converting practical consciousness knowledge into discursive consciousness knowledge. What happens when everything is perceived as arbitrary? What happens when the reflexive agent absorbs Foucauldian deconstructive style into the very heart of their being? They may become overcome with meaninglessness and a sense of self that goes into infinite regress like the elevator of nightmares, which falls into space.

Why does the modern pressure towards reflexivity not transform agents into lovers of ambivalence, as Bauman (1991) suggested that they might be? Building upon Heidegger, our being in the world is not separable from our interpretation of it. The essence of phenomenological insight is the realisation that we do not build a bridge between the self and the world out there as presupposed by the Cartesian world view. As Heidegger observes, the scandal of Western philosophy is not that we have failed to build a bridge between subject and object but that such a bridge was ever demanded. The unity of world and self is presupposed by being-in-the-world where objects exist ontically for our sake. When I see the table in front of me, I do not see an external object necessitating the construction of meaning through an epistemological bridge between me and it. Rather, it exists for the sake of me as meaning given. Its 'tableness' is inextricably bound up with my being-in-the-world, my particular ontology. If through some phenomenological *epoché*, I should decide to analyse the essence of chairness and, through radical Cartesian doubt, question the existence of the world out there, I would in the end be thrown back upon some meaning-constituted interpretative horizon which enables me to make sense of the world. If I were to interrogate this or that meaning, it could be done relative only to some other interpretative horizon. In the end there is no escape from ontology. The interpretative horizons with which we make sense of the world have, in the end, to be taken as given. There is no knowledge without ontic foundations beyond which there are more ontologies of meaning. The only general foundation that exists is a givenness that constitutes us as creators of order through meaning. In short, interrogation always ends with meaning and the conventionality that goes with it. This applies not only to that which is external but to the constitution of self-identity. Creating self-identiy means using the self as a carrier of meaning. These meanings do not exist on their own between signifier and signified as some form of correspondence. Rather, these meanings are constituted relative to a particular interpretative horizon. Meaning is relational within interpretative horizons. What happens if reflexive agents find themselves in an internalised ideal speech situation with nothing but layers upon layers of arbitrary conventions? They may become like Laing's description of schizophrenia.

Against infinite regress, the primordialness and naturalness of nations is a refuge from ontological insecurity. To the reflexive agent, the essence of Irishness and Norwegianness is an escape from ontological insecurity inspired by the arbitrariness of meaning. The ideological appeal of nationalism is that it offers an escape from the ontological insecurities of 'mere convention' created by reflexivity.

In Gellner's later work (1997), he wonders why nationalists have reacted so strongly to his constructivist model of nationalism. He is surprised by the fact that nationalists feel threatened by the idea that nationalism is culturally specific to modernity. He concludes that this is possibly because nationalists do not understand how important culture is. To say something is cultural is not, in the eyes of an anthropologist/sociologist like Gellner, equivalent to saying that it is trivial. However, Gellner has missed the point: if nationalism need not exist, if nationalist constructions of identity need not be, the reflexively constituted self faces the possibility of ontological insecurity inspired by the meaninglessness of infinite regress.

Not only does nationalism provide ontological security in terms of the constitution of self but it also provides this interactively. Structural reproduction presupposes both structuration and confirming structuration. Structuration without confirming structuration generates ontological insecurity. With regard to the relexive constitution of self, the position of creating a self who is not confirm-structured by others entails isolation and insecurity. In the case of negatively ascribed identities, actors may wish to pay the ontological costs of being a self whose identity is never confirm-structured. However, having an identity which others confirm-structure automatically is ontologically much more desirable. Hence, it makes ontological sense to buy into ready-made identities. Rather than risk living in a solipsistic universe of continual misunderstandings and misrepresentation, it is better to define the self in terms of Irishness or Norwegianness. Such an identity will be confirm-structured unproblematically and interaction will flow smoothly.

The desire for ontological security by avoiding either the potential infinite regress of arbitrary meaning or the interactive failure of non-confirming structuration is an internal force which feeds the ideological cravings for a nationalist primordialist certainty. However, in turn, they create external pressures toward others that reinforce the cycle of nationalism. The person who is not a nationalist is an inherent threat to those who are. Like Foucault, they are telling us that things could be otherwise. They are signifiers who, if internalised into the interpretative horizon of nationalists, have the potential to throw that nationalist back into an infinite regress of ontological insecurity. Nationalists have a direct ontological interest in the perpetuation of nationalism in others and, as a consequence, may well coerce or encourage others into nationalism. This is the reason that the universalism and internationalism of intellectual Jews posed a threat to German nationalism. Not only were they ambivalent beings, as argued by Bauman (1989), but also the living proof that nationalism is merely the embodiment of another set of arbitrary conventions invented at a certain time and in a certain place. They were signifiers that entailed ontological insecurity in a world desperately searching for foundations to reflexivity.

References

Anderson, B. (1983) *Imagined Communities: Reflections on the Origin and Spread of Nationalism* (London: Verso).

Bauman, Z. (1989) *Modernity and the Holocaust* (Cambridge: Polity Press).

Bauman, Z. (1991) *Modernity and Ambivalence* (Cambridge: Polity Press).

Beck, U. (1992) *Risk Society* (London: Sage).

Berger, P., Berger, B. and Kellner, H. (1973) *The Homeless Mind* (New York: Random House).

Berlin, I. (1981) *Against the Current* (Oxford: Clarendon Press).

Berlin, I. (1992) *Vico and Herder* (London: The Hogarth Press).

Bourdieu, P. (1986) *Distinction: A Social Critique of the Judgement of Taste* (London: Routledge).

Dworkin, R. (1977) *Taking Rights Seriously* (London: Duckworth).

Elias, N. (1978) *The Civilizing Process: The Development of Manners* (Oxford: Blackwell).

Fichte, J.G. (1968) *Addresses to the German Nation* (New York: Harper Torchbooks).

Foucault, M. (1979) *Discipline and Punish: The Birth of the Prison* (Harmondsworth: Penguin).

Foucault, M. (1988) *Michel Foucault: Politics, Philosophy, Culture* (ed. L.D. Kritzman) (London: Routledge).

Garfinkel, H. (1984) *Studies in Ethnomethodology* (Cambridge: Polity Press).

Gellner, E. (1983) *Nations and Nationalism* (Oxford: Blackwell).

Gellner, E. (1997) *Nationalism* (London: Phoenix).

Giddens, A. (1984) *The Constitution of Society* (Cambridge: Polity Press).

Giddens, A. (1990) *The Consequences of Modernity* (Cambridge: Polity Press).

Goffman, E. (1971) *The Presentation of Self in Everyday Life* (Harmondsworth: Penguin).

Habermas, J. (1984) *The Theory of Communicative Action, vol I, Reason and the Rationalization of Society* (Cambridge: Polity Press).

Haugaard, M. (1992) *Structures, Restructuration and Social Power* (Aldershot: Avebury).

Haugaard, M. (1997) *The Constitution of Power* (Manchester: Manchester University Press).

Haugaard, M. (2000) 'Power, Ideology and Legitimacy', in H. Goverde, P. Cerny, M. Haugaard and H. Lentner, *Power in Contemporary Politics* (London: Sage).

Heidegger, M. (1962) *Being and Time* (Oxford: Blackwell).

Jenkins, R. (1996) *Social Identity* (London: Routledge).

Mouzelis, N. (1999) 'Exploring Post-Traditional Orders', in M. O'Brien, S. Penna and C. Hay, *Theorizing Modernity* (London: Longman).

Wittgenstein, L. (1967) *Philosophical Investigations* (Oxford: Oxford University Press).

5   The Morphogenesis of Nation

Gordana Uzelac

One of the few, and most evident, points of agreement among the theories of nation and nationalism is that the nation is a social phenomenon. Hence, one could expect that social theory should be able to offer a starting point for the study of the nation. It would be too optimistic to say that the debates in social theory are more articulate than those debates in theories of nation and nationalism. However, while the current social theories at least use similar terminology, respect some basic epistemological assumptions, or share methodological approaches, an interdisciplinary approach to the study of nation and nationalism frequently opens a wide space for disagreements and misunderstandings among theoreticians. Without any aspiration to deal with or, even less, to resolve the current debates in theories of nation and nationalism, I will attempt to restrict my analysis to a single approach – a sociological approach. Hence, without offering any definition of the nation at this point it should be stated that the nation will be analysed as a particular social form with specific emergent properties. These properties have emerged as a result of a particular interplay of social structures and cultural systems among a given social group, and as such became a 'real' social phenomenon, that is, irreducible to its 'parts' – members of the nation – and inexplicable as an epiphenomenon.

Hence, an analysis of the process of nation formation and re-formation requires both theoretical and methodological frameworks which will serve as the basis for, firstly, an analysis of a distinctive social phenomenon – the nation; secondly, an analysis of the formation of a new social phenomenon; and, finally, an analysis of a specific social process.

The nation, it is easy to agree, emerges as a result of a social change. Sztompka (1993), however, indicates that any attempt to explain social change in terms of a single factor is insufficient. The factors of social change can be found in the domain of *ideas* – either as innovative technological ideas, political ideologies, or economic and religious doctrines; in the domain of the integration or malintegration of the different political, social or economic *institutions* of a society; or in the domain of the intended or unintended consequences of actions of individuals or different *social groups* in a society. Hence, one can conclude that any attempt to explain the phenomenon of social change must deal with the interplay between social structure, social culture and social action. An examination of the interplay between structure, culture and actions can not only systematise the factors of social change, but can also provide a framework for analysis of the mechanisms of social change. One theory which analyses the relationships between social structure, culture and action as a basis for social change is realist social theory.

Realist social theory

Realist social theory, most clearly expressed in the work of Margaret Archer (1988, 1995, 1996, 1998a, 1998b, 1998c) has been developed around the current debates in social theory regarding the relationship between structure, culture and agency. The common starting point of these theories is the understanding that social theories which present society in terms of dichotomies – such as 'the individual vs. society' and 'action vs. order' – have failed to explain an interplay between structure, culture and agency and hence the dynamics of an open system such as human society.

Margaret Archer developed realist social theory on similar assumptions. Archer claims that the fallacies of the so-called *myth of cultural integration*[1] and three types of conflation – 'downwards', 'upwards' and 'central' – marked the theorising of the relationships between structure and agency in social theory.

The *myth of cultural integration* can be described as 'one-way theorising', which conflates structure with agency. Theorising which reduces structure and culture to agency, that is, which denies their independence as different strata of social reality and explains them just as epiphenomena of the activities of agents, Archer calls *upwards conflation*. In contrast to this, theorising which reduces agency to structure and culture, that is, which explains agency as entirely determined and, hence, as their epiphenomenon, Archer labels as *downwards conflation*. These two versions of conflation, according to Archer, preclude any interplay between structure and agency. One level of social reality is always rendered inert: 'instead of interplay there was the one-way domination of either the logical (downwards account) or the causal (upwards account)' (1996, p. 97). However, epiphenomenalism, according to Archer (1996, p. 97), 'is not the only way in which the more general process of conflation operates'. The third type of conflation Archer calls *central conflation*, and this theorising is characterised by the elision of structure and agency. The best example of this type of conflation Archer finds in Giddens' structuration theory, which introduces the concept of duality and agency and structure as ontologically inseparable.[2] Central conflation deprives both structure and agency of their relative autonomy, 'not through reducing one to the other, but by *compacting* the two together inseparably' (Archer, 1995, p. 101). As a result of this elision, any analysis of the interplay between structure and agency is impossible.

Through the criticism of conflation theorising, Archer develops another approach to studying the relationship between structure and agency – *analytical dualism*. Analytical dualism is based on two premises:

> Firstly, it depends upon an ontological view of the social world as stratified, such that the emergent properties of structure and agents are irreducible to one another, meaning that in principle they are analytically separable. Secondly, it asserts that given structures and agents are also temporally distinguishable (in other words, it is justifiable and feasible to talk of pre-existance and pos-teriority when dealing with specific instances of the two), and this can be used methodologically in order to examine the interplay between them and thus explain changes in both – over time. In a nutshell, 'analytical dualism' is a methodology based upon the *historicity of emergence*. (1995, p. 66)

Hence, analytical dualism assumes the social world as made up of structure, culture and agents, which belong to different strata of social reality. Any reduction of one to the other or elision of one of them would preclude the exploration of the interplay between them.

Archer argues that it is *necessary* to separate structure and agency in order (a) to 'identify the emergent structure(s), (b) to differentiate their causal powers and the intervening influences of people due to their quite different causal powers as human beings, and, (c) to explain the outcome at all, which in an open system always entails an interplay between the two' (1995, p. 70).

The analytical separation of structure and agency provides a methodological tool for analysis of the interplay between them. According to Archer, agency always operates in some given structure.

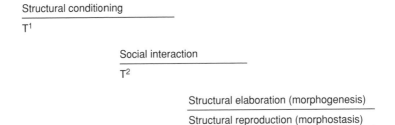

Fig. 1   The basic morphogenetic/static cycle of structure (Archer, 1995, p. 157)

So, structure 'necessarily pre-dates the action(s) which transforms it'; and this 'structural elaboration necessarily post-dates those actions' (1995, p. 76). Structures, as emergent properties, are 'irreducible to the doings of contemporary actors', yet they emerge from the 'historical actions which generated them, thus creating the context for current agency' (1995, p. 139). This process Archer calls a *morphogenetic circle*. Processes in which a system, state or structure is elaborated or changed as a consequence of social interaction Archer defines as *morphogenesis*. Conversely, processes in which 'complex system–environmental exchanges' tend to preserve or maintain a system's given form, organisation or state she defines as *morphostasis* (1995, p. 165).

The morphogenetic/static cycle offers an explanatory framework which acknowledges and incorporates (a) '*pre-existent structures* as generative mechanisms' – structural conditioning, (b) 'their *interplay* with other objects possessing causal powers and liabilities proper to them in what is a stratified social world', which happens at the level of social interaction, and (c) 'non-predictable but none the less explicable *outcomes* from interactions between the above', which can result as structural elaboration (morphogenesis) or as structural reproduction (morphostasis) (1995, p. 159). The morphogenetic/static analysis of structure is therefore based on four propositions:

(i)   there are internal and necessary relations within and between social structures (SS);

(ii) causal influences are exerted by social structure(s) (SS) on social interaction (SI);

(iii) there are causal relationships between the groups and individuals at the level of social interaction (SI);

(iv) social interaction (SI) elaborates upon the composition of social structure(s) (SS) by modifying current internal and necessary structural relationships and introducing new ones where morphogenesis is concerned. Alternatively, social interaction (SI) reproduces existing internal and necessary structural relations when morphostasis applies. (1995, pp. 168–169)

According to Archer, the method of analytical dualism based on separation and temporal analysis of the interplay between structure and agency can be directly applied to an analysis of the interplay between culture and agency. In this case, the basic propositions can be reformulated by stating that culture can be separated from agency, since culture possesses its own emergent properties, that is, it has its own irreducible and relatively enduring character and autonomous influence. Culture, therefore, necessarily pre-dates the action(s) that transform it, and cultural elaboration necessarily post-dates those actions. The relative autonomy of structure and culture means that 'they are not necessarily in synchrony with one another' (1995, p. 218). Archer argues that 'any form of socio-cultural conditioning only exerts its effects on people and is only efficacious through people' (1995, p. 184). Both cultural system and structural integration are creating a situational logic which motivates different forms of agents' actions. This *situational logic* is a consequence of the relationships between the elements of structure and culture.

At the structural level, which exists at any given time, relationships between the elements (institutions) can be either necessarily or contingently related to one another. Alternatively these relationships may be ones of complementarity or incompatibility (1995, p. 216). These relationships create four types of 'institutional configurations' which Archer calls the 'second order emergent properties' (1995, p. 216), and they create four possible situational logics.

First, when the institutions are in the relation of *necessary complementarity* they are 'mutually reinforcing, mutually invoke one another and work in terms of each other' (1995, p. 219). This relationship of high system integration creates a situational logic of *protection*, where the highest benefits for the agents are found in sustaining and supporting the established system, since alternative resources are unavailable. In this case morphostasis is the most probable outcome.

Second, the institutions can be in the relationship of *necessary incompatibility*. '[W]hen two or more institutions are necessarily and internally related to one another yet the effects of their operations are to threaten the endurance of the relationship itself, this has been referred to as a state of "contradiction"' (1995, p. 222). This relationship opens a space for changes, yet an unstable configuration creates the situational logic of *compromise*, since the outcome of any change is still uncertain.

Third, in the situation when contingent institutions are incompatible with each other, either because of internal or external influences (such as war), the agency finds itself in a situation when the greatest gains could be achieved by 'inflicting maximum injuries on the other side'. Hence, the institutional relationship of *contingent incompatibility* creates a situational logic of *elimination*.

Finally, the contingent institutions can be compatible with the interests of particular groups. This creates a situation of status quo, that is, a situational logic of *pure opportunism* where the agencies tend to preserve their already achieved gains and protect themselves from any losses. Still, this situational logic can be morphogenetic, with the emergence of new interests of the agency and new material means for institutional repatterning.

Just as at the level of structure the elements (institutions) can be in the relationship of contradiction or complementarity, so the elements of culture can be in similar relationships. The four 'second order emergent properties of structure' listed above correspond with four 'second order emergent properties of culture', and they create another four situational logics. At this point, culture is 'conceptualised as supplying directional guidance for agency' (1995, p. 229). Archer tries to analyse the possible relationships between the agencies which represent different theories, ideologies or beliefs. She argues that the 'maintenance of ideas which stand in manifest logical contradiction or complementarity to others, places their holders in different ideational situations' (1995, p. 229) (see Fig. 2).

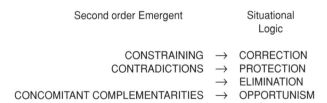

Second order Emergent		Situational Logic
CONSTRAINING	→	CORRECTION
CONTRADICTIONS	→	PROTECTION
	→	ELIMINATION
CONCOMITANT COMPLEMENTARITIES	→	OPPORTUNISM

Fig. 2   Cultural conditioning of strategic action

These second order emergent properties of structure and culture form a context which conditions the actions of the people within it – that is the first stage of every morphogenetic cycle, which Archer calls 'social and cultural conditioning'. However, only by analysing the second phase of the morphogenetic cycle – the level of socio-cultural and group interaction – is it possible to examine 'how the relationships between people are capable of changing or maintaining the relationships between ideas' (1995, p. 184) and institutions. Hence, these 'people' are not merely passive holders of ideas or puppets of their institutions, but active agents who transform and maintain them. Yet, through the process of changing their environment, the agency changes itself. A specific position of agency in society as a medium of all changes is produced by 'double morphogenesis'[3] – 'people collectively generate the elaboration of structure and culture, but they themselves undergo elaboration as people at the same time' (1995, p. 253).

Sociocultural conditioning of the groups does not direct behaviour of the agency. Rather, it is responsible for the distribution of resources amongst different agencies and hence creates a context in which agencies are rewarded for protecting and promoting their vested material and ideational interests. An agency positioned in this way has 'powers proper to itself ... Its typical powers are capacities for articulating shared interests, organising for collective action, generating social movements and exercising corporate influence in decision making' (1995, p. 259). Such agencies, which organise and articulate their interests, Archer calls *corporate agents*. On the other hand, Archer calls those which lack both organisation and articulation of their interests, and hence are unable to exercise their power in structural and cultural modelling, *primary agents*. Even though passive in direct social action, a primary agent 'reconstitutes the environment which Corporate Agency seeks to control' (1995, p. 260).

However, as mentioned before, the context of the second order emergent properties of culture and structure condition the regrouping of agency. In morphostatic situations the groups are mainly well defined where structural and cultural corporate agents are in control of resources and hence prevent primary agents from organising and articulating their ideas. These are situations which resemble those which Archer labelled the 'myth of cultural integration'. Yet, any alteration in an agent's situation redefines the categories of both corporate and primary agents. In a morphogenetic scenario 'progressive expansion of the number of Corporate Agents and divergence of the interests represented by them' results in 'substantial conflict between them' (1995, p. 263). This conflict alters the environment of primary agents by broadening the debate, which becomes an issue of 'popular agenda'. In conflicts between the corporate agents, their success becomes dependent on their success in the mobilisation of support amongst primary agents. The power of the primary agents in this context is what Archer calls 'co-action', where 'groups in roughly the same position (act) in approximately the same way' (1995, p. 267) and hence produce an aggregate effect which at the same time constrains and enables corporate agents. In this way primary agents present an 'environmental pressure of numbers'. Elaboration of social agency is thus the 'resultant of aggregate effects produced by Primary Agents in conjunction with emergent properties generated by Corporate Agents and thus does not approximate to what anyone wants' (1996, p. 265).

Hence, the proper answer to the question of when morphogenesis can happen can only be found in 'relations (interaction) between groups' (1996, p. 297) since social elaboration does not depend only on cultural proliferation or restratification of structure, but also upon their achieving social salience (1996, p. 304).

The distribution of resources and pre-grouping of agents determine their potential bargaining power. Finding themselves in the situations conceptualised by systemic complementarities and/or contradictions, these vested-interest groups are confronted with situational benefits or penalties. Their further actions, guided by existing situational logic, depend directly on the ability of corporate agents to 'organise mobilisation of the resources potentially available' (1996, p. 297). Depending on the success of this mobilisation, corporate agents will acquire a specific negotiating strength which positions them in a specific relationship to the other corporate agents involved.

However well positioned and defined groups are at this stage, it is difficult to 'predict' the outcome of this conflictual situation, since it occurs in an open system, that is, in human society. Anyway, as mentioned earlier, social changes can be identified only *ex post facto*. But the purpose of this theoretical exercise was not to equip a social scientist with a tool for prediction of social events in general. Archer's morphogenetic approach offers an explanatory methodology which results in an *analytical history of emergence*.

The purpose of this chapter is to offer an analytical history of the emergence of a nation. I believe that the morphogenetic approach can offer a methodological basis for such an analysis. Hence, in the next section I will attempt to offer a theoretical framework for the analysis of the history of emergence of any specific nation and to offer a definition of the nation as a specific social form.

Conflation in existing theories of nation formation

The most common classification of theories of the nation and nationalism has been centred around one question: what do the theories imply about the origins of the nation? The discussion between so-called primordialists and modernists has been based on whether the nation is 'invented, imagined or reconstructed' (Smith, 1991, p. 353). Even though this polarity is the most popular one, authors dealing with the classification and explanation of similar theories use other polarising classifications: Smith (1983, p. 12) – primordialism vs. instrumentalism, and perennialism vs. modernism; Comaroff and Stern (1994, p. 36) – primordialism vs. constructionism; and so on.[4] However they are named, one group of theories represents the attitude that 'nations and ethnic communities are the natural units of history and integral elements of the human experience' and the other group sees the nation 'as a purely modern phenomenon' (Smith, 1983, pp. 8–12). Alternatively, some theoreticians avoid using such terminology and present this distinction simply through the question as to whether a theory represents the idea of the creation of a nation before or after nationalism.

Theories dealing with the issue of the 'origins of the nation' assume a particular approach to the question of the process of social change, a result of which is the formation of a distinctive type of social form – the nation – and hence, directly involve issues regarding the necessary conditions, factors, mechanisms and scope of that change. Several of the most dominant theories of nation formation could be seen as examples of what Margaret Archer labels as 'conflation in social theorising'.

Today, one of the most prominent theories of the nation as a modern phenomenon is that of Ernest Gellner (1983; 1996; 1997). According to Gellner, the nation and nationalism are phenomena which originate from the process of transition from an agrarian society into a growth-oriented industrial society. Agrarian society was characterised by the existence of two horizontally differentiated (socially, politically and culturally) social strata. The first massive one was illiterate, food-production orientated, and static. The other was a literate, educated group which had all the economic and political power. These two groups, or as Gellner calls them, 'subworlds' (Gellner, 1983, p. 23), were sharply divided along cultural lines, separated by different ways of life, traditions, even language. Such a society, Gellner argues, cannot create or maintain either the nation or nationalism – 'an ideology' which is supposed to overarch all strata in a society.

On the other hand, a modern industrialised society is based on the idea of perpetual growth. It demands a highly mobile, literate, specialised workforce. The transition from the previous centralised, closed, and fused society into a decentralised, open, and specialised one (1983, p. 14) also transforms existing 'low culture' into a 'high culture'. High culture is 'a culture characterised by standardisation, a literacy- and education-based system of communication' (1983, p. 54). Gellner also labels this period of transition 'the age of nationalism'. 'Nationalism is not the awakening of an old, latent, dormant force, though that is how it does indeed present itself. It is in reality the consequence of a new form of social organisation, based on deeply internalised, education-dependent high cultures, each protected by its own state' (1983, p. 48).

Gellner's theory of nation and nationalism and their formation is a good example of 'downwards conflationism' in theorising the emergence of a social phenomenon. This theory implies that it is the social structure and the cultural system that not only provide the context of human action, but rather direct and limit it. Actually, the relationship between structure and culture, and agency, is of one direction. Structure and culture exercise their causal powers under which the sociocultural level, the level of their interaction with agency, is subsumed. Gellner's theory of nation formation is 'peopleless'. On the one hand, the changes in the structure and cultural system are seen as a product of contradictions within and between previous social structures and cultural systems; agency is only seen as their epiphenomenon. On the other hand, sociocultural cohesion is explained as a result of system integration and cultural cohesion.

Hence, in describing the 'nature' of the so-called agrarian society Gellner emphasises the structural and cultural contradictions within that society which, with the emergence of new technologies, brings them into direct conflict. New technology requires changed economic and political systems, which in return require a change in a cultural system. The sources of change are found exactly in these contradictions. Social change happens, and the nation emerges, as a result of the causal powers of social structures and cultural systems.

The result of this social change is, yet again, a fully integrated social system supported by cultural cohesion, now called 'national culture', achieved through a uniform educational system. The whole process is triggered from above. The members of the newly created nation are depicted as 'lemmings' whose actions and beliefs are shaped by a greater force. The mighty educational system teaches them to forget their old 'low' and 'high' cultures, and introduces a new 'national' culture of uniform language.

The nation described in these terms has to be explained as a new social phenomenon. It is a product of industrial and technological revolutions, which constitute a dramatic change of social systems. Hence, Gellner could ignore the question whether the nation 'has a navel' or not, since it is explained as a social form with a new integrated social structure and cultural system which, according to Gellner, have little in common with the 'low' and 'high' culture of agrarian societies. The nation emerges at a particular point in Gellner's unilinear evolutionist path of development after which a new era, the era of nationalism, starts, incomparable with previous stages of human development.

Gellner's theory of the nation and nationalism points to some of the most important processes of structural and cultural change which, one could easily agree, set the context for the formation of the nation. Yet, the picture of the process of nation formation is rather cloudy. The role of agency entirely disappears during this process. Hence, it leaves us wondering whether the industrial and technological revolutions and the introduction of a uniform state-sponsored educational system, besides being necessary, are also sufficient conditions for the formation of the nation.

One of the theories which is labelled 'primordialist', and stands in direct opposition to Gellner's, is that of Pierre van den Berghe. Along the lines of basic sociobiological assumptions, van den Berghe understands ethnicity as an extension of the idiom of kinship. Furthermore, here ethnic sentiments can be understood only as an extended and reduced form of kin selection. Like many other types of human community, an ethnic community, or as van den Berghe calls it, an *ethny*, is shaped endogamously and territorially.

In an attempt to explain the 'nature' of an *ethny*, van den Berghe reaches for the roots of human sociality. The basic units of human sociality are family, clan, tribe, i.e. small groups of interrelated individuals, who share common unilinear descent (patrilineal or matrilineal). This type of community has an 'evolutionary stable strategy'. Mutual interrelatedness is a guarantee for mutual max-imisation of inclusive fitness. A shared proportion of intrinsically selfish genes will always prefer kin over non-kin; nepotism will be the dominant kind of behaviour. Therefore, this mechanism can secure the immortality of the common gene, which is at the same time the basis of evolution.

At the moment when an exogamous basic group is transformed into an endogamous group, a breeding population of limited size whose members are related to each other, one can talk about an ethnic group. This 'ethnicity can be *manipulated*, but *not manufac-tured*' (van den Berghe, 1987, p. 27). Only with the developing of the political consciousness of an ethny, can an ethny develop into a nation: according to van den Berghe, 'the nation is a politically conscious ethny, that is, an ethny that claims the right to statehood by virtue of being an ethny. Such ideology is called nationalism' (1987, p. 61).

This biologically based explanation of the process of nation formation can be seen as an example of what Archer calls 'upwards conflation' in social theorising. Van den Berghe's starting point is the nature of human beings. Unlike Gellner, he rightly emphasises that humans as social beings create and then transform and maintain a specific set of relations known as social structure and cultural system, such as kinship, the family, the tribe, the ethny and, hence, the nation. All of these social forms are seen by van den Berghe as evolutionary stable strategies which secure human survival. Hence, the main rationale behind the creation and main-tenance of these social forms is not found either in human free will or in the 'nature' of social structure and culture, but in the internal driving force of genes. It would be unjust towards van den Berghe to say that he describes the whole richness of human society as deriving exclusively from genes. He recognises that human actions can be motivated by interests, principles and even curiosities. However, van den Berghe does not recognise the causal powers of those human 'creations'. Social structure and culture are not only transformed or maintained by agency, but they also provide a context and, at the same time, enable and condition human behaviour. Thus, for example, even van den Berghe cannot ignore the power of the taboo in directing the behaviour of a member of a tribe. This taboo could be seen as created by some members of a tribe in the past, but it is maintained by the following generations who live their lives according to the rules the taboo has set. These cultural and structural emergent properties always precede a particular agency, even though the same agency can transform them. This point can be even more clearly illustrated through another example of 'upward conflation' in explaining the process of nation formation.

With the aim of explaining the processes of nation formation, a group of theoreticians emphasised the role of social engineering 'which [is] often deliberate and always innovative, if only because historical novelty implies innovation' (Hobsbawm, 1983, p. 13). This approach also considers the creation of the nation as a modern process, but its methods are found in the so-called 'invention of traditions'. Eric Hobsbawm (1990; 1996) sees this set of practices as a method for the implementation of certain values and norms of behaviour simply by repetition. 'Inventing traditions ... is essentially a process of formalisation and institutionalisation, characterised by reference to the past, if only by imposing repetition' (1983, p. 4). This process occurs in moments of great social change, of rapid transformation in societies, when older traditions cease to fulfil the task they were designed for. '"New" traditions simply resulted from the inability to use or adapt old ones' (1983, p. 5). Such a rapid social change was most visible in the age of industrialisation and innovation – in a modern society. The creation of cohesion and stability in such a society can be achieved through three main modes of inclusion and control: (1) by establishing or legitimising institutions; (2) by the invention of new status systems and modes of socialisation, which will also provide modes for desirable beliefs, value systems, and behaviour; and (3) through the formation of a community such as the nation, which can provoke a sense of identification either with that community or with the institutions representing, expressing or symbolising it (1983, p. 9). Put in this way, the nation becomes a perfect means for the creation and stabilisation of modern societies, and it is constructed with that aim.

Hobsbawm's concept of 'invention' assumes the role of agency and yet it plays a crucial part in the process of nation formation. At the same time, agency is strongly influenced by radical changes of social structure and culture, which occur as a consequence of contingent contradictions between their 'parts'. However, it could not be said that Hobsbawm fully recognises the causal powers of structure and culture on human action. Following Hobsbawm's arguments, it seems that structural and cultural elaboration is entirely a result of agency's free will, which can invent a whole new set of 'traditions'. He does not recognise that even these 'new traditions' are set in the context of previous 'traditions' and other cultural emergent properties; that these 'new traditions' need a legitimisation for their introduction and are legitimised mainly by reference to the cultural system which preceded the changes.

Both van den Berghe's and Hobsbawm's theories of nation formation explain the emergence of the nation either as a result of agents' intentions and agendas or as genetically 'programmed'. At the same time both theories, though different in approach and context, fail to explain the influence of those necessary unintended consequences of human action in the form of stratified and complex social structure of a society, the richness of the cultural system, and above all, the interrelations between them. Even in the most turbulent periods it rarely happens that the whole social structure collapses, and that the entire existing cultural system proves unable to 'fulfil the task they were designed for'. New social forms mainly emerge as reflections of the old ones.

Several conclusions can be drawn from the examples of some of the most dominant theories of nation formation given above:

- any theory of nation formation which conflates one 'part' of social reality with another fails to explain the dynamics of the process of nation formation;
- such a theory cannot explain the stratified 'nature' of social structure, cultural system and agency and their causal powers;
- hence, such a theory fails to explain relations and interactions between structure, culture and agency on which the process of nation formation is based;
- such a theory cannot offer a sufficient explanation of necessary and sufficient conditions for morphogenesis to occur, the product of which would be a nation.

The morphogenesis of nation

The nation as a social form emerges through a process of social change. At the beginning of this chapter it was emphasised that in most cases it is difficult to predict when and if a social change will occur, and such a change can be detected and analysed only *ex post facto*. Nevertheless, even though subject to change, the relationships between structure, culture and agency are relatively enduring. It will now be argued that the process of nation formation can only be analysed by a closer examination of these relationships.

This analysis of the process of nation formation, based on the principles of analytical dualism, is necessarily historical in two senses: first, it assumes *historicity of emergence* (Archer, 1995, p. 66) where structure, culture and agency are not only analytically separable but also temporally distinguishable; and, second, the nation as a social phenomenon necessarily emerges in a specific historical period.

Following Margaret Archer's arguments, this analysis consists of three stages: first, it is necessary to analyse structural and cultural conditioning, that is, circumstances that preceded the emergence of the nation; second, an analysis of the dynamics of sociocultural and group interaction is necessary, in which contradictions between them can be explained; and, third, it is necessary to analyse the ways structural, cultural and group elaboration occur, which could ultimately result in the creation of the nation. Following Lockwood, Archer emphasises that agential interaction does not necessarily or even usually mirror systemic interaction (1996, p. 294). However, for a nation to emerge, a specific morphogenesis of structure, culture and agency has to occur in a relatively short period of time, and this can only be explained by individually analysing the three phases of emergence.

The aim of this section is not to offer a full account of the history of the emergence of the nation as a social phenomenon. Rather, it will be an attempt to construct a methodological framework for the analysis of the process of the formation or re-formation of a particular nation.

Structural and cultural conditioning

One of the common characteristics of all pre-national societies was the relation of necessary complementarity of structural emergent properties where the existing institutions were mutually reinforcing to one another. The system had developed institutions designed for reinforcing the rule of the monarch, protecting the existing distribution of resources, and preventing the emergence of any potential force which could contest it. One of the major forces required for the implementation of 'law and order' was the army, which served an individual, rather than a particular people or specific country. Even in situations where the rule of an existing monarch was contested by a pretender to the throne, the consequent system itself was not to be changed. Such a political system suited a mainly agricultural economy which, together with trade, small industry and occasional conquests, could sustain the existing political system. This high system integration produced a situational logic of protection, in which those involved would find sustaining the existing system to be personally beneficial.

While structural integration in these societies seems obvious, some authors, such as Gellner, question the level of its cultural integration. Indeed, in the way Gellner describes them, 'low' and 'high' culture have little in common. They represent two different life styles, sets of traditions, customs and mores, even languages. It was a period of low sociocultural integration. Yet, at the same time, at the level of the cultural system these two 'cultures' were in a direct logical relationship of 'necessary complementarity'. The 'high' culture of the elite would not have been possible or understandable without reference to so-called 'low' culture, and vice versa. However different in content these cultures were, reference to the 'low' culture necessarily invokes a 'high' one. The relationship between these two 'cultures' was regulated by the dominant doctrines, created in order to provide legitimisation for the existing distribution of resources. Hence, the ideas of a divine source of the monarch's sovereignty and of 'rights by birth' were equally accepted by both cultures, as too was the idea of a 'natural' division between those who rule and those who are ruled. Such a situation can be described as high cultural system integration.

This situation of high systemic (both cultural and structural) integration created a situational logic for agency and conditioned the creation of a single corporate agency in a society. This corporate agent managed to gain control over both ideational and material resources. Where structural and cultural emergent properties are in a relation of necessary compatibility, the cultural and structural corporate agents find an interest in sustaining and protecting the system. Hence, the cultural elite, mainly composed of, or controlled by, the clergy, found it beneficial to be sponsored by the political elite, thus securing their material interests. In return, the political elite adopted the doctrines promoted by the cultural elite, which provided its legitimisation. In contrast to these corporate agents, the vast majority of the unorganised population of primary agents, in a situation without many alternatives, were unable to articulate their interests. As Archer describes it:

> ... where there is unopposed cultural traditionalism and unchallenged structural domination, Corporate Agency tends to congeal into one, rather than developing fissiparous tendencies, and as a single group is even more empowered to mould and manipulate Primary Agents by controlling their opportunities for and attitudes towards greater social participation. (1996, p. 263)

Even though the primary agents are described as passive and unable to directly participate in reconstructing the structural system in which they live, they still constitute the environment in which the corporate agents act, and thus constrain them. What Archer calls 'cultural traditionalism' does not appear only at the level of the cultural system of the whole society. At the local level, independent from the corporate agents, primary agents are conditioned by their local 'low' cultures as well. While most of the corporate agents in a society share a similar 'high' culture, the primary agents are divided by their own traditions, maintaining their own local vernaculars, customs and mores, myths and symbols. Where these primary agents maintained a specific name for their group, and were attached to a specific territory, they were also recognised as a unique ethnic group.[5] Hence, unlike the corporate agents, the primary agents of a pre-national society are culturally conditioned in two ways – by the dominant doctrine which legitimises the position of the corporate agents, and by their local traditions. Even those who denied the legitimacy of the existing rule, either due to the lack of a competing doctrine, or to a lack of material resources, could not successfully contest its legitimisation.

In spite of the existing high level of systemic integration, factors such as strong divisions between corporate and primary agents, and division amongst the primary agents themselves, also prevented the creation of high sociocultural integration. Nevertheless, as long as the resources were concentrated in the hands of a single corporate agent, and as long as the cultural system was unable to produce alternatives, society continued to go through a series of morphostatic cycles.

According to Archer, these long periods of morphostasis are mainly responsible for the creation of a myth of cultural integration. However, every society undergoes some changes. The situational logic of protection, Archer explains, which is a result of necessary complementarities between structural and cultural 'parts', tends to strengthen pre-existing relations by both a systematisation of existing relations, and an adoption of systemic innovations. At the level of the cultural system, the systematisation of ideas results in a substantial increase in 'cultural density' (1996, p. 176). Thus it develops a specific vocabulary, distinctions, symbols and concepts, a tightly articulated set of ideas, which in return create 'natural boundaries' between cultures. Hence, while facing difficulties related to the adoption of further innovations, the systematised concept protects its stability by 'brooking no rivals from outside and repressing rivalry inside' (1996, p. 177). Such a protective closure strengthens the boundary maintenance of a particular culture. It is important to emphasise that the same process of cultural closure occurs at the levels of both 'high' and 'low' culture, yet not necessarily at the same time.

This is a rather simplistic picture of the structural and cultural conditioning of pre-national societies, mainly emphasising what was common in the majority of such societies. Of course, there are some significant differences between these societies as well. Without any wish to enter into a detailed discussion, it will be enough to emphasise the strategic differences between systemic conditioning of empires, monarchies and city states.[6]

Besides the structural differences in the management of societies due to their size, the most significant difference in the conditioning of agency was in the cultural domain. Even though the cultural systems of these societies were characterised by relations of necessary complementarities, not all of these systems had an equal success in systematising their main ideas, values and doctrines, or in protecting and reproducing them among their populations. Probably, in these terms, the most successful societies were those of the Western European monarchies. Here, the cultural elite, in co-operation with a structural one, managed to create and reproduce a unifying doctrine of legitimisation of their status which even at this stage prevented the formation of competitive corporate agents. On the other hand, the vast majority of population shared a similar local, 'low' culture. By protecting the 'intrusion' of any rival concepts from outside, which could contest the 'high' culture, the corporate agents were, at the same time, protecting any major disturbance of the local culture as well. As long as corporate agents were successful, the stability of the society was secured.

European empires faced bigger difficulties. Firstly, the main principle of the legitimisation of the dominant corporate agents, which was based on 'birth' and 'divine' rights, did not necessarily incorporate former elites of the conquered or 'inherited' societies, which had claimed their rights by the same principles. Moreover, these potential counter-elites were still perceived as corporate agents by their local populations. In spite of existing differences, the lack of resources, both material and ideational, prevented these former corporate agents from organising and articulating their interests. Secondly, at the local level, corporate agents were facing different environments created by culturally distinct primary agents. This conditioning, in turn, created the context in which corporate agents acted, and these agents inadvertently found themselves introducing instability into these local cultures.

In European city states, the situation was the opposite. Both 'high' and 'low' cultures found it difficult to 'protect' themselves from the influences of the surrounding cultures due to their closeness in space and context. Except in terms of a specific territory, these cultures could not successfully produce their own 'natural boundaries'.

As has been repeatedly emphasised, society is an open system and the protection from the 'intrusion' of novelties is always partial, even in the case of successfully systematised relations of necessary complementarities. By force of internal factors (e.g. pauperisation of the population) and external factors (like wars) the control of the corporate agents over the systemic configuration of society weakens. Hence, on the one hand, innovations in techniques and technologies implemented in the economy created a situation of contingent incompatibilities within the economic system which resulted in what some authors call the industrial revolution. On the other hand, ideas, doctrines and ideologies that could not be incorporated into the existing dominant core doctrine, were henceforth directly contesting it. These developments on both the structural and cultural levels necessarily conditioned the relationship between corporate and primary agents. As a result of the development of industrialisation, a redistribution of resources occurred. While the dominant elites were mainly engaged in agriculture, cultural reproduction and governing society, the primary agents entered into the sphere of industrialisation, both as managers and entrepreneurs, and as a newly urbanised workforce. A more complex economic system, along with the introduction of new technologies in war machinery, created a demand for stronger control over the structural system. Along with the industrialisation of society, a bureaucratisation occurred as well. These developments set the stage for possible socio-cultural interaction.

From this short overview of the systemic conditioning in pre-national societies, several methodological directions for an analysis of the emergence of a specific nation can be derived:

- any analysis of nation formation in a particular society has to take into account the specificities of developed structural and cultural systems;
- such an analysis has to explore relations between existing institutions which condition the distribution of material resources in a pre-national society;
- an analysis of the process of nation formation in a particular society must explain the relationships between the dominant set of doctrines, and the emergence of new doctrines and ideas which contest them;
- it is also necessary to analyse the level of sociocultural integration in that society, that is, the existence of separate cultural (ethnic) groups and the distribution of resources among them;
- an analysis, which offers an explanation of this specific structural and cultural conditioning, represents a starting point for the analysis of the sociocultural interaction of relevant agencies.

Sociocultural interaction

The structural and cultural conditioning described above created certain predispositions for the agency's actions. These conditional effects, 'to be socially efficacious ... have to be taken up, articulated and acted upon' (Archer, 1996, p. 253). As previously emphasised, systemic conditioning is mediated through agency, where it supplies the reasons for maintenance or change of the system. These reasons have to be recognised and accepted by an agency, and hence associated with its vested interests.

Newly created groups of entrepreneurs and bureaucrats were mainly recruited from primary agents. Both groups took over positions which enabled them to control material resources, by increasing their wealth or their power in governing the state. Yet, the strict distinction between the existing corporate agents and primary agents, as maintained by the dominant ideology, prevented these newly formed social groups from entering the ranks of dominant corporate agents. Certain ranks in the army, as well as in politics, like top positions in bureaucracy for example, were primarily reserved for the corporate agents themselves. Certain social circles were closed to the 'newcomers'. The education system, mainly controlled by the Church, was not open for all social strata. In addition, the existing corporate agents were controlling the taxation and customs systems, systems which were perceived as being restrictive to the newly developing industrialisation.

Even though the new agencies clearly recognised their own vested interests, they still could not directly challenge the legitimacy of the ruling elite. In order to accomplish this, these new agencies had to co-operate with a new cultural agency which could be able to create a counter-ideology. As Archer explains:

> Only if resources can be brought to bear to undermine the basis of domination, only if organisation can mobilise sufficient members to this end, and only if a counter-ideology challenging legitimacy and legitimating assertions is developed does a new Corporate Agent confront the entrenched Vested Interest Group. (1996, p. 266)

While the structural system produced new social actors usually labelled as the 'bourgeoisie', at the cultural level a new group of cultural agents emerged. Their emergence was the result of an inability of the cultural corporate agents to adopt and systematise new ideas within the dominant doctrines, since these newly created concepts and ideologies were in direct confrontation with the dominant ones contesting the same legitimacy of the corporate agents. The most dominant contesting ideology was that of nationalism. The 'core doctrine' of nationalism is summarised by Smith as follows:

1. the world is divided into nations, each with its own character and destiny;
2. the nation is the sole source of political power, and loyalty to it overrides all other loyalties;
3. everyone must belong to a nation, if everyone is to be truly free;
4. to realise themselves, nations must be autonomous;
5. nations must be free and secure if there is to be peace and justice in the world. (1999, p. 102)

As is apparent, the nationalist 'core doctrine' was built around the concept of popular sovereignty. The idea that the 'people' themselves have to be creators of their own destiny by forming their own government was presented as a 'natural law'. This concept was in direct opposition to the dominant doctrine, which recognised only one sovereign, the monarch. Yet, in order to successfully challenge the doctrine of the corporate agents, the term 'people' required further elaboration, and the demand for popular sovereignty further justification. Both were found in the concept of the 'nation'. The nation defined by a nationalist ideology is not an entirely 'new' concept created *ab ovo*. In this concept the nation is a delimited group, characterised by certain attributes. But the range of limitations and variety of attributions of such a group are necessarily constrained by pre-existing cultural and structural properties. On the one hand, those existing dominant doctrines and previously implemented structures, through the process of systematisation of their ideas and practices, had already formed a 'naturally bounded' agency. On the other hand, the broad population of these societies was not described as an agency just for the sake of being different from corporate agents. They were also adherents of their local cultures and structures. Nationalist ideologies defined the nation exactly around these specific properties – *their* culture. To be more precise: nationalist ideologies are not concerned with culture as a set of integrated ideas, concepts and doctrines, ways of life, symbols, myths and folk songs. Rather, they define a nation in terms of those cultural properties which could, first of all, be perceived by the majority of the given population as common and unifying, and second, as exclusive and unique. Only then can 'culture' be described as 'ours'. 'Our culture' is not only a marker of group boundaries. It is also a source of legitimisation for the group's existence and its rightful demands.

However, the vast majority of primary agents were disorganised and their demands were unarticulated, yet they formed the environment for the corporate agents' actions. Hence, newly emerging cultural agents could establish the idea of sovereignty among a specific population characterised by distinctive cultural characteristics. The idea of popular sovereignty was in a relation of necessary complementarity with the idea of the nation. This relation created a logical situation of protection and required further systematisation.

In order to challenge the position of dominant corporate agents, new structural agencies adopted the new nationalist ideology and hence made an alliance with the newly emergent cultural agency. At the same time, these new cultural agents, by collaborating with the new structural agents, found protection and sponsorship. Finding common interests, the new agencies acquired a structural organisation (either as political parties, movements or cultural groups) and an articulated legitimising ideology, which at the same time successfully challenged the legitimacy of the ruling elite, and hence they gradually established themselves as a new corporate agent. As such this new corporate agency put itself in the situation of direct confrontation with the old elite, each having its own bargaining powers.

Empires and city-state societies found themselves in an even more complex situation. In the case of empires, the redistribution of resources and the emergence of an alternative ideational concept – nationalist ideology – opened a space for the formation of several competing corporate agents. Those who managed to articulate their interests and organise themselves necessarily concentrated on challenging the legitimacy of the ruling elite. In addition, due to their competing vested interests, some found themselves in a direct confrontation with each other. The *concept* of the nation provided them with a tool for mobilising, not only their own culturally distinctive primary agents, but the local former elites as well.

The corporate agents of city states, who managed to define the structural but not the cultural boundaries of their societies, found themselves challenged by new corporate agents, who in turn had found a solution in the concept of the nation. As has already been emphasised, new cultural and structural agencies were mainly formed from the ranks of the primary agents. While corporate agents were still in possession of the bulk of resources, these primary agents could rely mainly on their human resources. The appearance of the new set of ideas, doctrines and ideologies, at the same time, opened a debate which put the issue of popular and national sovereignty on the 'popular agenda' (Archer, 1996, p. 267). The success of the new 'nationalistic' corporate agents now depended on the popular appeal of their proclaimed ideology.

Hence, in its second phase, an analysis of the formation of a particular nation has to examine developments of sociocultural interaction, conditioned by the structural and cultural systems in a pre-national society. A few methodological directions can be derived from this:

– for such an analysis it is necessary to determine all relevant agencies whose vested interests were in direct opposition to each other, due to the differential distribution of material and ideational resources;

- it is necessary to determine the main structural and cultural corporate agents and to explain the process of their emergence, and the relations between them;
- at the same time, the main characteristics of the primary agents have to be explained, especially with reference to their distinctive local cultures;
- special attention has to be given to the explanation of which cultural corporate agents developed a nationalist ideology, and how they went about doing this. This must include an analysis of the proposed definition of the nation in general and 'their own' nation in particular, the way it defined national culture, and proclaimed a political agenda;
- such an analysis has to examine the methods corporate agents employ for mobilising primary agents;
- therefore, an analysis of the sociocultural interactions of the main agencies in pre-national societies could underline the main processes which may eventually result in the formation of a particular nation.

Social elaboration

The main objective of this section, to paraphrase Archer (1996, p. 294), is to set out the conditions under which the morphogenesis of the nation might occur taking into account the developments in the sociocultural interaction conditioned in a prior social context. As Archer herself emphasises, bearing in mind that the nation emerges in a society defined as an open system, these conditions are only tendential. Moreover, the morphogenetic approach is not constructed with the aim of explaining the emergence of social phenomena, but rather to provide an explanatory methodological framework for an analysis of the emergence of a particular social phenomenon in a specific society at a defined time.

As has repeatedly been emphasised, even though conditioned by prior social structures and cultural systems, it is agency that changes or maintains them. Therefore, whether a sociocultural system will be reproduced or transformed depends exclusively on the developments in the sociocultural interaction of the corporate agents. Hence, as Archer explains (1995, p. 297) 'to specify the conditions under which changes are transacted is to indicate what, in addition to their initial bargaining position, gives a group *negotiating strength*'.

These initial bargaining positions of the groups are mainly determined by available resources and pre-groupings of agents. As was shown earlier, at the beginning the new corporate agents which adopted a nationalist ideology and agenda had limited access to material resources, which necessarily limited promotion of their demands. However, with the development of industrialisation, the division of labour, the development of bureaucracy and the systematisation of the new nationalistic doctrines, the availability and concentration of resources changed as well. These changes provided a new context for further interaction between conflicting corporate agents. The potential negotiating strength of the corporate agents in question depends on the availability of both material and ideational resources, but their real power depends mainly upon the social reception of their proclaimed ideology and political agenda by primary agents. These nationalistic corporate agents will occupy a better bargaining position only when they manage to successfully mobilise available material resources and gain the support of primary agents.

Primary agents were structurally and culturally constrained in a twofold manner: by their own local structure and culture and by those shaped and maintained by corporate agents. What defined them as primary agents was a lack of proper organisation and articulation of their own vested interests. This disorganisation was a direct consequence of the conditional influences of that dual set of structural and cultural emergent properties. Differences of gender, age, education, socioeconomic status, vernaculars, symbols, affinities, etc., in pre-national societies prevented them from forming an organised collectivity. At the same time, direct confrontation between 'old' and 'new' corporate agents forces them to seek support from primary agents. At this stage primary agents are still just 'recipients of struggles over decision-making between Corporate Agents' (Archer, 1995, p. 186). Even though unorganised and internally divided, these primary agents still present a substantial human resource which corporate agents will try to mobilise for their own purposes. However, through that process of mobilisation these primary agents '[a]s self-reflective agents, ... underwent regrouping in the process: in future time they were no longer a mere resource but have started to become a force – in a struggle which had now become their own' (Archer, 1995, p. 186).

To be more specific, new nationalist corporate agents formed their ideology around the principle of popular national sovereignty and consequently the principle of national self-determination, which directly challenged the legitimising principle of the 'old' corporate agents. In order to legitimise these claims, it was first necessary to define what is the nation and who are its members. Legitimisation is found in 'national culture'. Even though defined in *terms* of local cultures, these local cultures are not adopted as a whole into the new 'national' culture. Rather, local cultures provided already an existing set of cultural 'products', myths, memories, vernaculars, symbols, with which primary agents could identify. By carefully selecting specific cultural traits as markers of their nation, the corporate agents were politically organising fissiparous primary agents into a new community. However, it would be misleading to conclude that an appeal to common cultural traits alone is what mobilises primary agents. The appeal to the common 'national' culture defines the group which is to be mobilised, and offers a legitimisation for proclaimed demands. These proclaimed demands, and the stated political agenda of the nationalist corporate agents, are what will be decisive for the mobilisation of primary agents.

The beginning of this chapter also emphasised that the nation emerges as a result of a *process* of social change. According to the main principles of realist social theory a new social change occurs through the series of distinctive morphogenetic cycles. Any change which occurs in a structural or cultural system at the same time forms systematic conditioning for the following morphogenetic cycles. The morphogenesis of the nation has to be examined in the same manner.

Every redistribution of material and ideational resources available to the corporate agents is a product of some morphogenetic cycle. The existing distribution of resources conditions the actions of corporate agents involved. The level of availability of resources to nationalist corporate agents at their inception, the level of systematisation of their proclaimed ideology, and their direct relation to other corporate agents, condition the formulation of their demands. Therefore, for example, not all nationalist corporate agents set as their primary demand the formation of an independent nation state. Conditioned by the structural and cultural context, corporate agents have to deal with the issues they perceive as the most constraining or beneficial for the development of their bargaining power. Hence, nationalist corporate agents might include in their political programme, and make their primary aims, issues regarding the usage of their 'national' language in the education system, minority rights, equality of opportunity, parliamentary representation, and other similar issues. Even if corporate agents manage to define national culture and their nation in a form attractive to primary agents, their success in mobilising these primary agents will depend on the ways in which nationalist corporate agents have responded to pressing political, economic and social problems. With a changed set of structural and cultural circumstances, the corporate agents would have to redefine their ideology in order to sustain the broad support of primary agents. This does not just include a redefinition of priorities or the introduction of new political demands. Influenced by internal and external factors, the nationalist corporate agents will also have to redefine their national culture, their concept of the nation in general and 'their own' nation in particular. Like any other social form, the nation is an open system predisposed to change.

The question still remains: when does the nation emerge? Following the definition of the nation given earlier, it could be said that a specific nation emerges when:

- the nationalist corporate agents manage to institutionalise their activity through some kind of political, economic or cultural organisation;
- the nationalist ideology of corporate agents manages to clearly define the 'national culture';
- the nationalist corporate agents successfully mobilise the primary agents around their proclaimed ideology and political agenda;
- the primary agents regroup into a promotive interest group whose co-action supports the corporate agents' demands;
- the primary agents perceive each other as members of the same community;
- such a triple morphogenesis, that of agency, structure and culture, occurs at a roughly similar time.

When the conditions for the emergence of the nation are set in this way, a specific definition of the nation is imposed: hence, the nation will be defined as a social agency politically organised as a community which claims its rights on the basis of a culture defined as its own.

It is a political organisation that, on the one hand, re-stratifies a structural system (by forming political parties, a leadership, and ultimately state institutions); and on the other, offers a set of values, beliefs, ideas, etc., in a form of 'nationalist ideology'. Such a nationalist ideology offers a basis for mobilisation of the population around proclaimed national symbols, national values, national myths and memories, aims and agendas.

On the basis of this politicised culture the social agency perceives itself as a community. In this definition the term 'community' implies in and of itself, firstly, that its members *perceive* each other as members of the same social group and, hence, distinguish themselves from 'the other'. Secondly, being 'a community' assumes that this group *perceives* itself and is perceived by others as a group which possesses a set of unique characteristics. Finally, it implies that its members perceive each other as equals and that the group promotes solidarity amongst its members. This definition does not claim that the members of the same nation *are* equal or that the characteristics of this community *are* unique for that group. A perception of its members is what constitutes them as a community.

However, the social structure of the nation and nationalist ideologies are not formed *ex nihilo*. The structure of the nation is always formed with reference to previous existing structures; nationalist ideologies are always formed with reference to existing culture. Anyway, this diversity of structures and cultures which have *preceded* the formation of nations is what ultimately characterises these nations as 'Western' or 'Eastern', 'ethnic' or 'civic', 'state-seeking' or 'state-sustaining', 'cultural' or 'political', etc. Moreover, the formulation of a nationalist ideology is always contextualised by a form of social structure, and the structure of the nation is always reconstructed with reference to the proclaimed nationalist ideals.

Notes

1. For more about the myth of cultural integration, see Archer (1996, pp. 2–6).
2. For more about Archer's criticism of the structuration theory, see Archer (1995, pp. 93–134).
3. Archer defines agency as a product of 'double morphogenesis', as 'collectivities sharing the same life chances' (1996, p. 255). She distinguishes Agency from Actors and Persons where 'Agency stands as the middle element linking Person to Actors' (1996, p. 255). For more about the definitions and distinctions between Agency, Persons and Actors, see Archer (1996, pp. 255–257).
4. For a full explanation of these concepts see Smith (1998).
5. In order to keep the arguments as simple and clear as possible, at this point I will not further develop the relationship between the ethnic group and the nation.

6. I believe that parallels could be drawn with the non-European and colonial societies as well, but at this point, in order to keep the argument as simple as possible, I will not refer to these societies.

References

Archer, M.S. (1988) *Culture and Agency: The Place of Culture in Social Theory* (Cambridge: Cambridge University Press).

Archer, M.S. (1995) *Realist Social Theory: The Morphogenetic Approach* (Cambridge: Cambridge University Press).

Archer, M.S. (1996) 'Social Integration and System Integration: Developing the Distinction', *Sociology*, vol. 30, no. 4, pp. 679–699.

Archer, M.S. (1998a) 'Addressing the Cultural System', in M. Archer, R. Bhaskar, A. Collier, T. Lawson and A. Norrie (eds) *Critical Realism: Essential Readings* (London: Routledge).

Archer, M.S. (1998b) 'Introduction: Realism in the Social Science', in M. Archer, R. Bhaskar, A. Collier, T. Lawson and A. Norrie (eds) *Critical Realism: Essential Readings* (London: Routledge).

Archer, M.S. (1998c) 'Realism and Morphogenesis', in M. Archer, R. Bhaskar, A. Collier, T. Lawson and A. Norrie (eds) *Critical Realism: Essential Readings* (London: Routledge).

Comaroff, J.L. and Stern, P.C. (1994) 'New Perspectives on Nationalism and War', *Theory and Society*, vol. 23, no. 1, pp. 35–45.

Gellner, E. (1983) *Nations and Nationalism* (Oxford: Blackwell).

Gellner, E. (1996) 'The Coming of Nationalism and Its Interpretation: The Myths of Nation and Class', in G. Balakrishnan and B. Anderson (eds) *Mapping the Nation* (London: Verso).

Gellner, E. (1997) *Nationalism* (New York: New York University Press).

Hobsbawm, E.J. (1983) 'Introduction', in E.J. Hobsbawm and T. Ranger (eds) *The Invention of Tradition* (Cambridge: Cambridge University Press).

Hobsbawm, E.J. (1990) *Nations and Nationalism Since 1780: Programme, Myth, Reality* (Cambridge: Cambridge University Press).

Hobsbawm, E.J. (1996) 'Ethnicity and Nationalism in Europe Today', in G. Balakrishnan and B. Anderson (eds) *Mapping the Nation* (London: Verso).

Smith, A.D. (1983) *The Ethnic Origins of Nations* (Oxford: Blackwell).

Smith, A.D. (1991) *National Identity* (London: Penguin Books).

Smith, A.D. (1998) *Nationalism and Modernism* (London: Routledge).

Smith, A.D. (1999) Myths and Memories of the Nation (Oxford: Oxford University Press).

Sztompka, P. (1993) *The Sociology of Social Change* (Oxford: Blackwell).

van den Berghe, P.L. (1987) *The Ethnic Phenomenon* (New York: Praeger).

6 Cultural Variety or Variety of Cultures

Zygmunt Bauman

Radical change is taking place in the way we think and talk of 'culture' – that part of human condition which is 'human made': the part, that is, which has not been determined by the no-appeal-allowed verdicts of inhuman nature, but depends on past, present and future human *choices* and could be therefore, at least in principle, different than it is.

The idea of 'culture' is modern: it was born together with the modern spirit notorious for its bold and sometimes arrogant ambition to correct, improve and otherwise remake the setting of human life so that it would serve better the cause of decent life and human happiness. The term 'culture' appeared first in eighteenth century vocabulary as an exhortation, a clarion call, the name of a job to be done and a declaration of intent to see that job through. The concept conveyed a message: like plants in the field, orchard or garden, human beings need to be cultivated in order to develop in full their best qualities. The humanity of human beings is not something 'given', and will not develop of its own accord. Humanity lies still ahead: it is a task – one which has to be carefully designed, resolutely executed and vigilantly monitored all along.

Since culture, unlike 'nature', was a matter of choice – a sediment of choices made in the past and the outcome of choices currently made – it went without saying that the 'humanity' which the effort of cultivation (of teaching, training, educating, socialising, or whatever other name was used for that 'formative' influence) brings to bear may take various shapes and colours. There are many cultures: as Ruth Benedict famously put it, there are many cups with which different peoples drink from the stream of life.

The concept of 'culture' had an evaluating ring: it implied hierarchy – it suggested that 'being cultured' is a matter of degree, that there could be men and women who are better, worse or not at all 'cultured' (educated, refined), who come closer to, or stay distant from, the ideal which the labour of cultivation aimed to promote.

But it had also a differentiating edge: human collectivities differ from each other depending on the 'cultural patterns' by which they shape and obey their daily routines, setting apart the proper from the improper, good from evil, the beautiful from the ugly, the desirable from the resented, true from false and right from wrong. Each culture has its ideal standard, but what is considered to be ideal differs, and it is this difference between selected ideal patterns that makes human groups different from each other.

Our perception of the world is as a rule 'praxeomorphic'. We tend to see the world through the prism of the tasks we set for ourselves or the 'problems' which we recognise as calling for our attention and are struggling to resolve. At the time the idea of culture was coined, the human world was viewed from the perspective of the agenda set by the ruling and the learned classes engaged jointly in the complex task of 'nation building'. While setting that task, the governments of the emergent nation states, unlike the powers of the *'ancien régime'*, could not rely on the intrinsic wisdom of self-reproducing habits and routines: transformation of the many and varied types of 'locals' into the patriots of 'one nation' would not have occurred of its own accord.

Loyalty to the state claiming to embody the unity of the nation will not sprout and ripen by itself: its seeds have to be carefully selected and sown, fertilised, sheltered from inclement weather, protected against weeds and parasites. To replace the irritating randomness of the plurality of ways of life by an integrated and one-for-all national culture, not just intense indoctrination, but coercion had to be frequently used and a penal system had to be set in operation: under the French Third Republic, for instance, use of 'local dialects' instead of standard French was prohibited, and penalised, in schools (including the playgrounds), in the army and in public offices (Varnier, 1999, p. 69). Governments of the day treated their compatriots not unlike the populations of invaded countries were treated by their conquerors bent on colonising the captured territory and effacing its separate identity. Intended homo-geneity of national culture required stamping out local customs, dialects and calendars, consigning local histories to oblivion and tearing apart local bonds and loyalties. The confused and confusing variety of locally rooted traditional forms of life had to be thrown into a melting pot and recast as the spirit of the not-yet-existing nation. 'National culture' was nowhere else but at the horizon of the long and tortuous effort of cultivation.

Protecting the shared history, serving the shared interests and securing the shared future of the nation was to become the prime legitimating formula of modern states: the formula all governments of modern states would invoke whenever demanding from their subjects discipline to the law of the country, obedience to the powers of the state and sacrifice in the name of the shared goals as set out by state authorities.

Propagation of national solidarity, of the 'us' feeling (and so of the 'us versus them' perception of the world) provided the lens through which the role of culture was viewed and the cognitive frame in which the vision of culture was plotted. Like all other legal and institutional supports for nation-state sovereignty and for its claims to the citizens' obedience, culture had to be complete, distinctive and internally coherent and harmonious. No wonder it was visualised as a system – and a total and self-sustained system. Everything in a culture visualised in such a fashion was related to everything else, there was no room inside it for anything which jarred, or did not fit in with the rest, anything 'dysfunctional' or simply useless and devoid of function. It was feared that imported items would throw the totality out of balance, disturb or even incapacitate the system as a whole. Cultures basked in the reflected glory of nation-state sovereignty and like the state-made laws claimed a monopoly over the territory under the state's sovereign rule. In Ulf Hannerz's (1993, p. 68) description, cultures tended to be imagined as 'bounded, pure, integrated cohesive, distinctive, place-rooted and mapped in space'.

It is this image which has lost by now a lot of its past credibility. And no wonder – since the powers of the nation state (more exactly, of the modern state struggling to become a nation state), whose practices sustained the credibility of that image and made it look like a faithful replica of cultural reality, have been radically weakened, while the holders of state power have shed much of their previous normative-regulative ambition. Moreover, the state powers have found other, less costly, yet no less efficient means to legitimise the demands of the citizens' obedience to its much reduced authority than beefing up and then harnessing their patriotic sentiments. Governments ceded a large part of the social integration task to the seductive force of the consumer market, by its nature exterritorial and cosmopolitan; a force which unlike state sovereignty thrives on variety and difference and could not care less about the ideological preferences of its customers.

Thanks to the falling interest of political powers (and of the nation state in the first place) in regulating the movement of capital and commodities, and their diminishing ability to constrain and channel these resources, the global network of economic dependencies has acquired growing independence from the territory. A new 'global void' has emerged, in which departures occur that are crucial for the life condition of the residents of territorially circumscribed units, but which neither these residents nor their political representations can control. Even if they were the comprehensive, coherent, and self-enclosed systems as had been imagined in the nation-building and state-sovereignty era, 'cultures' would be unable under the new conditions to sustain the self-reproduction of communal, territori-ally plotted identities as they were supposed or imputed to do. The point is, though, that with the power-assisted intentions to secure and guard the purity of national cultures all but non-existent, and their pressures on daily life and life prospects ever less felt, there is little in the life experience of the denizens of the globalisation era to suggest, let alone to corroborate, the 'system-like' image of culture.

Indeed, we may say that the imagery of 'culture' inherited from the nation-building era undergoes currently a veritable 'paradigm crisis'. The mass of evidence contradicting the wholistic/systemic model of culture grows sky-high and can no more be set aside or dismissed as 'exceptions from the rule', anomalies or marginal dis-turbances of the pattern. An empirically sustainable model of culture, a model capable of incorporating and 'making sense' of current experience, needs to put paid to the idea of cultures as coherent, self-equilibrating and self-sustainable systems altogether. As Ronnie Lippens summed it up recently, the 'reading of contem-porary experience comes down to a reading of impurities, of hybridities' (2000, p. 11). Having coined the composite concept of (b)orders, which emhasises the fact that borders have at all times been by-products of ordering bustle, Lippens suggests that what we have come to realise nowadays better than ever before is that (b)orders tend to 'get thinner, while fixating' and that 'ours is a time when (b)orders ... have exploded. There are no clear (b)orders anymore' (pp. 11, 78).

Let us note that in order to make the new experience intelligible Lippens had to resort to concepts and images which have acquired their meaning from an experience now left behind and no longer available; for that reason, they are not well fitted to embrace the experience which has come to replace it – a predicament that further testifies to the condition of a 'paradigm crisis'. Terms like 'impurity' or 'hybridity' tacitly assume what the propositions formed with their help openly deny: that there could be such a thing as 'pure' (that is, free from 'foreign' intrusions) cultural totality and that each culture could be 'of one stock', 'monolithic'. And so even when the picture is meant to represent the 'normal' state of the cultural scene, now grasped thanks to our retrospective wisdom, it looks more like a collage of 'abnormalities'. We still deploy 'ghost' terms, 'zombie terms' (Ulrich Beck), and deploy them *'sous nature'* (Jacques Derrida) – lacking the vocabulary fully adequate to the task of narrating our kind of life – a life lived 'in a flow' rather than amidst fixed objects.

Perhaps the time is ripe to abandon the term 'culture' altogether. The meanings which this term was coined to convey have lost a good deal of their experiential grounding: the hierarchical, evaluating meaning has lost much of its sense since there are no more 'ideal patterns' to promote and no agencies wishing or able to promote them, let alone hoping for the ultimate success of the undertaking, while the differential meaning has lost much of its use in view of the notorious porousness of all boundaries and the glaring impotence of the border guards. In addition, the opposition between 'culture' and 'nature' (between 'human made' parts of the world and all the rest) has lost much of its previously assumed sharpness; aspects of the world once believed to stay firmly beyond the reach of human transforming capacity, like heredity, are increasingly the objects of purposeful manipulation – while on the other hand many phenomena once considered to be unaffected by human actions, like weather patterns, are found to be the outcomes of human activities – even if only as their unanticipated consequences.

All this is not meant to imply that the global flow of free-floating cultural tokens (objects as well as behavioural patterns) which are no longer system-riveted nor space-bound, signals the levelling-up of cultural distinctions and the demise of separate 'culturally shaped identities'. As Nigel Rapport convincingly argues, the emerging picture is ambiguous. On the one hand, there is growing evidence to support Lee Drummond's (1980, pp. 352–374) suggestion that in view of the abundance of 'creolisations', cultural patterns of mixed origin and often incoherent composition, we can no longer sensibly speak of 'distinct cultures', only of 'intersystemically connected, creolizing Culture': one might agree therefore with Ulf Hannerz (1993) that the time has arrived to conceive of culture as a 'flow' or a 'diversity of interrelations': and one should accept Clifford Geertz's metaphor of the 'Kuwaiti bazaar' for all 'local points', which are constituted as 'global collages' (Geertz, 1986, pp. 105–122). Indeed, all local or group-oriented 'condensations' are products of the creolisation of heterogenic items drawn from a worldwide pool of cultural offerings and can no longer claim their uniqueness, their own history independent of the 'global flow' or a separate and autonomous logic of development. On the other hand, however, Rapport points out that 'advocates of different selections' tend to be 'exclusionary if not hostile', and that the result of such an 'exclusionary tendency' is 'cultural compression', 'an insistence of socio-cultural difference'; 'a piling up of socio-cultural boundaries, political, ritual, residential, economic, which feel experientially vital, and which people seek to defend and maintain' (Rapport, 1997, p. 71). Homogenising pressures proceed hand in hand with a new diversification. They are both effects, closely intertwined and interdependent effects, of the pressures of, and responses to, globalisation.

Deprived of the protective, even if stiff and often constricting, armour of nation-state sovereignty, no place can now claim immunity from global pressures, the right to resist them, or the capacity to withstand them. As the place becomes a meeting point for shifting and restless global powers, and so fast loses the meaning it once carried of 'secure home', it paradoxically acquires new and enhanced significance; however illusionary the protective capacity of the place might have become, people buffeted by forces they can neither understand nor control tend to cling, in their desperate search for security, to 'the place' as the sole entity that stands still while everything else – sources of livelihood and the skills they require, partnership and neighbourhood, objects of desire and causes of fear – seems to be on the move and to change shape with constantly increasing speed.

Whatever the enthusiasts of globalisation may say about the impending unification of humankind that it is bound to bring in its wake, its immediate effect is quite the opposite; not only is the anticipated species-wide solidarity slow to materialise, but in many places the prospect of 'one humanity' seems to arouse a great deal of anxiety and resentment. In her essay on Karl Jaspers, Hannah Arendt predicted such a reaction and explained why it would happen:

> It is difficult to deny that at this moment the most potent symbol of the unity of mankind is the remote possibility that atomic

weapons used by one country according to the political wisdom of a few might ultimately come to be the end of all human life on earth. The solidarity of mankind in this respect is entirely negative. It rests ... on a common desire for a world that is *a little less unified*. (Arendt, 1996, p. 83, italics added)

The collapse of the *'ancien régime'*, the weakening of the balancing and integrating powers of traditional community-based institutions, and the sudden exposure to the inexplicable, apparently haphazard impact of distant and poorly understood as well as completely uncontrollable powers, must have exerted a similar psychological effect on the generations witnessing the birth of the modern order. But at that time a new dense network of state-run and state-administered institutions was quick to fill the void and mitigate the fears emanating from this. State institutions were set up to provide a collective and nationwide insurance against individual and local misfortune; since the time of the French Revolution the modern state had asserted itself as the embodiment of what would later be described as the 'politics of pity', and which was bound to underlie the emergent sentiments of national unity and a shared national home. Nothing comparable however is happening so far, on the global scale this time required, to fill the void opened by the demise of the state-bound warrants of existential security. Under the circumstances, there is little to prompt and add vigour to the species-wide solidarity; more often than not, 'mankind' (indeed, everything 'global') is suspected of being the factory of known and as-yet-unimaginable risks, and thereby acts as a prolific source of apprehension and suspicion, while the orphaned and unanchored hopes of security drift in search of a 'locality' small and cosy enough to offer the feeling of a home-like safely.

The dreamt-of and feverishly sought stable and secure place has however no officially confirmed and legally protected location. Designating and manning the boundaries, once the institutionalised prerogative of the state, has now become for all practical intents a do-it-yourself job, left by-and-large to local initiative. Since the borders can count on no other protection than the vigilance, dedication and determination of people who draw and patrol them, the assertion and defence of borders become highly emotional affairs – manifestations of patriotic loyalty instigated by well-settled and entrenched nation states seem bland and lukewarm by comparison. The do-it-yourself border derives whatever reality it can count on from the perpetual tug-of-war with neighbours and a never lapsing vigilance again the 'fifth column', 'the enemy inside', not so much the admittedly alien foreigners as those 'among us' who are indifferent to the zeal for purification or not strongly enough committed to the cause of purity .

The urge to draw boundaries is not the result of the perception that the heartfelt difference is threatened and therefore needs defence. It is, rather, the other way round: the overwhelming desire to wall off one's abode from the storms of globalising forces prompts the search for orientation points around which turrets could be erected and moats dug. Differences, genuine or putative, are given new salience, are drawn into the focus of attention and assigned 'topical relevance' (Alfred Schutz) in as far as they promise, or are hoped, to serve as such orientation points. We may say that given the intensity of the separation-exclusion urge, were there no differences they would have to be invented. There is, however, no shortage of distinctive marks around which boundaries can be drawn and defensive lines built. The inventiveness of commodity merchants is itself more than sufficient to assure a constant supply of differences to choose from.

Imagination needs to defy the realities of life in the globalising world to endow a modicum of credibility to the cohesive 'communities of fate' it conjures. The defiance can never lapse, since the postulated communities tend to fall apart as quickly as they are assembled and the stories of unity, however long may be the stretch of history they invoke, hold only as long as they are told, heard and listened to. As Nigel Rapport puts it, community-bound identities tend to be temporary and fickle products of the 'dialectic between movement and fixity'. 'It is in and through the continuity of movement that human beings continue to make themselves at home' (Rapport, 1997, p. 77). Identity is, like the people who seek it, constantly on the move; to use Paul Ricoeur's terms – the '*ipséité*' (distinctiveness that makes the difference) needs constant renegotiation, readjustment and reassertion in order to secure a degree of '*mêmeté*' (continuity over time); it can never stand still, it cannot be defined once and for all, though this is precisely what the spokesmen of communal identities have to and do aver. One can apply to cultural identity Jon Berger's description of home as 'no longer a dwelling but the untold story of a life being lived' (Berger, 1984, p. 84; Rapport, 1997, p. 73). The story needs to be endlessly reiterated, and always in terms likely to catch the attention of the audience.

The stories are likely to change with each successive repetition, yet telling them will hardly stop; after all, as Robert Dunn points out, 'the politics of identity and difference are only a manifestation of a generalized and structurally induced *destabilization* of identity in the West and perhaps through the world' (Dunn, 2000, p. 110) – and since destabilisation is a permanent condition of the world undergoing globalisation in its present and apparently durable form, factors that add urgency and impetus to the politics of identity and difference will not be in short supply in the foreseeable future. Given that the audibility of the message must be set to a high and rising pitch not to drown in the cacophony of competitive offering, the stage on which the drama of identity is played is likely to remain for a long time full of sound and fury.

There is nothing remotely reminiscent of a 'global culture' in the sense of a cultural choice shared by the whole of the human species; neither is it certain that such worldwide 'cultural sameness', were it to become reality, would necessarily be a good thing. 'Global culture' is neither desirable nor, fortunately, on the cards, though this is what some observers, taking *pars pro toto*, imply when quoting the worldwide spread of various 'globalised localisms', such as the 'basic English' of Internet addicts, car salesmen and car-park attendants, McDonald's burgers, Coca-Cola bottles, pizza parlours, explosive births and instant deaths of Pokemon/Digimon crazes, mourning for Princess Diana, American soap operas, or the Sydney Olympics beamed across the world by television channels.

There is, though, a new phenomenon of the 'globality of culture' – worldwide 'virtual travel' and worldwide display of locally born forms of life. The totality of human cultural invention constitutes today the pool from which cultural items deployed in the construction of difference, prompted by the politics of identity and recognition, are picked. Globality of culture is sustained by the worldwide communication between locally born and bred traditions; it proves, if proof is needed, that cultural inventions gestated in localities that are isolated and remote from each other are mutually comprehensible, and that the bond that tied them historically to a particular location is contingent and relative and does not bar them from being adopted and enjoyed by others. By the same token, globality of culture holds a promise that all cultural creations may, conceivably, gel into a common property of humankind and become a shared treasure chest from which the stuff from which individual and collective identities are formed can be drawn by all.

Globality of culture is a scene: scenes limit the range of scenarios which can be staged, yet do not determine which scenario will eventually be chosen, nor the style of production. The most seminal of choices is that between *cultural variety* and *variety of cultures* (or between cultural pluralism and plurality of cultures); between *multicultural* and *multicommunitarian* policies. The first assumes, to quote Alain Touraine, that culture stops being seen and treated as a 'system', a self-sustained order, being recognised instead as an 'orientation of individual conduct'; in other words, that it is admitted both in theory and in practice that cultural choice is a matter which should be left to the discretion of individual men and women and that the choices individuals make should be respected. To stand a chance, however, this scenario needs to 'break up the communities' formed after the pattern of social systems, that is such communities as aspire to pre-empt cultural choices by the conjunction of institutionalised power and communal consensus. The 'multicultural society' Touraine recommends is possible only if the prospect of 'multicommunitarian society' (the second of the alternative scenarios) is rejected and resisted (Touraine, 1997, pp. 306, 312). Multicommunitarianism is not the fulfilment of multiculturalism, but its principal adversary.

Cultural plurality carries a tacit assumption of human rights – that is, of the right of every human individual to be different and to have her or his difference respected. As Jürgen Habermas alerts, the promotion of human rights cannot be 'focused on safeguarding private autonomy' while 'the internal connection between the individual rights of private persons and the public autonomy of the citizens who participate in making the laws is obscured from view ... Safeguarding the private autonomy of citizens with equal rights must go hand in hand with activating their autonomy as citizens ...' (Habermas, 1994, pp. 114, 116). There is no autonomy of the individual without an autonomous society, and the autonomy of society means fully-fledged citizenship. The right to be different cannot be fulfilled unless the equality of individuals as citizens is institutionally entrenched and practised. The right to citizenship is the preliminary condition for human rights to be honoured and observed: for the forms of life chosen through private autonomy to be respected and recognised.

The preliminary, though not the only condition: political equality won't suffice if it is not supported by the capacity of citizens to act on their preferences and practise the form of life of their choice. And to do that, citizens need more than the absence of interference and legally guaranteed tolerance – they need the resources which would allow them to make choices and to 'make them stick'. As I argued in *Liquid Modernity* (Bauman, 2000), we are all now individuals *de jure* – deemed responsible for our choices and charged with responsibility for their consequences: we are praised for success and blamed for failure, and if our efforts do not bring the results we wish, we are told that this is due to lack of trying, or to not trying hard enough. We are, so to speak, 'individuals by decree' – but the decree assumes, counterfactually, that we are all equally able to shape our life trajectory, attend to life challenges and solve life problems on our own; and that we possess, individually, the tools allowing us to do just that.

None of these assumptions, however, holds much water. The era of 'liquid modernity' is the time of precarious, insecure and uncertain existence, of increasingly fragile and ineffective interhuman bonds and – last though not least – of rapidly rising inequality of the individually available resources for action and ranges of realistic choices. Perhaps a minority of 'individuals *de jure*' can practise the strategy recommended to us all: seek and find *biographical* solutions to *systemically* produced problems and eke out a satisfying and stable existence despite the endemic insecurity of your condition; or even: use the uncertainties which haunt most people to your own individual advantage. The rest, however, may at best watch and envy. For that rest, choices are made by default rather than design. To rub salt into the wound, even if the choice happens to be satisfactory there is no knowing for how long it will stay so and how great its holding power will prove to be; and to add insult to injury the enjoyment of a good choice is likely to be poisoned, and the pain inflicted by the wrong choice made more acute, by the awareness that whatever happens, for whatever reason, it is the victim who will be blamed, and that when it comes to the passing of a verdict no allowances will be made for the victim's powerlessness to change the course of their fate.

The distance separating individuality *de jure* from individuality *de facto* relatively few people find easy to negotiate, once the network of public transport has been phased out line by line, and the few remaining bridges spanning the gap carry a warning: 'entry for private cars only'. It should not come as a surprise, therefore, that the resulting anxiety and anger may turn against lonely travel as such; against the no-choice precept to choose individually which

178   Making Sense of Collectivity

evidently serves a few well while handicapping all the rest. The very idea of 'doing it alone', of taking decisions on one's own responsibility, becomes suspicious and off-putting.

Since the prospect of joining the privileged few who feel at home in the unstable and fluid environment (that is, the prospect of acquiring enough individual power for self-confident action) seems remote and nebulous, another ostensible remedy – cutting down on the number and reducing the gravity of choices to be individually made, and simplifying thereby the equation that needs be solved at every step – becomes ever more alluring. 'Multicommunitarianism' promises just that: rather than amplifying the individual choice and putting it within reach of all those who have been thus far denied the capacity of practising it (and so making the merely formal rights real and lifting the 'individuals *de jure*' to the status of 'individuals *de facto*'), it sets about sparing the individuals the trials and tribulations which have accompanied so far the necessity to choose. Instead of offering a way to bridge the gap between individuality *de jure* and individuality *de facto*, 'multicommunitarianism' suggests that the gap, and so the need to cross it, can (and should) be taken off the public agenda by the simple expedient of reducing the scope of individual choice and deleting some choices altogether from the inventory of individual rights.

John Gray (1997, pp. 80–81) rightly points out that 'in the context of the past two decades or so ... communitarian thinking is a response to the conception of the sovereign individual chooser that has been advanced or presupposed, in recent liberal thought both of the Left and the Right'. Communitarianism in its present form capitalises on the increasingly evident hypocrisy of 'abstract individualism' which mistakes legal equality for the 'equality of sovereign choosers' and refuses to take account of the factual inequality of the conditions under which individuals make their choices. There is little doubt that the ailments to which communitarianism offers itself as a remedy are genuine. The problem, though, is whether the remedy does indeed attack the causes of the sufferings it promises to cure, and how painful the side-effects of the therapy are likely to be.

Gray warns that 'communitarian thought will be fruitless or harmful if it engages in any project of propping up traditional forms of social life or recovering any past cultural consensus'. He is right, since even if restoration of the self-enclosed enclaves of 'cultural consensus' were feasible, it would come nowhere near to making innocuous or palatable the condition that prompted the search for a remedy. The precariousness and insecurity that haunt individual life would stay by and large unaffected and unmitigated. The loss of individual rights which the implementation of the communitarian programme is bound to incur won't be compensated for by the gain of confidence and self-assurance. The riskiness of life won't go away, while the opportunities that the new human freedoms may offer are lost or surrendered.

Something else is required: instead of trying to make the burden of individual rights lighter by cutting down on the right to choose, what is needed is to optimise the conditions under which choices are made, and to make those conditions available to those who have been thus far denied access. And that, in turn, calls for a number of essentially political steps about which the communitarian programme keeps silent and which 'multicommunitarianism' would do little, if anything at all, to facilitate. To quote Gray once more:

> reforming the central institutions of the free market so that they *are friendlier to vital human needs* for *security and autonomy* ... *preventing social exclusion* by enabling all to participate in productive economy ... developing institutions, countervailing or complementary to those of the market, which *foster common life* where the workings of markets risk furthering exclusion. (Gray, 1997, pp. 80–81, italics added)

All in all, these and other measures of this kind, unlike the multi-communitarian programme, may use the opportunities for communication and mutual comprehension provided by present-day cultural plurality for the sake of the peaceful, solidaristic and mutually enriching coexistence of forms of life, varied and different yet united in their humanity. Cultural plurality and plurality of cultures are names of alternative political responses to the challenge of 'liquid modernity'; responses which carry widely divergent consequences for the prospect of a good society and a humane life.

References

Arendt, H. (1996) *Men in Dark Times* (New York: Harcourt Brace).

Bauman, Z. (2000) *Liquid Modernity* (Cambridge: Pluto Press).

Berger, J. (1984) *And Our Faces, My Heart, Brief as Photos* (London: Writers and Readers).

Drummond, L. (1980) 'The Cultural Continuum: a Theory of Intersystems', *Man*, no. 5, pp. 352–374.

Dunn, R.G. (2000) 'Identity, Commodification and Consumer Culture', in J.E. Savis (ed.) *Identity and Social Change* (London: Transactions Publishers).

Geertz, C. (1986) 'The Uses of Diversity', *Michigan Quarterly Review*, vol. 25, no. 1, pp. 105–122.

Gray, J. (1997) *Endgames: Questions in Late Modern Political Thought* (Cambridge: Polity Press).

Habermas, J. (1994) 'Struggle for Recognition in the Democratic Constitutional State', in A. Gutmann (ed.) *Multiculturalism: Examining the Policy of Recognition* (Princeton: Princeton University Press).

Hannerz, U. (1993) 'The Cultural Role of the World Cities', in A.P. Cohen and K. Fukui (eds) *Humanising the City* (Edinburgh: Edinburgh University Press).

Lippens, R. (2000) *Chaohybrids: Five Uneasy Pieces* (Lanham, Md.: University Press of America).

Rapport, N. (1997) *Transcendent Individual: Towards a Literary and Liberal Anthropology* (London: Routledge).

Touraine, A. (1997) 'Faux et vrais problèmes', in M. Wieviorka (ed.) *Une societé fragmentée? Le multiculturalisme en débat* (Paris: La Découverte).

Varnier, J.-P. (1999) *La mondialisation de la culture* (Paris: La Découverte).

7 A Disagreement about Difference

John A. Hall

Throughout the halls of contemporary academe – and in many of the contributions to this volume – can be heard, again and again, assertions that we are diverse, that difference rules. My own initial response to this was bafflement. Surely the sensation of solipsism, of being trapped inside one's own skin, is not unique to me? In fact, this reaction is unfair for what is at issue is less individual difference than cultural pluralism. It is worth noting that such pluralism is held to be desirable, especially in comparison with homogeneity – purportedly achievable only by force, and held to be the result of the imposition of a particular rather than a universal set of standards. This seems to be the language of tolerance, even liberty. Let a thousand flowers bloom! Surely no decent person could argue a contrary case?

I do claim decency yet reject a good deal of this general position. Mild jokes might be in order at the start. For one thing, it is noticeable that the cry for difference is uniform, singular and homogeneous! For another, claims for difference often go hand-in-hand with assertions that the world is becoming globalised! More seriously, there is certainly a good deal to be said against difference insofar as it fades into relativism, surely the last refuge of the scoundrels of the modern world. Though I will touch on that, my principal contribution will be sociological, that is, descriptive rather than prescriptive. The argument that follows can best be seen as offering scepticism towards the claim that social processes are such that multicultural loyalties are replacing more national identities. Attention focuses in turn on concepts, the United States, the history of nationalism in Europe, and – all too briefly – on the character of nation building elsewhere. It should be said immediately that what is on offer is a sustained scepticism rather than a full account of any of these very varied topics.

How homogeneous must we be?

Conceptual clarity can be gained by considering in turn the 'how', 'must' and 'we' of this question. We can do no better than to begin by commenting on the 'how' by dissecting the celebrated notions of civic and ethnic nationalism, not least because this will suggest a schema differentiating options of belonging.

We should not accept everything that is implied in the formula ethnic/bad, civic/good. For one thing, there is nothing necessarily terrible about loyalty to one's ethnic group – and this sentiment in fact underlies the supposedly civic nationalism of the French. For another, civic nationalism is not necessarily nice: its injunction can be 'join us or else'. This was certainly true of the way in which Paris treated the Vendée during the early years of the revolution, and it remains at the back of the contemporary *'affaire des foulardes'*. Differently put, civic nationalism may be resolutely hostile to diversity. This suggests the following scheme:

Ethnic

(Non-)liberal Caging   Civic

Civil

Moving clockwise around this circle allows a series of theoretical points to be made. Ethnic nationalism is indeed repulsive when it is underwritten by relativist philosophies that insist that one should literally think with one's blood. Much less horrible is the combination of ethnic and civic nationalisms represented by France – that is, a world in which one is taken in or allowed in as long as one absorbs the culture of the dominant ethnic group. Civic nationalism becomes more liberal when it moves towards the pole of civility, best defined in terms of the acceptance of diverse positions or cultures. Whether this move is, so to speak, sociologically real can be measured by asking two questions. First, is the identity to which one is asked to accede relatively thin, that is, does it have at its core political loyalty rather than a collective memory of an ethnic group? Second, are rates of intermarriage high? Differently put, is the claim that one can belong, whatever one's background, borne out by the facts? All this is obvious. Less so, perhaps, is a tension that lies at the heart of multiculturalism. In the interests of clarity, matters can be put bluntly. Multiculturalism properly understood *is* civil nationalism, the recognition of diversity. But that diversity is – needs to be, should be – limited by a consensus on shared values. Difference is acceptable only so long as group identities are voluntary, that is, insofar as identities can be changed according to individual desire. What is at issue is neatly encapsulated when we turn to the notion of caging.[1] If multiculturalism means that groups have rights over individuals – if, for example, the leaders of a group have the power to decide to whom young girls should be married – then it becomes repulsive. Such multiculturalism might seem liberal in tolerating difference, but it is in fact the illiberalism of misguided liberalism, diminishing life chances by allowing social caging. This view is of course relativist, and it is related to ethnic nationalism in presuming that one must think with one's group. Importantly, the link to ethnic nationalism may be very close indeed. If there are no universal standards, and ethnic groups are held to be in permanent competition, then it is possible, perhaps likely, that one group will seek to dominate another.

If these are ideal typical positions, a powerful stream of modern social theory in effect suggests that some have greater viability than others. A series of thinkers, interestingly all liberal, have insisted that homogeneity, whether ethnic or civic, is a 'must' if a society is to function effectively. John Stuart Mill made this claim when speaking about the workings of democracy, insisting that the nationalities question had to be solved in order for democracy to be viable (Mill, 1862, Chapter 16). The great contemporary theorist of democracy Robert Dahl (1977) has reiterated this idea. The notion behind all this is straightforward. Human beings cannot take too much conflict, cannot put themselves on the line at all times and in every way. For disagreement to be productive in the way admired by liberalism, it must be contained – that is, it must take place within a frame of common belonging. Very much the same insight underlies David Miller's view (1995) that national homogeneity is a precondition for generous welfare regimes. This is correct: the generosity of Scandinavian countries rests on the willingness to give generously to people exactly like oneself. But the great theorist of the need for social homogeneity was of course Ernest Gellner. As it happens, the explanation he offered for this ever more insistently – that of the necessity of homogeneity so that industrial society can function properly – is rather question begging.[2] But even the most cursory consideration of his life suggests that he captured something about the character of nationalism. Born into Kafka's Czech-German-Jewish world and forced into exile in 1939, he returned in 1945 to find the Jews murdered and the Germans being expelled. A second period of exile ended when he returned when communism fell – to witness on that occasion the secession of the rich majority from the Slovaks. Visceral experience underlay his image of political space moving from the world of Kokoschka to that of Mondrian – that is, from a world in which peoples were intermingled to one in which national homogeneity was established (Gellner, 1983, pp. 139–140).

This brings us to the 'we' in the title of this section. The claim of those variously stressing the need for homogeneity amounts to saying that we are very unlikely to have civil nationalism, that is, that multinational entities are an impossibility. This is to say that constitutional schemes – federal, confederal and consociational – from which civil nationalism hopes so much are very unlikely to work. That has certainly been a key part of the experience of Europeans. In general, this has been the dark continent of modernity, as Mazower (1998) stresses, for homogeneity was often achieved through repulsive means – through population transfers, ethnic cleansing and genocide much more than by voluntary assimilation. Will the rest of the world follow the European example? If so the future of world politics looks set to bring us catastrophe, given the complex ethnic intermingling of many states, particularly some of those in the developing world. As noted, some consideration of this crucial issue is given below.

The melting pot

There are at least two obvious and powerful reasons for turning to the United States. First, the United States deserves far more study than it receives, and not just in relation to the topic presently under analysis. For America is the greatest power that the world has ever known. At present it spends more than 50 per cent of the world total of military expenditure, giving it continuing power over the international market – that is, over such economic rivals as Japan and the European Union. Secondly, it is the world within which talk of difference is insistent, even deafening. This may of course be no accident. The historic uniqueness of the United States perhaps lies in the fact that it was formed through immigration, that it is a polity created from difference. Of course, that very formulation suggests that America has been a melting pot, homogenising the many into a single unit. Was that true? Is it still true today?

The answer to that question must be wholly affirmative.[3] But recognition of a sociological reality does not require moral endorsement. Hence consideration is offered to begin with of the harsh side of the melting pot, before then turning to fundamentally meritorious social practices that allow American nationalism to move beyond its dominant civic core towards elements of genuine civility.

The United States is not a social world favouring diversity. An initial consideration to that effect lies in the simple fact that white Anglo-Saxon settlers more or less exterminated the native population, thereby establishing their own hegemony.[4] Further, the creation of the new state placed a very strong emphasis on uniformity. For one thing, a constitution was formed, a singular set of ideals created, which thereafter was held to be sacred.[5] For another, the United States was created by means of powerful acts, usually directed from below, of political cleansing. A significant section of the elite – in absolute numerical terms larger than those guillotined during the French Revolution, and from a smaller population at that, that had supported the Crown – was forced to leave (Palmer, 1959, pp. 188–202). Canada thereby gained an element of that anti-Americanism which comprises the key part of its national identity.

Perhaps the most striking general interpretation of American history and society, namely that proposed by scholars such as Richard Hofstader, Daniel Bell and Seymour Martin Lipset, is that which insists on the power of these initial ideas, of continuity through continuing consensus.[6] That is not quite right. If some alternatives were ruled out at the time of foundation, others were eliminated as the result of historical events. The two most important examples deserve at least minimal attention.

First of all we ought to remember that the United States remained unitary only as the result of a very brutal civil war. The Constitution had of course recognised the different interests of the slave-owning southern states, but the difference between North and South grew in the early years of the republic. The works of John Calhoun amount to a myth of hierarchy on the basis of which a new nation might have been formed. War destroyed that diversity, with Lincoln trying at the end of the conflict to create unity by means of such new institutions as Thanksgiving. Of course, the South did not lose its cultural autonomy simply as the result of defeat in war, maintaining a key hold on federal politics well into the 1930s. Nonetheless, over time the South has lost its uniqueness, especially in recent years as the result of political change and of population and industrial transfers from North to South. And in this general area of nationalism, it is well worth noting that there is no possibility of the United States becoming a multinational society. No one wants a second civil war of visceral intensity. Further, all evidence shows that Americans are overwhelmingly opposed to the idea that Spanish should be recognised as a second official language. The toughness of American civic nationalism is well expressed in the quip used in a Texas gubernatorial election some years ago: 'If English was good enough for Jesus Christ, it is good enough for Texas.' This is surely one element ensuring that Spanish is being lost as a second language as fast as was the case for the languages of other immigrant groups in the nineteenth century.

The second alternative vision was that of socialism, in one form or another. Revisionist history makes it equally clear that there was a genuine socialist stream of ideas and institutions in American history, represented most spectacularly in the militant unionism of the International Workers of the World. Further proof of the strength of working-class activism can be found in the bitterness of labour disputes – whose end result was a very large number of deaths, second only to those at the hands of the late Tsarist empire.[7] This is all to say that American ideals of individualism and enterprise were not so powerful or so widely shared as to rule out a challenge. The ascendancy of these ideals came about for two fundamental reasons. On the one hand, the fact that citizenship had been granted early on meant that worker dissatisfaction tended to be limited, to be directed against industrialists rather than against the state – thereby limiting the overall power of the working class. On the other hand, and crucially for this argument, socialism was literally destroyed – as is made apparent by that very large number of working-class deaths. The recipe for social stability is often the combination of political opening with absolute intolerance towards extremists. Certainly this mixture worked in the United States, ensuring that it would thereafter be bereft of any sort of social democratic tendency.

The rosier and milder face of the coin of American homogeneity can be seen at work in American ethnic relations. A warning should be issued before describing what is a remarkable American achievement. Everything that will be said excludes Afro-Americans, whose position inside the United States remains heavily marked by racial discrimination. The hideousness of what is involved can be seen in the desire of the vast majority of Afro-Americans 'to get in', with great bitterness being shown by middle-class blacks who 'make it' economically only to find that integration does not exist in the suburbs to which they move (Hall and Lindholm, 1999, Chapter 10). But for the majority of Americans, ethnic identity is now – as Mary

Waters' (1990) superb *Ethnic Options* makes clear – a choice rather than a destiny imposed from outside. Rates of intermarriage are extremely high, not least for the first generation of Cuban-Americans in Florida, more than 50 per cent of whom marry outside their own group.[8] Ethnic identity has little real content. It is permissible to graduate from kindergarten wearing a sari as long as one does not believe in caste – that is, as long as one is American. There are severe limits to difference.

Societies are complicated, so it makes sense to summarise what has been said by placing the United States at several points of the schema that has been provided. It is not the case that the United States has been completely free from ethnic nationalism. The colonists destroyed the native inhabitants. Further, some part of the identity enshrined in the Constitution reflects the British background of the initial majority. Nonetheless, the United States does score firmly in the civic camp. The harshness of its civic culture can be seen in the destruction of alternative visions. Against this can be set the fact that the United States does allow movement towards a civil position: American identity is less Anglo-Saxon than it was – not least because of the astonishing rates of intermarriage – for all but Afro-Americans, whose life chances remain scandalously impoverished. In contrast to these points of reference must very clearly be set a particular absence. All those books and treatises, the polemics of despair, asserting that the United States is falling apart because multiculturalism is becoming – in our terms – caging and illiberal are woefully misguided. It might very well be terrible were the relativism of politicised identity cages so complete as to destroy any sense of a common culture. But that is not the case. What matters about identity claims in the United States is that they are at once without content and so very generally made. They represent yet another moment of America's startling ability to create a common culture. This is a remarkable society, but it is not one of great difference and diversity. The powers of homogenisation in the United States – deriving as much from Hollywood and consumerism, of course, as from the factors examined here – remain intact. The melting pot still works.

No essence but existences

Although it is well known that the great theorists of nationalism came from the world of Austro-Hungary, insufficient attention has been paid to a thinker from that world whose thought provides us with a key insight. I have in mind here Sigmund Freud. What matters about his work is less the particular views expressed in *Moses and Monotheism* than an argument that can be made on the basis of his view of the libido. That peculiar substance is seen to be sticky, capable of attaching itself to different objects which then lend it a particular character. So it is with nationalism. This protean force is licentiously labile, gaining its character from the social forces with which it interacts. In a nutshell, nationalism has no essence but very varied existences. Let us consider three highly stylised, ideal typical moments of nationalism in modern European history since to do so will advance the argument.

The first stage is that of simplicity and innocence. In a nutshell, nationalism is linked with liberalism. The old regime represents a common enemy, and its incursions into civil society as geopolitical conflict intensifies in the late eighteenth century means that the definition of the people involves both national and electoral issues. A typical figure in this regard is John Wilkes, the editor of *The North Briton* and the somewhat flawed champion of popular representation. To mention the Highland Clearances in Scotland is to note that nationalism at this time had some hideous moments of forced homogenisation. Nonetheless, this period, best represented by Britain, was relatively benign. The sociology of the situation was simple: the state had come before the nation. The centralisation of feudalism played a large part in the creation of a single language early on to which varied groups acceded over a long period of time.

The second stage is that of horror and viciousness. One key sociological consideration is that nation came before state in the composite monarchies of the Romanovs and the Hapsburgs. In these empires – and in that of the Ottomans – varied ethnic groups gained self-consciousness, thereby turning ethnic diversity into genuine multinationalism. Gellner is certainly right to argue that this often made for great difficulties, notably when national and social inequalities were combined. Nonetheless, multinational arrangements were not necessarily doomed by socioeconomic pressures coming from below. To the contrary, many nations merely sought the affirmation of their historic liberties, with the Slavs being somewhat scared of secession given their geopolitical placement between Russia and Germany. But exit became attractive in the course of time given state policies directed at them. For a second sociological variable at work was the desire to catch up.[9] One element to this variable was the belief at the time, held most notably in Russia but present too in the Ottoman and Austro-Hungarian realms, that strength would come through linguistic and cultural homogenisation, that is, by copying the leading powers so as to make nation states out of diverse materials. A second element to catching up was the belief that secure sources of supply and secure markets were necessary for state strength. Differently put, in this period nationalism came to be associated with imperialism (Kaiser, 1990). Both these elements ensured that the stakes of any war, should it come, would likely be very great. Such proved to be the case during the First World War, with the pressures thereby released creating tensions – revolution, irredentism, paramilitary mobilisation – that led to a second round of conflict in the course of which massive processes of national homogenisation took place.

The third period is one of modesty. Two factors lie at the back of a considerable achievement. On the one hand, Europe's security dilemma was solved as the result of American engagement in NATO. On the other hand, the genius of French bureaucrats whose memories were of catastrophic wars with Germany led to the creation of agreements of economic interdependence, that is, led to a world in which the leading states gave up their capacity to autonomously produce their own secure supply of weapons. Europe – and Japan – thereby at last became trading states, replacing heroic adventure by economic advance.[10] This is not for a moment to accept the claim, made so often these days, that the nation state is dead (Milward, 1992; Anderson, 1997a; 1997b; Moravcsik, 1998). To the contrary, at the back of every agreement in the recent history of European institutions has been agreement between France and Germany, with broader international bargaining being clearly present recently in the agreements made at Nice about the future of the European Union. But the mood of the nation state has changed. Abandoning the attempt to be complete power containers in fact increased security. Less proved to be more.

This last stage has sometimes allowed for a measure of European self-congratulation. This should be avoided. To begin with, Gellner was absolutely right at a purely factual level. In 1914 something like 65 million lived in states not ruled by their own co-culturals. Today, there are very few examples of successful multinational regimes west of the Ukraine – Spain for sure, idiosyncratic Switzerland as well, but with Britain, Belgium and Canada in the midst of fairly severe challenges. More generally, democracy works more easily in most of Europe, including much of Central Europe and the Balkans, precisely because forced homogenisation has taken place. Much of the discussion of multiculturalism is in a sense hypocritical: we speak the language of tolerance now that we have no great national divisions to deal with. We can hope that the complex consociational agreements designed for Northern Ireland will work, but it is by no means as yet sure that they will.

None of this is to say, let it be noted once again, that Gellner's principal explanation for national homogenisation is correct. At a theoretical level, I have suggested that a more political account – stressing that the desire for secession comes from political exclusion and that the desire for catch-up led nationalism to be clearly linked both to ethnic cleansing and to imperialism – is needed to complement his overwhelmingly socioeconomic account.[11] This is to say that there is a chance that changed political circumstances could allow for greater pluralism, and this is certainly something that Gellner sought and which I would welcome. But if we can hope, we should also continue to fear, for at least three reasons. First, there have as yet been few successful transitions from agrarian and authoritarian multinational entities to their industrial and democratic equivalent. Second, it may be that the political force driving national homogenisation is nothing less than democracy itself – with the least one can say being that popular politics often has the temptation to take a dark route (Mann, 1999). Finally, there may be new and negative factors to set against such positive developments as have been singled out, notably the breaking of the link between imperialism and nationalism. If there is anything to the notion of a third wave of democracy, then a major concern of politics in the near future will be that of the exit of authoritarian leaders from power.[12] It may be that a more globalised capitalism will allow some leaders to find a way to maintain advantage – by joining a larger world and leaving their compatriots behind. Party membership declined dramatically in Hungary before 1989 in much this way, as leaders found the economy a more secure route to advantage than political power. But not all leaders are economically capable. Milošević was not. There was an air of opportunism about the way in which he played the nationalist card – but an air that makes one fear, given that others may act in exactly the same way.

Hopes and fears for the majority of humankind

Most general sociological schemes have at their core the notion of the less developed seeking to catch up the more advanced. This applied within Europe, with both nationalism and industrialisation, and probably socialism, being best seen as late development strategies.[13] It is all too easy to imagine that this logic will apply to what is after all best known as the less developed world. The result can only be appalling, as noted, if nationalising homogenisation becomes the norm of the world's polities.

Remarkably, there are grounds for hope that this may not generally be the case: the non-European world may manage its affairs better, by invention rather than by imitation. The clearest and most important example is that of the way in which linguistic diversity has not led to nationalist secessions in India. David Laitin has argued that this is best explained by the 'three plus or minus one' linguistic repertoire available to – and in fact often possessed by – Indians (Laitin, 1992). The three is reached in this manner. One official all-India language is Hindi. A second is English. The reason for this dual situation is that Nehru's attempt to linguistically homogenise the newly independent nation failed because of the resistance it encountered from his own civil servants – whose cultural capital very largely lay in their mastery of a world language. The third language necessary is that of one's state – that is, of one's province. It is possible to subtract a language if one's state is Hindi-speaking, but necessary to add a language if one is a minority in a non-Hindi-speaking province. There can be no doubt about the diversity of life within India, yet – incredibly to European eyes – the situation is rather stable, a sort of Austro-Hungary that works. None of this is to say that Indian life is without tension. It may yet be the case, for instance, that religious division will tear India apart – although there are reasons to doubt this. Still, what has been achieved does allow hope.

This sort of linguistic repertoire is equally present in much of Africa. Since the future of that continent is often seen in a wholly negative light, it makes sense at least to note two further factors that may constrain national homogenisers. One is simply the presence of a large number of ethnic groups, perhaps 120 in Tanzania alone, none of which is close to demographic dominance. In these circumstances, political parties tend to be formed of multiethnic coalitions, none of which dares to play the ethnic card. Secondly, Africa has by and large seen little sustained interstate war since decolonisation, for all that it has been plagued by low intensity internal strife – and by more recent resource-driven conflicts. A negative side of the absence of sustained geopolitical conflict has been relative failure in state building – so much so, indeed, that there is not much discussion of 'failed states' in Africa (Herbst, 2000). But there is another, more positive side to the picture. One factor that intensified ethnic cleansing in Europe was competing claims to a single piece of territory.[14] Near-absolute endorsement of the principle of nonintervention has meant that this factor has by and large been missing in Africa. Of course, none of this is to say, once again, that sweetness and light can be guaranteed. The darkest alternative is of course represented by the genocide in Rwanda. Further, it looks likely that the war in Congo-Zaire will do nothing but harm – neither state nor nation building, merely reliable destruction.

Since so much reliance has been placed on Laitin's analysis, it is worth looking at his more recent analysis of the erstwhile Soviet sphere (Laitin, 1999). By and large, the optimism found in the developing world – that is, the demonstration that many nations can share political space – is abandoned when dealing with the Baltics. All that the beached Russian diaspora can hope in those countries is genuine civic nationalism – that is, the creation of a homogeneous monolingual society in which their desire to join is accepted. The rather different situation in Kazakhstan seems no more likely to lead to diversity. Perhaps, Laitin argues, the Ukraine will do better. One can hope, but one must also fear given the debilitating failure to undertake political and economic reform.

Conclusion

The schema presented is merely a heuristic tool. But it does allow us to realise that the pole of civil nationalism has been difficult to achieve in practice. The recognition of real diversity demands a great deal of human beings. A corollary of this deserves especial highlighting. Life is hard, with our desires by no means being, or being able to create, social reality. Civil nationalism may be (and in the view of this author is) desirable, but it remains – let it be said again – very difficult to achieve. Philosophical desires are not necessarily social realities.

Notes

1. The notion of caging is of course that of Michael Mann. It is variously used in the first two volumes of his *Sources of Social Power* (1986; 1993).

2. For a series of critical reviews on this point, see most of the essays in J.A. Hall (ed.) (1998).
3. The arguments that follow are presented in greater detail in J.A. Hall and C. Lindholm (1999).
4. I have learnt a great deal in this regard from a forthcoming book by Michael Mann dealing with ethnic cleansing.
5. It may seem that the diversity allowed in religious practice contradicts the point being made. That is not really so, as is most evident once we note that Americans today trust those who have a religion – any religion – whilst showing suspicion of those who have none.
6. The clearest statement of this view is now S.M. Lipset (1996).
7. This point is well made by Mann (1993, Chapter 18). The rest of this paragraph is indebted to Mann's analysis.
8. I rely here on the research of Elizabeth Arias of the State University of New York at Stony Brook.
9. For a superb account of the late nineteenth-century pressures on the Russian, British, Ottoman and Austro-Hungarian empires, see Lieven (2000).
10. I am playing here with the title (*Traders and Heroes*) of Werner Sombart's (1915) analysis, at the start of the century, of Germany's geopolitical choice.
11. Mann's manuscript on ethnic cleansing adds to this a detailed analysis of other political elements which help explain murderous ethnic cleansings.
12. This last point is the theme of J. Snyder (2000).
13. For an interpretation of socialism in this light, see R. Szporluk (1988).
14. Mann argues this in his manuscript on ethnic cleansing.

References

Anderson, P. (1997a) 'Under the Sign of the Interim', in P. Gowan and P. Anderson (eds) *The Question of Europe* (London: Verso).

Anderson, P. (1997b) 'The Europe to Come', in P. Gowan and P. Anderson (eds) *The Question of Europe* (London: Verso).

Dahl, R. (1977) *Polyarchy* (New Haven: Yale University Press).

Gellner, E. (1983) *Nations and Nationalism* (Oxford: Blackwell).

Hall, J.A. (ed.) (1998) *The State of the Nation: Ernest Gellner and the Theory of Nationalism* (Cambridge: Cambridge University Press).

Hall, J.A. and Lindholm, C. (1999) *Is America Breaking Apart?* (Princeton: Princeton University Press).

Herbst, J. (2000) *States and Power in Africa* (Princeton: Princeton University Press).

Kaiser, R. (1990) *Politics and War* (Cambridge: Harvard University Press).

Laitin, D. (1992) *Language Repertoires and State Construction in Africa* (Cambridge: Cambridge University Press).

Laitin, D. (1999) *Identity in Formation* (Ithaca: Cornell University Press).

Lieven, D. (2000) *Empire* (London: John Murray).

Lipset, S.M. (1996) *American Exceptionalism* (New York: Norton).

Mann, M. (1986) *The Sources of Social Power, Vol. I: A History of Power from the Beginning to AD 1760* (Cambridge: Cambridge University Press).

Mann, M. (1993) *The Sources of Social Power, Vol. II: The Rise of Classes and Nation-States, 1760–1914* (Cambridge: Cambridge University Press).

Mann, M. (1999) 'The Dark Side of Democracy', *New Left Review*, no. 235.

Mazower, M. (1998) *The Dark Continent* (London: Allen Lane).

Mill, J.S. (1862) *Considerations on Representative Government* (New York: Harpers).

Miller, D. (1995) *On Nationality* (Oxford: Oxford University Press).

Milward, A. (1992) *The European Rescue of the Nation-State* (Berkeley: University of California Press).

Moravcsik, A. (1998) *The Choice for Europe* (Ithaca: Cornell University Press).

Palmer, R. (1959) *The Age of Democratic Revolution* (Princeton: Princeton University Press).

Snyder, J. (2000) *From Voting to Violence: Democratization and Nationalist Conflict* (New York: W.W. Norton).

Sombart, W. (1915) *Händler und Helden* (Leipzig: Dunckler und Humblot).

Szporluk, R. (1988) *Communism and Nationalism* (Oxford: Oxford University Press).

Waters, M. (1990) *Ethnic Options* (Berkeley: University of California Press).

8   Identity: Conceptual, Operational and Historical Critique

Siniša Malešević

Identity is not something tangible, material or visible. Yet many claim that its presence is felt everywhere today. Television, radio and newspapers bombard us on an everyday basis with the information that 'the very identities of numerous ethnic groups are threatened'. We hear over and over again, not only from right wing politicians, how our national identity has to be preserved from the 'the flood of immigrants'. Romantic writers and organic intellectuals demand of us that we discover and awaken our cultural identities; the advertising industry seduces us daily with consumerist messages that seek to manupulate our sense of belonging to various status identities; and so on. As numerous studies and publications demonstrate, identity has become a dominant idiom in contemporary academic and activist discourse. Even Internet search engines give us over four million entries for the term 'identity'.

This concept has not only acquired such a near universal acceptance but it has also become a normative straitjacket. Today, a person is expected and required to have an identity. Even though there is profound popular disagreement on whether identities are essential or existential, primordial or constructed, singular or multiple, there is almost no dispute over the question of whether identities exist or not. It is assumed that everybody has at least one identity and not having an identity might be regarded as suspicious, threatening or immoral. Being identity-impaired today might be perceived socially as more problematic than being mentally or physically impaired.

In this chapter I intend to question this unproblematic use of the concepts of 'identity' and in particular 'ethnic identity'. I argue that the vague nature of the concept has deep implications for the quality and value of research conducted in the social sciences. The first part of the chapter discusses conceptual problems with the use of the terms of 'identity' and 'ethnic identity'. Here I focus on and question the two dominant ways of how identity has been conceptualised in the social sciences: as sameness and as difference. In the second part I present examples from my previous work in order to highlight and explore the empirical consequence of conceptual ambiguities surrounding the ideas of identity and ethnic identity. In the final part I sketch some possible historical and sociological reasons why the concept of identity has acquired such a powerful and privileged position today.

The idea of identity

Social scientists in general and sociologists in particular are renowned for their inexhaustible hunger for analogies, metaphors and images which enable them to capture the 'essence' of social reality in a single word. In order to interpret and explain the nature of social change, individual and group behaviour or the outcome of unpredictable social events, social scientists are very often eager to look for meaningful and generalisable categories outside their respective disciplines. More often than not these categories of generalisibility are found in the natural or technical sciences (with examples ranging from Durkheim's mechanic and organic solidarity to Parsons' equilibrium to Castells' network society or Beck's risk society). The concepts 'identity' and hence its derivative 'ethnic identity' also have their origins outside the social sciences – more precisely in mathematics.

According to Goddard (1998) identity is defined in mathematics simultaneously in two ways – as absolute zero difference and as relative nonzero difference.[1] The absolute definition of identity relates to 'the unconditional nature of a thing that is not derived from external relation – the product of internal self-similarity', while the relative definition of identity implies 'the conditional nature of a thing, n, derived from the difference between n and not(n) – the product of external other-difference'. An example of zero difference is the logical statement 'he must be John since he is the same as John', whereas an example of nonzero difference is 'John is best since he earned more than the others'.

After its incorporation into the discourse of the social sciences the concept 'identity' preserved its dualistic mathematical meaning.[2] Having an 'identity' meant being on the one hand identical (or in less extreme versions, similar) to members of a group/category and on the other hand it also meant being different from members of another group/category (John = John, John ≠ Mary). For example, a working-class identity simultaneously implied that individuals who share this form of identity have more or less identical class position (e.g. being manual workers, dependent on similar wages, living in similar housing estates, having the same educational qualifications, sharing the same cultural values, etc.) and at the same time that this group differs from other classes (e.g. the middle or upper classes) and their respective identities.

However, this dual application of the concept in the social sciences was paradoxical from the very beginning. While mathematics can operate with an absolute and total concept (e.g. absolute zero) which cannot be reduced further to anything else (2 = 2), sociology and the social sciences do not have such a privilege. On the contrary, the events and actors in the social world are, as most social scientists now agree, highly dynamic, flexible, constantly changing, fuzzy, unpredictable and in the continuous process of creating unintended consequences of their action (Giddens, 1984). In other words, there is no absolute zero difference in the world of humans. This paradox implies that the concept of 'identity' could legitimately be used in two ways only – by maintaining solely the mathematical concept of relative nonzero difference or by treating identity in a nonmathematical way altogether. Opting for one over the other of these uses of identity has profound implications for the nature of research strategies employed. If one preserves a strict, mathematical concept of identity as a relative nonzero difference (John ≠ Mary) this dramatically reduces the scope of sociological analysis to the behaviour and attitudes of individuals, that is to what is generally known as methodological individualism. This implies not only very rigorous definitions of the entities involved (e.g. what exactly 'John' and 'Mary' stand for) but also adherence to very strict methodological procedures of sampling, experimentation, validation and so on through which one could develop reliable and testable tools to generate verifiable findings on the nature of identity and ethnic identity.

If one alternatively chooses to opt for a nonmathematical concept of identity, one is forced to operate with a metaphorical level of analysis. This strategy entails giving up the ambition of producing statistically reliable and testable hypotheses on the nature of identity claims and as such raises a question about the relevance and validity of the entire concept of identity. In other words, if identity is used as a metaphor only how can one justify its use over the alternatives?

It seems that most social scientists, explicitly or implicitly, have opted for the uses of the concepts of identity and ethnic identity in a nonmathematical, that is a metaphorical way. This raises an important question, which is: Is it useful to employ the concept of identity in either of these two ways? I argue in this chapter that neither one of the two options is constructive and that we should if not abandon the concept of identity then at least disregard it as a major research tool.

The concept of identity

Brubaker and Cooper (2000, pp. 6–8) have recently identified five dominant ways in which the concept of identity is currently used in the social sciences and the humanities: (a) identities as noninstrumental forms of social action; (b) identities as collective phenomena of group sameness; (c) identities as deep and foundational forms of selfhood; (d) identities as interactive, processual, contingent products of social action; and (e) identities as fluctuating, unstable and fragmented modes of the 'self'. They argue that these five understandings of identity range from 'strong' to 'weak' uses of the concept – while the first two conceptions operate with the common-sense, 'hard' uses of the term, the remaining three, which are often found in social constructivist approaches (particularly in cultural studies, anthropology and sociology) work with very 'soft', flexible and contingent understandings of identity. However, focusing on the classical mathematical use of the concept one can point to an important rearrangement of these categories which will allow us a closer scrutiny of the concept.

Hence, these five distinct uses of identity can be closely observed if we categorise them in relation to the original mathematical use of identity. So, one can argue that the uses of identity as 'noninstrumental forms of social action' and 'interactive, processual, contingent products of social action' refer in our mathematical classification to relative nonzero difference, while the 'collective phenomenon of group sameness', 'deep and foundational forms of selfhood' and 'fluctuating and fragmented modes of the "self"' refer in a literal or metaphoric sense to absolute zero difference.

Relating identity to social and political action means defining a group or category from the outside in. In mathematical terms the conditional nature of a thing, n, is derived from the external relation which in this case is social action. The authors who operate with the concept of identity in this tradition define identity in firm opposition to self-interest or alternatively as a ground for possible social action. The idea is that actions of individuals and groups are not determined only by their instrumental rationality but also by shared cultural values reflected in common cultural or political identities. In contemporary sociology of ethnic relations one can find numerous examples of this form of identity use.

A good and readily available example is a debate in *Sociological Research Online* (1996, vol. 1, issues 2–4) on 'national identity, citizenship and multicultural society' between J. Rex and G. Delanty. While the authors express profound disagreement on whether interests or identities are at the core of 'new nationalism' in Europe, they both share the understanding that identities are something opposed to interests. So for example, Rex[3] writes how

> Delanty also seems to want to argue that the banal nationalism of the masses is now no longer about the pursuit of interests as, I think, was the case with classes, but is now primarily concerned with identity ... *therefore* [they] become concerned above all to achieve identity. They will surely still have *interests* which they pursue and which affect the structure of their organisations. (Rex, 1996, para. 1.5)

and furthermore, 'Whether we are talking about interests or identity, however, we should be clear that the "banal" interpretation of the immigrants' role may be challenged' (Rex, 1996, para. 1.8). In addition, Delanty also operates with the concept of identity as a base for social action, arguing that 'identity' not 'ideology' is a key motive of social action. So we read that nationalism 'no longer appeals to ideology but to identity. ... This of course does not mean that ideology has come to an end, but that it has fragmented into a politics of identity: ideology is being refracted through identity' (Delanty, 1996, para. 2.3). There are three crucial problems with this use of 'identity'. Firstly, there is no obvious reason why all forms of noninstrumental motivation and action should be categorised as being based on 'identity'. As we can learn from Weber (1968) and others, social action can originate from a variety of motives: those that are predominantly rational (instrumental or value rational), traditional, habitual, emotional and so on. The use of the term 'identity' here is extremely counterproductive because by not differentiating between all these different forms of action it explains very little. Instead of pinpointing the exact type of motive or action taking place and thus providing an explanation, it obscures the entire explanatory process by simply conjuring up the word 'identity', like pulling a rabbit out of a hat.

Secondly, there is no self-evident reason why any form of social action should be characterised as having a basis in 'identity'. One can straightforwardly explain certain types of social and political action without making any reference to 'identity'. If we look at our previous example of 'new nationalisms' in Europe one can develop a similar argument to Delanty's without invoking the concept of identity at all. So one could argue that nationalism no longer appeals to ideology but to group membership, self-understanding, self- or group perception, a sense of commonality, shared values and so on.

Thirdly, there is no empirical evidence that it is 'identity' that motivates individuals to form groups. If identity is understood as a form of a value-driven action then following the principle of methodological individualism[4] one has no empirical tools to measure the intensity of values. As Hechter argues,

> values cannot readily be imputed from behaviour ... usually we do not know if such behaviours result from the fear of sanctions ... or directly from deeply held value commitments. Since both mechanisms produce the same outcome, it is impossible to tell which of them is responsible in the usual case. (1995, p. 56)

The uses of identity in relation to 'group sameness', 'foundational forms of selfhood' and as 'fluctuating modes of the self' entail defining a group or category from the inside out. The strategy used here is a literal[5] or metaphoric understanding of identity with reference to its unconditional nature, which is not derived from an external relation. This is most clearly visible in the work of authors who operate with strong concepts of group membership and thus write about 'gender', 'cultural', 'ethnic', 'national' and other identities. For example, H. Isaacs and A. Smith operate with very strong and definite concepts of cultural, ethnic and national identity. While Isaacs' conceptual framework incorporates the relation to 'group sameness' and 'foundational forms of selfhood', Smith's theory works with all three understandings of identity ('group sameness', 'foundational forms of selfhood' and as 'fluctuating modes of the self') as an absolute zero difference. Isaacs' concept of 'basic group identity' represents the most straightforward case of understanding identity as an absolute zero difference. According to Isaacs:

> this is the identity derived from belonging to what is generally and loosely called an 'ethnic group'. It is composed of what has been called 'primordial affinities and attachments'. It is the identity made up of *what a person is born with* or *acquires at birth*. (1975, pp. 29–30, my italics)

Even though Smith uses more subtle concepts, his terminology is still firmly rooted in understanding identity as an absolute zero difference. With clear reference to 'group sameness' and 'foundational forms of selfhood' he writes how 'the *attempt to create new* communities and *cultural identities* is likely to prove painfully slow and arduous, especially where the *new identities lack clear boundaries* and must compete with *well established and deep rooted identities* and communities' (1999, p. 19, my italics); or how 'identities are forged out of shared experiences, memories and myths in relation to those of other collective identities' (1999, p. 247). Furthermore he defines nationalism as 'an ideological movement for *attaining and maintaining identity*, unity and autonomy of a social group some of whose members deem it to constitute an actual or potential nation' (1999, p. 18, my italics). Smith finally incorporates the third understanding of identity ('fluctuating modes of the self') by making a distinction between individual identities which are seen as changeable, situational and optional, and collective identities (e.g. ethnic, religious and national identities) which 'tend to be pervasive and persistent' (1999, p. 230).

These uses of identity are even more problematic than the previous one. Firstly, the concept is reified to the extreme. Both Smith and Isaacs operate with the idea of identity as something tangible, visible or touchable. As we can read in their works, identities just like other material things have 'clear boundaries', they are 'acquired' and 'well rooted', should be 'attained and maintained' and so on. Identities are truly perceived as things. They are seen as something firm, stable and given and not as a product of social action, contingent events, human agency and so on. In this way a concept (that of identity) acquires attributes and property that only the material world can have – boundaries, action or will. This view is not only analytically problematic but it can also have serious practical implications when used in popular discourse for the political mobilisation of groups or individuals. Hence, people are incited to kill or die in order to 'preserve, maintain or acquire their identities'.

Secondly, by using the concept of identity with reference to 'group sameness' and 'foundational forms of selfhood' in such a reified way, we are unable to provide an explanation of individual or group behaviour. Instead of focusing on the job of explaining why individuals reify their group membership and perceive other groups and categories as homogenous things with single wills, we engage in the creation, maintenance or reproduction of the reified view of the social world. As Brubaker and Cooper (2000, p. 5) following Bourdieu (1990) rightly point out, academics who take on this type of reasoning do not distinguish between the categories of practice ('lay', 'folk', 'native' concepts) and the categories of analysis. If the social actors in their everyday life operate with terms such as 'identity', 'ethnic identity' or 'national identity' as something self-evident and unproblematic this does not mean that a researcher should treat these categories in the same manner.

Thirdly, even when researchers such as Smith (1999, p. 230) acknowledge occasionally that some forms of 'identity' are contingent, situational and instrumental (as typical of 'fluctuating modes of the self'), there is no self-evident rationale for why, or explanation of how, the concept of identity is necessary to explain individual's and group's multiple and fragmented perceptions and understandings of 'selves'. What some theorists and researchers do here is to invoke 'identity' to explain 'modernity', 'postmodernity' and other grand concepts. Thus, one (reified) metaphor is used as a shortcut to explain the other (grand) metaphor. This strategy leads to a very soft understanding of the concept which produces extreme vagueness and as such is empirically of very little value. If the concept of 'identity' is used theoretically to mean anything and everything (as in some works from poststructuralism and cultural studies) than it empirically means nothing.

To recap, neither of the two theoretical models (relative nonzero difference and absolute zero difference) and none of the five conceptual approaches (non-instrumental forms of social action, interactive and contingent products of social action, collective phenomenon of group sameness, deep and foundational forms of selfhood, and fluctuating and fragmented modes of the 'self') to the study of identity has theoretical or heuristic legitimacy. On the one hand the concept is not indispensable nor necessary while on the other hand it is either vague and all-inclusive or reified and excessively inflexible. However, what is most significant here is that such a conceptual wilderness has profound consequences when one attempts to apply this concept in the empirical world. Let us explore this link more closely.

Measuring the invisible

Conceptual problems with the use of 'identity' have direct implications for research strategies and methodology. In other words, in order to explain, analyse and 'measure' identity claims one needs to have a clearly defined understanding of what identity is. Empirical studies on identity (ethnic and national in particular) range from strictly conducted quantitative studies using surveys and experiments to qualitative ethnographic research focusing mostly on in-depth interviewing, observation or textual analysis. Since academics oriented towards qualitative research recognise, explicitly or implicitly, that their empirical use of the concept of identity is rather on the metaphorical level, I will focus here only on quantitative studies that work with the nonzero difference concept of identity.

A great number of surveys on 'identity' claims were devised and conducted on common-sense assumptions of identity as something unproblematic. A typical example is the highly influential and often cited study by J. Linz and A. Stepan (1992) on national and ethnic identities in Spain, the Soviet Union and Yugoslavia. The main argument of the authors (the crucial importance for the preservation of multiethnic states emerging from authoritarian regimes) of holding democratic elections first at the state or federal level before holding them at the regional level is based on the results of surveys employing simplified and stereotypical distinctions, such as 'being proud to be' Spanish, Catalan, Basque etc. On the one hand the concept of identity is understood in a very strict way as something everybody necessarily possesses, and on the other hand the entire concept has been reduced to a single variable 'being proud of'. Why should this variable be regarded as measuring 'identity' at all and not the intensity of proudness of being a member of a particular category or group? And furthermore how do we know that the respondents' answers are not just a stereotypical reaction to a colloquial question? Even if one intends to find out about the intensity of 'being proud to be Spanish' this information can certainly not be acquired from a single question.

However this example is only the tip of the iceberg. There are cases of serious empirical research that employ a much more complex definition and operationalisation of identity. I will concentrate here on two such attempts which I found useful in my own research on ethnic identity – the works of W. Isajiw and P. Weinreich.

Two examples

W.W. Isajiw (1990, p. 35) analyses ethnic identity by deducing it from membership of a concrete ethnic group. He makes a distinction between ethnic groups which develop: social organisation – an objective phenomenon which supplies the structural basis for an ethnic community; and identity – a subjective phenomenon which gives to individuals a feeling of belonging, and to a community a feeling of unity and historical importance. Ethnic identity is seen as the way a person, on the basis of his/her ethnic origins, psychologically locates her/himself in relation to one or more social systems, and also the way in which s/he understands and locates others in relation to these systems. Ethnic identity is defined as a level of socialisation in one particular ethnic group, or through the perception of the existence of ancestors, the real or symbolic members of the (particular) ethnic group.

Isajiw (1990, p. 36) distinguishes between external and internal aspects of one's ethnic identity. External aspects indicate observed behaviour, cultural and social: speaking an ethnic language, the practice of ethnic traditions, etc.; participation in ethnic personal networks (e.g. family, friends, etc.); participation in institutionalised ethnic organisations (for example, churches, schools, firms, media, etc.); participation in voluntary ethnic organisations (for instance, clubs, 'societies', youth organisations, etc.); participation in events sponsored by ethnic organisations (such as, excursions, trips, dances, concerts, etc.).

Internal aspects of ethnic identification can be divided into at least three categories: cognitive, moral, and affective. The cognitive dimension incorporates 'self-image', knowledge of one's own group, knowledge of the group's own heritage and historical past (real or fictional) or of some selected aspects of its past, and knowledge of those values of the group that are part of its heritage. The moral dimension is understood as the existence of feelings of group obligations (for example, teaching descendants their ethnic language, endogamy within the ethnic group, ethnic nepotism, etc.). The affective dimension of ethnic identity includes feelings of attachment to the group. The most important feelings according to Isajiw are: the feeling of security and sympathy (mutual under-standing, associative preference for members of one's own group rather than members of some other ethnic group); and the feeling of safety and comfort within the culture of one's own group and opposition to accepting the cultural traits of other groups or societies.

Different combinations of the above-mentioned aspects of ethnic identification lead to different forms of ethnic identity (see Schema A). Loosely applying this theoretical framework to a representative sample of a population of university students (using a survey technique) I have empirically identified the existence of three dominant types of 'ethnic identity': ritualist-affective based ethnic identity, cognitive ethnic identity and identity of rebellion or non-ethnic identity (Malešević, 1994; Malešević and Malešević, 2001).[6]

SCHEMA A – Ethnic Identity 1

Theoretical model – Isajiw's ethnic identity retention model

External features
speaking an ethnic language
the practice of ethnic traditions
participation in ethnic personal networks
participation in institutionalised ethnic organisations
participation in voluntary ethnic organisations
participation in performances sponsored by ethnic organisations
Internal features
Cognitive
self-image
knowledge of one's own ethnic group
knowledge of the ethnic group's own heritage and historical past (real or fictional)
knowledge of values of one's ethnic group which are part of the group's heritage
Moral
teaching descendants the ethnic language
ethnic endogamy
ethnic nepotism
Affective
feeling of security and sympathy

feeling of safety and comfort within the culture of one's own ethnic group

Empirical application

'ethnic identity perceptions' instrument – 20 variables (Likert-type scale)

Principal component analysis

1. **ritualistic-affective based ethnic identity**
2. **cognitive ethnic identity**
3. **identity of rebellion/non-ethnic identity**

In the same set of surveys I have also developed a research instrument based on the definition of ethnic identity proposed by P. Weinreich.[7] Weinreich has developed what he calls a metatheoretical framework which incorporates elements of various theories of identity (the psychodynamic approach of Eriksen and Marcia, the symbolic interactionism of Mead and Goffman, the personal construct theory of Bannister and Mair, the social identity theory of Tajfel, etc.). Weinreich believes that a general grand theory of ethnic identity that would be able to explain all forms of ethnic identification is not possible, and as a result he opts for this 'open metatheoretical framework' which enables us to 'generate an empirically grounded particular theory within its framework (Weinreich, 1986, p. 315). This framework is articulated through what he terms Identity Structure Analysis – a set of research devices to measure intensity and salience of identity. Weinreich defines identity in the following way:

> One's identity is defined as the totality of one's self-construal, in which how one construes onself in the present expresses the continuity between how one construes onself as one was in the past and how one construes onself as one aspires to be in the future. (Weinreich, 1983, p. 151)

In accordance with social identity theory he perceives ethnic identity as a segment of a general social identity. Hence his definition of ethnic identity is largely deduced from the definition of general social identity and he states that ethnic identity is 'that part of the totality of one's self-construal made up of those dimensions that express the continuity between one's construal of past ancestry and one's future aspirations in relation to ethnicity' (Weinreich, 1986, p. 308). So the emphasis is on the temporal dimension in defining an ethnic identity: perceptions of the past (ethnic ancestry) and the future (individual or group aspirations).

In my research I have operationalised Weinreich's definition of ethnic identity and have attempted to establish an empirical link between the respondents' perceptions of their ethnic origins (ancestors) and their future life aims (see Schema B). The survey results revealed the existence of a single dominant type of 'ethnic identity' which linked together the factor 'strong affective identification with ethnic ancestors' on the one hand with the factor 'altruism as a main life goal' on the other hand to produce the type of ethnic identity provisionally called 'the ideal of sacrifice for an ethnic collectivity' (the identity of ethnic altruism) (Malešević, 1993).[8]

SCHEMA B – Ethnic Identity 2

Theoretical model – Weinreich's model of ethnic identity

Definition: ethnic identity is 'that part of the totality of one's self-construal made up of those dimensions that express the continuity between one's construal of past ancestry and one's future aspirations in relation to ethnicity' (Weinreich, 1986, p. 308).

Empirical application
'Life aims/aspirations' instrument – 25 variables (Likert-type scale)
'Attitudes towards ethnic ancestors' instrument – 18 variables (Likert-type scale)
Principal component analysis
Life aims/aspirations – 6 principal components
1. respect for elementary ethical principles
2. ecological-humanistic orientation
3. family values
4. knowledge and creativity oriented aspiration
5. altruism as a main life goal
6. aspiration to consumerism and ownership
Attitudes towards ethnic ancestors – 4 principal components
1. strong affective identification with ethnic ancestors
2. ignoring the links with ethnic ancestors
3. ritualistic-pietistic identification with ethnic ancestors (non-affective identification)
4. elements of the biological identification with ethnic ancestors

Canonical analysis – **The identity of ethnic altruism** (strong positive correlation between 'altruism as a main life goal' and 'strong affective identification with ethnic ancestors')

What is interesting here is that the two highly sophisticated and carefully elaborated theoretical models and definitions of ethnic identity, when empirically operationalised and applied to the same sample, have produced different research results. Although there are vague similarities between Isajiw's ritualist-affective ethnic identity and Weinreich's affective identification with ethnic ancestors, there are much greater differences between the two research results. So what do these results tell us?

Firstly, they show us empirically what we have argued theoretically, that in the social sciences one cannot operate with a nonzero difference model of identity. If one could, then the definitions of the two applied models would produce the same or very similar results. And they have not. Although I have used the same sample and applied strict empirical criteria in the sampling, conceptualisation and operationalisation of these models of ethnic identity, I have ended up with very different answers to the same question relating to the existence of ethnic identity types. Not only has this research produced contradictory findings on how many types of ethnic identity exist in this particular population (one or three), but also the contents of these 'ethnic identities' greatly differ as well.

Secondly, the research results indicate that the two operationalised models in fact measure two different things. Although both conceptual models claim to measure and are designed to measure 'ethnic identity', the research results clearly show that either one or both of them are flawed, or more likely that the concept in itself is problematic. Because of its conceptual vagueness the term identity is able to accommodate very different research designs. While this conceptual looseness might be perceived as an advantage in the qualitative-metaphoric tradition, it is no less than a disaster for quantitatively oriented research.

'Identity' in the historical vacuum

Although, as persistently argued in this chapter, the concepts of identity and ethnic identity appear to be theoretically and empirically deficient, one cannot dispute their astonishing popularity within and outside academia. Although the concept was steadily gaining prominence from the 1960s, it was really during the late 1980s and through the 1990s that 'identity' acquired an almost hegemonic position in both academic and popular discourse. While mass media and scholarly journals and books made very sporadic references to 'identity' or 'ethnic identity' in the 1940s and 1950s, today it is impossible to skim through articles, news bulletins or books on cultural or political difference without noticing tens and often hundreds of references to 'identity'. This fact in itself raises a question: Why has such a clearly ambiguous concept become so dominant in popular and academic discourse in a relatively short time?

There are probably many sociological and historical reasons why the concept of identity has acquired such a dominant position. However, I will focus here only on one which I consider to be the most important. The astonishing popularity of the concept comes primarily from the fact that 'identity' has filled the role that the three other major social concepts have vacated – the concepts of 'race' 'national character' and 'social consciousness'.

The master concept used to make sense of human difference and similarity from the late eighteenth until the first half of the twentieth century was the concept of 'race'. Charles Linne was the first who used the concept of race in an academic and diligent way to produce the following and at the time very influential typology of human races: 1. Americans – reddish, obstinate, and regulated by custom; 2. Europeans – white, gentle, and governed by law; 3. Asians – sallow, severe, and ruled by opinion; and 4. Africans – black, crafty, and governed by caprice (Wolf, 1994, p. 4). What Linne started, the use of quasi-biological concepts to define, select and order human difference, the social sciences of the nineteenth and early twentieth centuries has developed to the level of perfection. As Banton (1983, pp. 35–50) explains, the use of the concept of 'race' has shifted from the initial emphasis on descent to a taxonomic and eventually to an explanatory level: it was very much the responsibility of scientific discourse that race has become conceived of as a stable, permanent, definite and unchangeable biological and cultural entity. De Gobineau, Lubbock, Morton, Knox and other 'scientific racists' perceived races as different species (in a zoological sense) and had a belief that 'a person's outward appearance was an indicator of his place in the natural order'. Darwin's theory of evolution has only strengthened the authority of the 'scientific concept of race' while social Darwinism has fully co-opted the concept for the social sciences and the general use. Banton (1983, p. 52) and Dickens

(2000) document well how the concepts of race and racial inequality were dominating public discourse of the nineteenth and early twentieth centuries and how very few if any intellectuals were immune to belief in the superiority of their ('white') race. The general belief was that one should 'preserve racial hygiene', races had to be 'maintained' and their purity 'attained', it was seen as legitimate to 'fight for one's race' or to 'awaken racial consciousness'. It was only the military defeat of the Nazi state and its racist ideology that has largely delegitimised academic and consequently popular concepts of race. Although the term has survived the Second World War and is still used, it has lost most of the scientific and popular appeal it had before the war. The post-Nuremberg world had to look for and adopt another social concept that would deal with cultural and physical difference and would at the same time guard its users against being seen as in any way resembling the Nazi project.

In the 1950s and 1960s there was no clear winner to replace 'race' – whereas European and left-leaning intellectuals and after them journalists and the general public in Eastern (but also in Western) Europe switched to the master concept of 'social consciousness', centrist and right-wing intellectuals as well as the general public in America opted for the master concept of 'national character'.

Like 'race', these two concepts provided enough elasticity to cover many distinct processes and forms of cultural, political or physical difference. The Marxist-inspired idea of 'social consciousness' gained prominence together with the discourse of class politics. While racial unity and racial consciousness were now seen as dangerous concepts, proletarian unity and class consciousness were not only accepted but were considered highly desirable ideas throughout communist and non-communist Europe. Following Marx it was regularly argued that classes can fully exist only when they develop 'full class consciousness' (class *'für sich'* and class *'an sich'*). Class consciousness and workers' unity had to be 'awakened', 'attained' and 'maintained'. One had to fight using revolutionary means to 'preserve and acquire' social consciousness. Class consciousness was also regarded as superior to 'national consciousness'. Marcuse (1964) and other Frankfurt School theorists believed that capitalism and mass culture produce 'false needs' and false or in Marcuse's terms 'unhappy' consciousness and that the proletariat and other disadvantaged groups have to liberate themselves to discover their 'true consciousness'.

Similarly, following the influential culture-and-personality school of anthropology (M. Mead, R. Benedict) the concept of 'national character' largely replaced race in a quasi-biological sense in America in the 1960s. As Gleason emphasises:

> the new era of scientifically respectable study of national character was inaugurated in World War II by a group of scholars who were called upon by agencies of the United States government to apply their skills to such questions as how civilian morale could best be maintained or what kind of propaganda could be most effectively employed against the enemy. (1983, p. 24)

The term caught on in the public eye and academics, politicians and journalists embraced it in language such as that 'national character has to be preserved' or that nations strongly differ in terms of their 'characters'; McCarthy's Committee on Non-American Activities declared that 'communism is not part of the American national character', that one had again 'to fight for the true national character', to prove worthy of being 'a part of the American national character', and so on.

Although fairly different, the master concepts of 'social consciousness' and 'national character' had a great deal in common. They were both vague and inclusive enough to accommodate many distinct processes, events or social actors and as such quickly secured popularity. They both answered the need of cold war politics to present a unified front to the enemy side by perceiving its citizens as belonging to close-knit entities with singular and clearly recognisable wills – 'we may all be different individuals but we share an American/British/French national character' or 'Soviet class consciousness is above petty individual differences'. As such they were both also deeply collectivist, analytically inflexible and strongly prone to reification. Hence, whereas the master concept of 'race' was now abandoned in form, it fully persisted in its content, meaning and function – only the term was rejected – as 'character' or 'consciousness'.

With the emergence in the West of youth, ethnic, gender and other radical politics in the late 1960s and 1970s, and in the East Gorbachev's policies of openness in the mid-1980s, the domination of 'the national character' and 'social consciousness' has started to erode. The new social movements could not easily fit into the old cold war concepts of class and nation state. 'Identity' politics was slowly taking over. The absolute collapse of communist ideology and the break-up of supranational federal states in Eastern Europe has ultimately delegitimised the notions of class consciousness in the East and of stable and predictable national character in the West. 'Identity' emerged as a new and all-inclusive master concept to simultaneously define and 'explain' the current situation of dramatic social change. The popularity of this master concept has come precisely from its ambiguity and its ability to accommodate different processes, structures, actions and events. 'Identity' provided an illusion that dramatic social change is under control: we know what is happening – 'people are only fighting to preserve, awaken, maintain, etc. their identities'. Identity has thus emerged as a grand umbrella term to contain all the unexplained and constantly emerging phenomena of our times in a single word – just as 'race', 'national character' and 'social consciousness' had earlier possessed the elasticity and aloofness to make easy sense of difference and similarity. 'Identity' and its derivatives, ethnic and national identity, have today become a legitimate political tool in academic and popular discourse just as 'race' was at the end of the nineteenth century and the beginning of the twentieth, and as 'national character' and 'social consciousness' were during the Cold War. This time again the form ('national character', 'social consciousness') has been sacrificed to the content. One communitarian, reifying, stultifying concept has just been replaced with another similar one.

Furthermore, the vagueness and aloofness of this master concept correspond even more with the times than did the previous three master concepts. 'Identity' is a fuzzy term for fuzzy times. The speed and intensity of social and political change have prevented development of more analytical, more precise or empirically more useful concepts. In the postmodern spirit of the times every social problem is easily and quickly labelled and 'explained' as an identity problem, and since it is now commonly acknowledged (at least in academia) that identities are fluid, complex, multiple, dynamic, then no full explanation of this or that social problem is possible. 'Identity' is the tautology for our times.

However, what is important to emphasise here is that just like 'race', 'national character' or 'social consciousness', 'identity' is not an innocent concept. Exactly as 'race' was uncritically borrowed from biology, with the theory of evolution being crudely applied to the world of humans to justify political goals – colonialism or Nazi expansion, and 'national character' and 'social consciousness' were borrowed from medicine (psychiatry in particular) and used to delegitimise ideological (class or national) enemies, so was 'identity' appropriated from mathematics to serve political goals. These goals may now be multiple – to acquire political autonomy or an independent state for an ethnic group ('to maintain cultural identity'), to gain the power or to uphold the political status quo in the state ('to attain or keep democratic political identity'), to win public or media support against asylum seekers ('to preserve national identity') and so on, but the reason for its borrowing remains as political as it was before, if not more so. Individuals and groups are still politically mobilised to fight, to die or to kill for the preservation and defence of their 'identities', just as they were before for the protection of racial hygiene or class unity.

Conclusion

Most general studies of identity emphasise that identity implies sameness and difference at the same time. So, for example, Jenkins (1996, pp. 3–4) argues that 'the notion of identity simultaneously establishes two possible relations of comparison between persons and things: similarity, on the one hand, and difference, on the other'. And indeed this is exactly what the original mathematical meaning of the term is all about. However, as argued in this chapter, the definitional simplicity and seductive crispness of the concept as developed in mathematics is, for better or for worse, unachievable in the social sciences. Both attempts to transfer the concept, either in its original mathematical way or in a more popular metaphoric manner, have proved futile. The term 'identity' (as well as its derivatives 'ethnic' or 'national identity') covers too much ground to be analytically useful. Instead of theoretical and methodological clearance the concept has brought upon us more confusion and opened the door for possible manipulation. Its conceptual ambiguity prevents clear and transparent operationalisation, which has profound methodological implications, whereas its methodological aloofness leads to analytical paralysis. And finally its quasi-scientific use brings popular recognition, and this has the potential for devastating political outcomes.

'Identity' is no more than a common name for many different and distinct processes that simply need to be explained. Wrapping all these diverse forms of action, events, actors under a single expression can only generate more misunderstanding and will not help us in any way to explain the extraordinary social change that has started taking place in the last few decades. 'Identity' is an ill-suited concept for such a giant task.

Notes

1. The mathematical example would look something like this: because 2 is the same as 2 the difference between 2 and 2 is 0. This implies that this 2 is simultaneously defined by its difference from not(2) and its similarity to itself (2). According to Goddard (1998) this entails that difference (from zero difference to nonzero difference) defines the whole structure of identity.
2. As Gleason (1983) and Brubaker and Cooper (2000, p. 2) point out, the concept of identity was introduced into the social sciences only in the late 1950s and the 1960s, primarily through the work of the psychologist E. Erikson. There were almost no references to 'identity' in social sciences dictionaries and encyclopaedias before the 1950s.
3. To be fair, John Rex shows some degree of scepticism towards the concept of 'identity', nevertheless he still operates with that concept in his work.
4. As explained earlier in the text, if 'identity' is understood in a non-metaphorical way, that is in a strict mathematical sense as a relative nonzero difference, then methodological individualism seems to be the only legitimate conceptual and methodological research strategy on offer. For my criticism of this particular research strategy as applied to the study of ethnic relations see Malešević (2002).
5. A literal understanding of the concept of identity (as an absolute zero difference), as already clarified, has no legitimate theoretical foundation in the social sciences.
6. These three factors have been generated with the help of factor analysis. For more about the methodology and sample structure used in this research see Malešević (1993; 1994) and Malešević and Malešević (2001).
7. Although Weinreich has developed his own set of research tools designed to study identity ('Identity Structure Analysis' – ISA) I have not used this empirical tool here but have only operationalised his definition and theory of ethnic identity. This has been done with the purpose of securing methodological compatibility with Isajiw's concept of ethnic identity.
8. These factors have been generated with the help of factor analysis, while the relationship between the two factors has been established with the help of canonical analysis.

References

Banton, M. (1983) *Racial and Ethnic Competition* (Cambridge: Cambridge University Press).

Bourdieu, P. (1990) *The Logic of Practice* (Cambridge: Polity Press).

Brubaker, R. and Cooper, F. (2000) 'Beyond "identity"', *Theory and Society*, vol. 29, no. 1, pp. 1–37.

Delanty, G. (1996) 'Beyond the Nation-State: National Identity and Citizenship in a Multicultural Society – A Response to Rex', *Sociological Research Online*, vol. 1, no. 3, http://www.socresonline.org.uk/1/3/1.html.

Dickens, P. (2000) *Social Darwinism* (London: Oxford University Press).

Giddens, A. (1984) *The Constitution of Society: Outline of the Theory of Structuration* (Cambridge: Polity Press).

Gleason, P. (1983) 'Identifying Identity: A Semantic History', *The Journal of American History*, vol. 69, no. 4, pp. 910–931.

Goddard, I.W. (1998) *The ID Matrix and the Conservation of Identity*, http://dev.null.org/psychoceramics/archives/1998.02/msg00002.

Hechter, M. (1995) 'Explaining Nationalist Violence', *Nations and Nationalism*, vol. 1, no. 1, pp. 53–68.

Isaacs, H. (1975) 'Basic Group Identity: The Idols of the Tribe', in N. Glazer and D. Moynihan (eds) *Ethnicity: Theory and Experience* (Cambridge, Mass.: Harvard University Press).

Isajiw, W. (1990) 'Ethnic Identity Retention', in R. Breton, W. Isajiw, W. Kalbach and J. Reitz (eds) *Ethnic Identity and Equality: Varieties of Experience in a Canadian City* (Toronto: University of Toronto Press).

Jenkins, R. (1996) *Social Identity* (London: Routledge).

Linz, J. and Stepan, A. (1992) 'Political Identities and Electoral Consequences: Spain, the Soviet Union and Yugoslavia', *Daedalus*, vol. 121, no. 2, pp. 123–139.

Malešević, S. (1993) 'Percepcija "etničkog porijekla" i "životnih ciljeva" kao determinanti etničkog identiteta', *Revija za sociologiju*, vol. 24, nos 1–2, pp. 87–99.

Malešević, S. (1994) 'Percepcija etnickog identiteta: Aplikacija jednog modela', *Migracijske teme*, vol. 10, no. 1, pp. 31–55.

Malešević, S. (2002) 'Rational Choice Theory and the Sociology of Ethnic Relations: A Critique', *Ethnic and Racial Studies*, vol. 25, no. 2, pp. 193–212.

Malešević, S. and Malešević, V. (2001) 'Ethnic Identity Perceptions: An Analysis of Two Surveys', *Europa Ethnica*, vol. 58, nos 1–2, pp. 1–16.

Marcuse, H. (1964) *One-Dimensional Man: Studies in the Ideology of Advanced Industrial Society* (Boston: Beacon Press).

Rex, J. (1996) 'National Identity in the Democratic Multicultural State', *Sociological Research Online*, vol. 1, no. 3, http://www.socresonline.org.uk/1/4/rex.html.

Smith, A. (1999) *Myths and Memories of the Nation* (Oxford: Oxford University Press).

Weber, M. (1968) *Economy and Society* (New York: Bedminster Press).

Weinreich, P. (1983) 'Psychodynamics of Personal and Social Identity: Theoretical Concepts and their Measurement', in A. Jacobson-Widding (ed.) *Identity: Personal and Socio-cultural* (Stockholm: Almqvist and Wiksell International).

Weinreich, P. (1986) 'The Operationalisation of Identity Theory in Racial and Ethnic Relations', in J. Rex and D. Mason (eds) *Theories of Race and Ethnic Relations* (Cambridge: Cambridge University Press).

Wolf, E.R. (1994) 'Perilous Ideas: Race, Culture, People', *Current Anthropology*, vol. 35, no. 1, pp. 1–12.

Notes on Contributors

Zygmunt Bauman is professor emeritus in the Department of Sociology and Social Policy, Leeds University. He is the author of numerous very influential books including *Legislators and Interpreters* (Polity, 1987), *Modernity and the Holocaust* (Polity, 1991), *Modernity and Ambivalence* (Polity, 1993), *Globalization* (Polity, 1998), *In Search of Politics* (Polity, 1999) and *Liquid Modernity* (Polity, 2000).

S.N. Eisenstadt is professor emeritus in the Department of Sociology and Anthropology at the Hebrew University of Jerusalem. He is the author and editor of many prominent books including *The Origins and Diversity of Axial Civilizations* (State University of New York Press, 1986), *Society, Culture and Urbanization* (Sage, 1987) and most recently *Power, Trust and Meaning* (Chicago University Press, 1995), *Japanese Civilization* (Chicago University Press, 1996) and *Fundamentalism, Sectarianism and Revolution: The Jacobin Dimensions of Modernity* (Cambridge University Press, 1999).

John A. Hall is a professor in the Department of Sociology, McGill University, Montreal. He is the author of many path-breaking books and articles on nationalism, the state, war and social theory including *Powers and Liberties* (Penguin, 1985), *Liberalism* (University of North Carolina Press, 1987) and more recently *Coercion and Consent* (Polity, 1994), *International Orders* (Polity, 1996), *Is America Breaking Apart?* (Stanford University Press, 1998) and *The State of the Nation* (Cambridge University Press, 1998).

Mark Haugaard is a lecturer in the Department of Political Science and Sociology, at the National University of Ireland, Galway. He is the author of *The Constitution of Power* (Manchester University Press, 1997) and *Structures, Restructuration and Social Power* (Aldershot, 1992), co-editor of *Power in Contemporary Politics* (Sage, 2000), and editor of *Power: A Reader* (Manchester University Press, 2002).

Richard Jenkins is a professor in the Department of Sociological Studies, Sheffield University. He is the author of many influential books and articles on ethnicity, racism, transition to adulthood, nationalism and social theory including *Pierre Bourdieu* (Routledge,

1992), *Social Identity* (Routledge, 1996), *Rethinking Ethnicity* (Sage, 1997) and *Challenging Sociology: Towards a Better Understanding of Human Society* (Palgrave, 2002).

Siniša Malešević is a lecturer in the Department of Political Science and Sociology at the National University of Ireland, Galway. He is the author of *Ideology, Legitimacy and the New State* (Frank Cass, 2002) and of many articles on ethnicity, nationalism and sociological theory. He is also co-editor of *Ideology after Poststructuralism* (Pluto Press, 2002) and editor of *Culture in Central and Eastern Europe: Institutional and Value Changes* (IMO, 1997).

John Rex is professor emeritus in the Department of Sociology at Warwick University. He is the author and editor of many highly influential books and articles on ethnic and race relations, nationalism and sociological theory including *Race and Ethnicity* (Oxford University Press, 1986), *Theories of Race and Ethnic Relations* (Cambridge University Press, 1987), *Ethnic Minorities in the Modern Nation-State* (Macmillan, 1996) and *The Ethnicity Reader* (Cambridge University Press, 1999).

Gordana Uzelac is a lecturer in the Department of Sociology at the University of North London. She is the author of articles on the perception of the nation, nationalism, ethnic distance and war.

Index

Compiled by Sue Carlton

Africa 45, 66, 77, 113, 191–2
Afro-Americans 106, 186, 187
agency 58, 59–60, 129, 148–50
    corporate and primary 144–5,
        153–4, 155–6, 157–8, 159–64
    and culture 142–3, 144, 147
    and structure 139–44, 147
    see also structure, culture and
        agency
agrarian society/pre-national societies
    146–8, 152–3
analytical dualism 140–2, 152
Anderson, Benedict 10, 21, 98, 125
Andhra 55
anthropology 10, 15, 16
Arabic language 97
Archer, Margaret 8, 139–45, 146, 149,
    152
    Corporate Agency 153–4, 158, 161,
        162
Arendt, Hannah 172–3
Aristotle 124
Armenia 66
army 152, 157
assimilationism 114, 115–16
    see also homogeneity; melting pot
associative relations 89–90, 91
Assyria 44, 45
asylum seekers 112–13, 115, 213
attachments 90–1, 94
    see also kinship
Austro-Hungarian empire 104, 189
axial age civilisations 3, 7, 40, 46–53
    religions 37, 47, 49–52
    vernacularisation 55–8
    see also Japan
Ayudhya 55
Aztecs 45

Balkans 77
Banks, M. 100
Bannister, D. 206
Banton, M. 209–10
barbarism 67, 68
Barth, Fredrik 16, 20, 30, 31, 95
basic group identity 200–1

Basques 203
Baumann, Z. 134, 136
Beck, Ulrich 125, 128, 171, 196
behaviour, common 6–7, 18, 19, 21
being-in-the-world 135
Belgian empire 104
Bell, Daniel 185
Benedict, Ruth 167, 210
Bentham, Jeremy 126
Berger, Jon 174
Berger, P. 20, 127–8
Berlin, Isaiah 126
(b)orders 170
boundaries 30–1
    construction of 33–7
    crossing 36, 45
    fuzziness 13, 23–4, 93, 95
    institutionalisation of 40–1
    maintenance 20, 21
    need for 173–4
    organisational/institutional 33, 35
    perpetual renewal 16, 17, 28, 29–30
    symbolic 33, 35
    see also collectivity/collectivities;
        identity
Bourdieu, P. 2, 129, 133–4, 202
bourgeoisie 158
Brazil 70, 71
Britain, and multiculturalism 114
British empire 104
Brubaker, R. 198, 202
Buddhism 50, 53, 54, 77
bureaucracy, development of 156,
    157, 162
Bush, George W. 5
Byzantine empire 52

Calhoun, John 185
Cambodia 66
Canada 185
    Huron ethnicity 103
capitalism 122
Castells, Manuel 196
Catalans 102, 203
categories and groups 18
Chalukayas 55

chaos, fear of 34–5
China 52, 73, 74, 75
Chinese language 56, 57–8
Cholas 55
Christian X 26
Christianity 50, 77, 78
church, national 25
citizenship 63, 66, 176
city-states 156, 160
civic nationalism 5, 9, 182, 186, 192
civil nationalism 5, 9, 182, 184, 192
civilised man 62
civility/civic consciousness 37–8, 41
class consciousness 122, 210, 211,
    212
class-for-itself/class-in-itself 2, 16, 18
Clifford, J. 113
Code Napoléon 73
Cohen, Anthony 16, 20
collective consciousness 6
collective identities
    and codes/themes 36–8, 41–2, 45–6,
        64
    construction of 7, 33–82
        in axial age civilisations 46–53
        in contemporary world 76–82
        and destructive potential 42–3,
            66
        disintegration and reconstruc-
            tion 43–4, 49–51
        and intersocietal interaction
            43–4, 48–9
        in Japan 53–5
        in Latin America 68–71
        in modern societies 58–76
        in pre-modern societies 45–58
        and social movements 65–6
        in United States 71–3
    and continual contestation 60–1,
        63, 67
    different modes of 67–76
    distinctiveness of 36, 39, 40, 41
    and equality 41
    and exclusion 43, 67, 68
    and influential social actors 40–2,
        47, 50, 61, 65
    new types of 77–8
    and political order 61–2
    and religion 78
    secular codes 61
    and symbolism 41

collectivity/collectivities 2–3, 6
    and class consciousness 122
    classificatory orders 19–20
    and common behaviour 6–7, 18,
        19, 21
    cultural programmes 38–9, 40,
        47–8, 50, 51, 52
    as culture 15
    forms of 3–4
    and imagination 21, 27, 33, 97–8
    intentionally created 1–2, 4
    and longevity 14, 23, 24–5, 28–9
    materiality of 19
    and membership 3, 4, 5, 13, 21–2,
        45
        similarity of members 36, 39–40,
            41
    more-than-the-sum-of-the-parts 1,
        12, 16, 21, 22–3, 28, 30
    problems in conceptualising 12–14,
        15
    as product of interaction 16–23,
        33–5
    shared knowledge 6, 17–18, 19, 20,
        21
    shared objectives 16
    shared symbolism 27
    in social sciences 14–17
    social-constructivist approach
        16–17, 18, 21
    as symbolic complexes 6, 17, 20–1,
        28
    see also boundaries
colonial societies 88, 104, 105
Comaroff, J.L. 146
communism 73–4, 79, 211
community/communities 88, 89–95
    and association 89–90, 91
    closed 93
    and ethnicity 93–4
    nation and 165
    and primordial relations 45, 89–94
    see also ethnies
conflationism 8, 139–40, 146–51
    see also realist social theory;
        structure, culture and agency
Confucianism 50, 51, 53, 54, 75
Congo-Zaire 192
constructionism, and nation
    formation 146
Cooper, F. 198, 202

corporate agents 144–5, 153–4, 155–6, 157–8, 159–64
creolisations 9, 171–2
Cuban-Americans 187
culture 6, 9, 31
  and agency 142–3, 144, 147
  and choice 167, 176–9
  and coercion 168
  creativity 40, 48
  cultural integration 153–5
  cultural programmes 38–9, 40, 47–8, 50, 51, 52
  and distinctiveness 40
  and globalisation 170–5
  globality of 175–6
  ideal standard 168
  national 9, 163, 168–70
  paradigm crisis 170–1
  pluralism 181
    see also multicommunitarianism; multiculturalism
  traditionalism 154
  and variety 9, 167–79
  and vernacularisation 57
  see also structure, culture and agency

Dahl, Robert 183
Danishness 3, 24–9
Dannebrog 25, 26
Darwin, Charles 209
Davy, G. 46
Delanty, G. 199, 200
democracy 183, 190
democratisation 129
Denmark 23–9
Derrida, Jacques 171
developing countries, and nationalism 191
devolution 102
dialect 97, 98, 168
diaspora 107, 113, 192
  see also immigration; migrant communities
Dickens, P. 209–10
difference 181–92
Drummond, Lee 171
Dunn, Robert 175
Durkheim, E. 1, 6, 10, 89, 105, 122, 123
  and kinship 91, 92
  solidarity 5, 16, 36, 196

Dutch empire 104
Dworkin, R. 124
Dybbol, defeat of Prussians 26

education, state control of 122, 124, 147, 148
Egypt 44, 45, 46
Elias, Norbert 36, 62, 128, 129
emancipation 129, 131
empires 88, 103–7, 155–6, 160
  breakdown of 106–7
  establishment of 104–6
  and imperial control 104–5
Engels, Friedrich 105
England 67
Enlightenment 67, 72, 73, 126, 127, 128
epiphenomenalism 139–40
equality 41, 124, 125
Eriksen, T.H. 100
Erikson, E. 206
ethnic cleansing 9, 184, 190
ethnic identity 10, 195
  and altruism 207–8
  and ancestors 207, 208
  cognitive 205, 206
  definition of 206–7
  emergence of concept 208–13
  empirical research on 10, 203–8
  external aspects 204, 205
  identity of rebellion 205, 206
  internal aspects 204–6
  ritualistic-affective based 205, 206, 208
  and social sciences 196, 197, 202
  see also ethnicity; identity
ethnic nationalism 8, 9, 88, 101, 103, 182, 183
ethnic nations 99–100, 107
  and nation state 101–3
ethnicity 7, 88–117
  attributed and self-chosen 94–5
  and class 100
  community and 93–4
  instrumentalist view of 95, 96
  and kinship 94, 99, 148–9
  and migration 99, 107–13
  as primordial 44, 58, 65, 88
  and reflexive identity 95
  and religion 94, 99
  role of intellectuals 100

ethnies 88, 96–9, 148–9
    and functional relationships 98–9
    institutional structure of 96–7
    see also ethnic nations
Europe
    economic interdependence 189
    homogeneity 184
    modes of collective identity 67–8,
        73
    and multinationalism 189–90
    and nation state 66, 189
    pluralism 51, 65
    unity 9, 28
    vernacularisation 57
European Union 4, 27, 77, 78, 189
Europeanness 4
exclusion 43, 67, 68
existential anxiety 34–5

Faroe Islands 27
Faubian, J.D. 58–9
feminism 125
Fenton, S. 100
feudalism 99, 124, 125, 188
Fichte, J.G. 126
Finland 27
First World War 66, 122, 189
Firth, R. 91
Folkekirke 25
Foucault, Michel 62, 128, 129, 131,
        133, 134
France 67, 73, 78, 189
French Revolution 66, 101, 103, 182
Freud, Sigmund 188
fundamentalist movements 77, 78–82
    and modernity 79
Furnivall, J.S. 105

Garfinkel, H. 130
Gastarteider policy 114
Geertz, C. 38, 90, 91, 171–2
Gellner, E. 107, 153, 183–4, 188,
        189–90
    and Marxism 102
    and modernising nation state
        101–3
    nationalism and modernity 8, 10,
        122–4, 134, 135–6, 146–8
Gemeinschaft 5, 7, 8, 89, 91, 123
Geneva Convention 112, 115
Genghis Khan 49

genocide 66, 184, 192
Germany 27, 29, 189
Gesellschaft 5, 8, 89, 91, 123
Giddens, A. 3, 127–8, 129, 140
Gillen, F. 91
Gilroy, P. 113
Gleason, P. 211
globalisation 8–9, 29–30, 76, 190
    cultural 80, 170–6
    and difference 181
    as form of collectivity 2, 3–4
    reactions to 172–4
Glücksborg, House of 25
Gobineau, J.-A. comte de 209
Goddard, I.W. 196
Goffman, Erving 16, 19, 130, 206
Gorbachev, Mikhail 211
Gray, John 178, 179
Great Chain of Being 124, 132, 133,
        134
Greek language 56
Greenfeld, L. 103
Greenland 27, 28
groups 2, 4, 18, 19
    group identification 21–2, 27
Guibernau, M. 99

Habermas, Jürgen 132, 133, 176
habitus 2–3, 4, 6, 129
Haider, 116
Hannerz, Ulf 169, 171
Hapsburg empire 104, 188
Hayek, F. von 15
Hechter, M. 200
Heidegger, M. 134–5
Herder, J.G. von 126
Herzog, T. 70–1
Hindi 191
Hindu identity 50, 52
Hinduist movement 77
Hobbes, T. 15
Hobsbawm, E. 8, 103, 150–1
Hofstader, R. 185
Holland 67
Holocaust 66
homogeneity 62–3, 64, 78, 181–4,
        189, 190
    forced homogenisation 9, 168, 190
    see also United States, melting
        pot/homogenisation

human biological programme,
    openness of 33, 34, 35
human rights 9, 176, 178–9, 183
Huron 103

Iceland 27, 28
Iconoclasts 50
ideal speech situation 132, 133
identity 10, 195–214
    ambiguity of concept 213–14
    and collectivity 5–6
    conceptual approaches 198–203
    and confirm-structuring others
        131–2, 136
    cultural 6, 174–5, 195
    definition of 206–7
    emergence of concept 10, 208–13
    empirical studies on 10, 203–8
    as fluctuating modes of self 198,
        200–2
    and foundational forms of selfhood
        198, 200–2
    and globalisation 174–5
    and group sameness 198, 200–2
    and interests 199
    mathematical concept of 10, 196–7,
        198, 213
    metaphorical concept of 197–8
    and political goals 212–13
    and reflexivity 128
    reification of concept 201–2
    and similarity and difference 196–7,
        213
    and social action 198–200
    and social sciences 196–203
    see also boundaries; ethnic identity;
        self
Identity Structure Analysis 206
imagined communities 21, 33, 97–8
immigration
    migrant workers 114
    official policies on 115, 117
    popular responses to 116–17
    responses and attitudes to 114–17
    see also migrant communities
India
    and identity 51–2
    linguistic diversity 191
    vernacularisation 55, 57
individual order 19, 28

individuals 13, 14, 15, 126, 176–8
    interaction between 16–23, 28, 33–4
    see also social interaction
Indonesia 105
industrialisation, and nation
    formation 146–8, 156, 162
Inkeles, Alex 59
institutional order 19, 28
institutions 6–7, 19, 21, 28
    contingent incompatibility 143
    necessary complementarity 142,
        152–3
    necessary incompatibility 142–3
    pure opportunism 143
    shared 14
instrumentalism, nation formation
    and 146
interaction order 16, 19, 28
    see also social interaction
Isaacs, H 200–1
Isajiw, W.W. 204–6, 208
Islam 50
    fundamentalism 77

Jacobin movements 67, 79
Japan
    collective identity 53–5, 62, 74–6
    trading state 189
Jaspers, Karl 172
Java 55
Jenkins, R. 100, 131, 213
Jepperson, Ron 62
Jews
    fundamentalism 77
    identity 49, 50
    threat to German nationalism
        136–7

Kadiri 55
Kannada 55
Kant, Immanuel 126
Karnataka 55
Kawakami Hajime 75
Kazakhstan 192
Kelamite revolution 103
kinship 45, 91–2, 94, 98, 99, 148–9
    fictive 96
knowledge
    and discursive consciousness
        129–30, 132, 134

and meaning/interpretation 126,
    129–31, 133–5
shared 6, 17–18
tacit/practical consciousness 2–3, 4,
    6, 129–30, 131, 134
and unconscious 129
see also meaning
Knox, R. 209
kokutai 75
Kosovo 66
Kotuku Shusui 75
Kuhn, T.S. 14
Kuper, L. 106

labour, division of 92, 97, 122, 124,
    162
Laing, R.D. 135
Laitin, David 191, 192
language 22, 45, 92, 99, 126–7, 188
    in Americas 69
    Danish 26
    and dialect 26, 97, 98, 168
    in India 191
    and small communities 93
    Spanish 186
    vernacularisation 50, 52, 55–8
Latin 56
Latin America, collective identities
    68–71
Le Pen, Jean-Marie 116
Lerner, Dan 59
libido 188
Lincoln, Abraham 185
Linne, Charles 209
Linz, J. 203
Lippens, R. 170
Lipset, S.M. 185
'liquid modernity' 177, 179
Lockwood, D. 152
Lubbock, J. 209
Luckmann, T. 20

McCarthy, J.R. 211
Mair, M. 206
Majapahit 55
Malaysia 107
Marcia, J.E. 206
Marcuse, H. 210
Marx, Karl 6, 10, 16, 18, 89, 105, 122
Marxism 2, 75, 102
Massey, D. 108

Mayas 45
Mazower, M. 184
Mead, G.H. 6, 16, 22, 206
Mead, M. 210
meaning 126, 129–31, 133–5
Meiji state 74, 75
melting pot 9, 105–6, 116, 184–7
meritocracy 122–3, 124–5, 128
Meso-American societies 44, 45
Mexican Revolution 71
Meyer, John 62
migrant communities 88, 99, 107–13
    assimilation 110, 114
    boundaries 109
    cross-border migrants 111–13
    economic and political migrants
        111–13
    extended family 109, 111
    and homeland society 108–9
migrant communities *continued*
    and land of first settlement 109–10
    onward migration 110
    religion and language 111
    return home 112
    and separate immigrant culture
        109–10
    transnational 111, 113
    see also immigration
Mill, James 126
Mill, John Stuart 126, 183
Miller, David 183
Milosevic, Slobodan 190
Miskitu Indians 71
modernity
    cultural and political programme of
        58–76
    destructive forces of 66
    hegemony of centres of 78
    and increased civilisation 128
    multiple modernities 81–2
    nationalism and 8, 10, 58, 65, 101,
        122–37, 146
    and progress 66
    and reflexivity 58, 59
    reinterpretations of 79–82
Moret, A. 46
morphogenesis 8, 151–65
morphogenetic cycle 141–2, 143–5,
    163
morphostasis 141, 142, 154
Morton, S. 209

multicommunitarianism 9, 176, 178–9
multiculturalism 9, 88, 176, 181, 182–3, 190
    forms of 114–15
    and human rights 9, 176, 183
    and political migrants 115
    and social caging 183
    in United States 115–16
multinationalism 188–9, 190
Muslim schools 114
myths and legends 26–7

nation
    and community 165
    conditions for emergence 164–5, 168–9
    defined by nationalist ideology 159, 164–5
    morphogenesis of 8, 151–65
    and national culture 163
    origins of 146
    as social phenomenon 138
nation formation 8, 9, 146–51
    and corporate agency 153–4, 155–6, 157–8, 159–64
    role of agency 148–50, 157, 159–60, 161
    role of social engineering 150
    social elaboration 161–5
    sociocultural interaction 152, 157–61
    structural and cultural conditioning 152–7
nation state 1, 3, 61–2, 88, 99, 101–3
    borders 3, 30–1
    collective memories 63, 64
    constitution 27, 28
    defining 101–2
    and indoctrination 103
    institutionalisation of 66
    Japan 74–5
    loyalty to 168–9
    and national culture 9, 168–70
    and primordiality 4–5, 63, 64–5, 69
    revolutionary states 73–4, 76, 77–8
    see also ethnic nations
national anthems 24–5, 28–9, 98
national character 10, 209, 210–11
national flag 25, 98
National Front, France 116

nationalism
    appeal of 8, 122–4, 134, 135–6
    core doctrine 158–9
    developing countries and 191
    diasporic 107, 113
    and false consciousness 123, 125, 127
    and hermeneutic insight 126–7
    and identity 199, 200, 201
    as ideology 125–6, 132, 134, 149, 199
    and imperialism 189, 190
    and language 127
    and liberalism 188
    and modernity 8, 10, 58, 65, 101, 122–37, 146
    normative claims of 125–7
    post-imperial 106–7
    and primordiality 44
    and social theory 138
    stages in 188–90
    and threat from non-nationalists 136–7
Native Americans 72
NATO 27, 189
nature 133
Nazism 125, 210
Nehru, Jawaharlal 191
neighbours 91, 96
Netherlands 78, 114
new social movements 65–6, 76–7, 79–80
Northern Ireland 190
Norway 27, 29

Oommen, T. 100
Organisation of African States (OAS) 115
Ottoman empire 103, 104, 188, 189

Pakistan 95
Pali 57
Parsons, Talcott 89, 196
patrimonial authority 98–9
People's Party, Austria 116
perennialism, and nation formation 146
Persian language 56
pillarisation 114
plantation system 105–6
Plato 123, 124

political system, Denmark 25–6
Polynesian society 45
Popper, Karl 15
popular sovereignty 158–9, 160, 162–3
Portuguese empire 70, 104
post-colonial societies 107
postmodern movements 79–80
practical consciousness 2–3, 4, 6
primary agents 144–5, 153–4, 156,
    157, 159, 162, 164
primordiality 37–8, 41, 45, 88, 89–94
    nation formation and 4–5, 63,
        64–5, 69, 146, 148
    reconstruction of 44, 50, 55–8, 65
    types of primordial attachment 91–2
print capitalism 98
Protestantism 50, 67
    fundamentalism 77
Puritanism 72

race 10, 26, 45, 209–10, 212, 213
Radcliffe Brown, A. 91
Rapport, Nigel 171, 172, 174
Rashtrakutas 55
realist social theory 8, 139–46, 163
    see also conflationism; structure,
        culture and agency
reason 126–7
reflexivity 34, 58–9, 128–9, 130, 131,
    134
religion 91–2, 93, 96–7, 99
religious movements 77, 78–82
revolutionary states 73–4, 76, 77–8
Rex, J. 199
Ricoeur, Paul 174
ritual 16, 35, 38, 43
Roman empire 52
Romanov empire 188
Roniger, L. 70–1
Roosens, E. 103
royal house, Denmark 25
Ruritania and Megalomania, parable
    of 122–3
Russia 189
Rwanda 66, 192

sacredness (transcendence) 34–5, 36,
    37, 39, 41–2, 50–1
Sanskrit 56, 57
Sartre, Jean-Paul 34
Scandinavia 67

schizophrenia 135
Schlesinger, A. Jr. 116
Schneider, D.M. 36
scientific racism 209–10
Scotland 102
    Highland Clearances 188
secession 188, 190
second order emergent properties
    142–4
Second World War 66, 211
self
    and meaning 130–1, 135
    and membership of collectivity 5
    and others 16
    and world 134–5
    see also identity
self-awareness 34, 35
    see also reflexivity
Shiite Islam 50
Simmel, G. 6, 16, 22
Singhasari 55
Sinhala 55
slavery 124
Slavs 188
Smith, A.D. 98, 101, 107, 146, 200,
    201, 202
Smith, M.G. 105–6, 107
social change
    factors of 138–9
    and nation formation 146–8, 150,
        151, 163
social consciousness 10, 209, 210, 211
social interaction (SI) 16, 33–4, 141–2
social order 47, 50, 124–5
    arbitrariness of 42–3, 133–4
    and collective rituals 38–9
    essentialist view of 124–5
    and practical consciousness 2–3,
        132
    and sacred and profane 36
social sciences
    and analogies 196
    and collectivity 14–17
    and ethnicity 88–9
    and identity 196–203
society 1, 14–15, 17, 28
    and autonomous human agency 60
    and intersocietal contact 43–4
    nation state model 29–31
    sociological model of 29–30
    worship of 92

solidarity 16, 33, 36, 102, 169
    mechanical and organic 5, 36, 196
South Africa 106
sovereignty
    popular 158–9, 160, 162–3
    state 169, 172
Soviet Union 73, 74, 203
    former republics of 66, 77, 192
Spain 203
Spanish empire 69, 70, 104
Spencer, B. 91
Sri Lanka 55, 66
Stepan, A. 203
Stern, P.C. 146
structuration, confirming and non-
    confirming 130–2, 136
structure, culture and agency 8,
    139–46, 147, 151–65
    see also agency; conflationism;
        culture; realist social theory
Sukhotai 55
Sunni Islam 50
Sweden 27, 29, 115
Switzerland 67
symbolic interactionism 15
symbolic universes 20, 21, 28
symbols 39, 97–8, 100
Sztompka, P. 138

taboo 149
Tai 55
Tajfel, H. 206
Tamil Nadu 55
Tanaka, Stefan 75
Tanzania 191
Telugu 55
territory 24, 28, 62, 96, 98, 99
Thailand 55
Thanksgiving 185
Thatcher, Margaret 1, 30, 116
Thomas, W.I. 21
Tokugawa period 53–5
Tönnies, F. 5, 89, 90–1
Touraine, Alain 176
tradition 133
    invention of 8, 150–1
truth 133

Tsarist empire 104
Turkey 103

Ukraine 192
United Kingdom 78
United Nations 23
United States
    and civic nationalism 5, 186
    civil religion 71–2
    Constitution 185, 187
    and ethnic identity 186–7
    hegemony 78
    illegal immigrants 116
    individualism 72
    and language 116
    melting pot/homogenisation 9,
        105–6, 116, 184–7
    and multiculturalism 115–16
    patterns of collective identity 71–3
    and racial discrimination 186, 187
    and socialism 186
    and unity 185–6
Urry, J. 15, 29–31

van den Berghe, P. 8, 106, 148–9, 151
vernacularisation 50, 52, 55–8
Vico, Giambattista 126
Vlaamse Blok, Belgium 116

Waters, Mary 186–7
Weber, Max 1, 6, 16, 37, 89, 199
    associative relations 90–1
    modernising nation state 101
    modernity 10, 58–9, 129
    patrimonial authority 99
    unmerited suffering 92
Weinreich, P. 204, 206–8
Werblowski, J.R. 53
Wilkes, John 188
Wittgenstein, L. 133
Woon, L. 95

Yugoslavia 77, 203

zero difference/nonzero difference
    196–7, 198, 200, 202
Zolberg, A. 94